BUSINESS ETHICS

Also by Norman Barry

Hayek's Social and Economic Philosophy
An Introduction to Modern Political Theory
On Classical Liberalism and Libertarianism
The New Right
Welfare
Classical Liberalism in the Age of Post-Communism
The Morality of Business Enterprise

Business Ethics

Norman Barry

First published 1998 by
MACMILLAN PRESS LTD
Houndmills, Basingstoke, Hampshire RG21 6XS
and London
Companies and representatives throughout the world

ISBN 0–333–55185–0

A catalogue record for this book is available from the British Library.

This book is printed on paper suitable for recycling and made from
fully managed and sustained forest sources.

10 9 8 7 6 5 4 3 2 1
07 06 05 04 03 02 01 00 99 98

Printed in Great Britain by
Antony Rowe Ltd
Chippenham, Wiltshire

For
L.J.H.

Contents

Preface

Over the last 30 years business ethics has become an established academic discipline, especially in the USA. It has attracted philosophers, economists, management consultants and members of the clergy of all denominations.

While it is probably true that very few people today are old-fashioned socialists, favouring the abolition of private property, the nationalization of industry and comprehensive central planning, it is the case that practitioners of business ethics are more sceptical of capitalism than the original founders of the social and economic doctrine of market economics. Of course, this scepticism has been provoked by some well-publicized business scandals which have led to a bout of self-analysis and introspection on the part of the business community itself. Business agents sometimes even feel the need to absorb some controversial, but still fashionable, doctrines from social philosophy, such as social justice and communitarianism in the public justifications they occasionally give for their activities.

The critics of business may accept the efficiency properties of the market, and even commend it for the freedom that it encourages, but they tend to test the practice of business against more or less universal standards of morality. It must find some validation in a set of moral principles which are external to the activity of commerce itself. The social responsibility of business is a constant theme and business agents are often urged to forgo profit in order to fulfil some social goal which is not intrinsically a part of business enterprise. Thus they must not only satisfy the basic rules of morality, which apply to all aspects of social life, but they should purge themselves of the grosser forms of self-interest and act communally wherever that is consistent with the survival of the enterprise.

That is why a lot of books on business ethics are kinds of 'advice' books that attempt to indicate appropriate forms of conduct for business personnel; social duties which may not be apparent to them in their daily activity. Furthermore, the lure of the profit motive, and the pressure of competition, may distract personnel from even the basic moral duties. No business scandal occurs without journalists, clergymen and academics informing business agents of the duties they had neglected or the promises they had breached. The point here is that scandals are public and the details of them are easily presented in suitably lurid terms.

However, the fact that business activity goes on daily in perfectly respectable moral ways in capitalist society is seldom noticed. Nor should it be: behaving morally, following the rules of just conduct and respecting contract and property, should not be a reason for congratulation. But neither should the latest business outrage be presented as if it were a regular feature of market activity. Yet contemporary business moralists often assume that trade and commerce do not provide their own standards of probity and that their personnel have to be constantly reminded of how to behave ethically.

The business class is certainly affected by moral criticism. Indeed, its members often feel the need to sanitize their activity by indulging in public displays of virtue; as if they needed to compensate for the apparent wrongs, or at least dubious displays of self-interest, to which their activity might give rise, by outward displays of altruism. Despite the obvious success of capitalism in the production of wanted goods and services, and in job creation, many of its critics still feel that all these good things could be generated without some of the less attractive features of business enterprise. Some moral philosophers regard it as their duty to remind business personnel not only of their basic ethical duties but also to encourage them to go beyond the minimal requirements of moral conduct, even if that leads to a reduction in efficiency.

This book is not written in the style of a censor of commerce, of the moral critic anxious to impose on business personnel moral duties which exceed those required of ordinary agents. Indeed, it specifically rejects the idea that there is some special business ethics which imposes on business people and entrepreneurs moral standards that would not be expected of non-business personnel. It is maintained that the language of ordinary morality is adequate to condemn, or to praise, the actions of business agents. For example, it is maintained that the fact that firms and corporations *appear* to have special privileges and powers is not a reason to burden them with extra social duties.

Furthermore, the book is written with a particular purpose in mind: to defend a particular form of capitalism, the Anglo-American type. This is the kind of market economics that is practised primarily in the English-speaking world, and is exemplified by the commercial and financial systems of Wall Street and the City of London. It is, of course, not the only type of successful capitalism and rival forms have attracted the critics of individualistic, profit-based commerce. For example, the more communally-based and less individualistic economies of Germany and Japan seem to combine economic success with a more caring and less ruthlessly profit-orientated approach to commerce. They are often the models for critics of Anglo-American business. Although I shall cast some doubt on the validity of all this, my main concern is not comparative but is an attempt to outline the defining characteristics of the Anglo-American model and to indicate its moral strengths and shortcomings. Hence a lot of the book is taken up with an analysis of the corporation, of the ethics of the stock market, and of the morality of takeovers, and the problem of business and the environment. In this enquiry I shall discuss some of the scandals that have occurred and try to indicate the moral issues that were at stake. In some examples I indicate where there is reason to doubt the cogency of the censure that was directed against the personnel involved.

The book itself is the product of some reflection and valuable conversations with friends and colleagues. It arose out periods of time spent researching the subject at the Center for Social Philosophy and Policy at Bowling Green State University, Ohio and I am grateful to the Directors of the Center, Fred Miller, Ellen Frankel Paul and Jeffrey Paul for their excellent facilities and congenial intellectual atmosphere. I am also grateful for the David Hume Institute, Edinburgh, for permission to reproduce parts of an earlier book I wrote on the subject, *The Morality of Business Enterprise*, which was published under its auspices. Chapter 5 of the book, on insider dealing, is based largely on a pamphlet I wrote for the Foundation for Business Responsibilities, London, and I thank Simon Webley, its director, for permission to use some of that material. I also owe a special debt to my friend and colleague at the University of Buckingham, Martin Ricketts, for his helpful advice on the economic aspects of business ethics. I am particularly grateful to Mrs Norma Prout, also of Buckingham, whose wizardry with computers saved me from many a crisis at the keyboard. I should also like to thank my research assistant, Miss Faye Merchant, for her invaluable assistance.

Buckingham, 1997 NORMAN BARRY

1 Business and Moral Philosophy

WHY BUSINESS ETHICS?

Business ethics as an academic discipline is a comparative newcomer to the typical university curriculum, and one which was at one time geographically limited to the United States; though, of course, the ethics of business, the morality of capitalism, the profit motive and the justice (or injustice) of free markets are topics that have been explored repeatedly since the beginnings of the commercial civilization in sixteenth-century Europe. Capitalism itself may be said, not inaccurately, to have a morally tainted biography in that its mainsprings tend to derive from the baser human motives, self-interest and the desire for personal profit. Its success, to many people, seems to depend on the suspension, if not outright rejection, of those moral constraints on individual gratification that are said to be integral to Western morality. Furthermore, the cultivation of some of the traditional moral virtues, honesty, integrity, self-sacrifice and the charitable instinct, seems to be hampered, if not made impossible, by the competitive impulse which is the driving force of the enterprise of business. Many people would regard the peroration in favour of 'greed' (a motivation to be cultivated to the exclusion of conventional moral imperatives) delivered by the Wall Street arbitrageur, Ivan Boesky, to a group of business students in 1986, as only a slightly hyperbolic description of the egoistic psychology and amoral attitudes that drive the business community. Boesky said that: 'Greed is all right by the way. I want you to know. I think greed is healthy. You can be greedy and still feel good about yourself.'[1]

Indeed, many of the well-publicised scandals of recent years, 'insider dealing' in the stock market (for which Boesky was eventually convicted), the Bank of Credit and Commerce International and the Robert Maxwell affairs have all lent a superficial credence to the popular view of capitalism. Even though those phenomena involved straightforward crimes, and are clearly not illustrative of normal business activity, the 'myth of amoral business' persists. Even in America, although capitalism itself is not regarded as morally condemnable, the activities of business corporations and their senior employees are regarded with some cynicism by the public at large and even more so by the intellectual community.[2] Religious groups especially have sedulously stressed the anti-social and amoral (if not immoral) nature of business.

The 'ethics' of competition have, at least since the end of the nineteenth century, been regarded as no more than Social Darwinism; a social application of the biological doctrine of the 'survival of the fittest', in which it is 'right' that inefficient firms, organizations and individuals should be sacrificed in the relentless and remorseless competitive process. To impose social duties on business enterprises and individual entrepreneurs, either by coercive law or by conventional morality, would weaken competition and place arbitrary obstacles in the way of progress.

Despite philosophical objections to the assimilation of the 'good' to whatever has emerged through competition, the doctrine that business is self-justifying has historically not been unimportant. It was given a superficial moral gloss by the attribution of indefeasible moral rights to individuals, so that, irrespective of the question of social progress, government action that violated an individual's right to exchange, to enjoy the products of his or her own labour and to accumulate wealth were in principle condemnable. This idea was as much a part of Herbert Spencer's social philosophy as was his doctrine of evolution: indeed, the two ideals – rights and social progress – were claimed to be harmonious. This view is echoed in some *laissez-faire* arguments today. Thus, even though business activity looks, superficially, justifiable only in terms of the social benefits it brings, it may ultimately be validated by individualistic conceptions of rights and freedom.

For most of the twentieth century little was done to counter the egoistic image of capitalism, an image cultivated by intellectuals. In fact, capitalism was attacked on two fronts. One argument, from orthodox Marxists, claimed that, irrespective of their moral failings, capitalism and the market were destined for extinction by inexorable social 'laws'; competition between firms would drive down the rate of profit, causing industry to be concentrated in a few hands; increasing mechanization would create a revolutionary 'reserve army' of the unemployed; and the succession of booms and slumps in an undirected market would eventuate in a final 'crisis' from which socialism (and ultimately communism) would emerge triumphant. The manifest failure of socialist planning and the recent rush into market arrangements in formerly communist regimes in Eastern Europe, however, has not as much validated the morality of capitalism as it has decisively negated the Utopianism of collectivist planning; capitalism may not be 'just' but it works. Thus the second, and now more fashionable, critique of capitalism centres almost entirely on its moral failings. Business ethics as a discipline is very much concerned to evaluate capitalist enterprise by reference to morality. Critics say that capitalism is not self-justifying and it has therefore to be validated by external moral criteria. Those moral values, such as trust, honesty and fair dealing, that are intrinsic to business are not sufficient for its moral credibility.

The failure of socialism has led erstwhile critics of capitalism to concentrate their fire on one particular form of capitalism – the Anglo-American (sometimes called Anglo-Saxon) variety. This may be briefly characterized as an economic order in which corporations (where managements are normally separated from owners) compete to satisfy consumer demand for goods and services in order to maximize returns to investors and wages for employees. The participants in this are treated as 'anonymous' agents motivated by the desire for profit; they have no formal responsibility to society at large. This form is often contrasted with the German[3] (and Japanese) models, which are apparently less investor-driven and where other values than profit-maximization are effective; perhaps the pursuit of market share or some more socially appropriate goal. Firms are also said to be more concerned about employee well-being than those in Anglo-American capitalism. The emphasis here would be on the importance of establishing a consensus between the participants in a commercial enterprise and this is contrasted favourably with the individualistic self-interest that is supposed to characterize Anglo-American capitalism. There is less faith in the proposition derived from Adam Smith that the public good will emerge from private action subject only to minimal constraints.

Often the arguments here are purely about efficiency. It is said, for example, that in German and Japanese companies the managements can take a long-term view of investment opportunities because they need worry less about fluctuating share prices. But whether this does lead to improved use of resources is a matter for economic history, not business ethics. However, a moral gloss is put on the argument when it is claimed that participants in these economies take the wider interests of the community into account in such matters as plant relocation, employment policy and industrial reorganization. Thus the disdain they show for the takeover mechanism is thought to have a moral dimension as well as an alleged efficiency advantage.

It is true, of course, that market economies can take various forms. Indeed, the limited liability public corporation is only one type of enterprise: there are privately-held corporations, partnerships and so on. The moral strictures that are raised against the corporation are applicable to all these forms to the extent that they rely exclusively on the profit motive. Indeed, there are many complaints made about behaviour in them. If business ethics is to be a coherent critical discipline it cannot be arbitrarily confined to conventional corporate capitalism. What all forms of free enterprise have in common is the system of private ownership on which they are founded. This distinguishes them from all types of socialism, including market socialism.

The recognition of the efficiency of free enterprise has a long and honourable history in the writings of political economists, but even from this perspective the credit accorded to it was provisional; the efficiency ethic had to be supplemented by morality if it were to be acceptable. Thus when business ethics began to be taken seriously in the USA, at the beginning of the 1960s, the dominant *motif* of the writers was that commerce had to be restrained by an appeal to justice, rights, social utility and other concepts drawn from the traditional Western moral vocabulary. Thus firms were urged to serve the community and not just the stockholders; to refrain from activities which, although lawful, might have an adverse effect on society at large; to honour justice by adopting hiring policies which, although technically inefficient, favoured deprived minorities; to refrain from bribery in international dealings even though that might be an accepted practice in the countries with which they are involved; to be honest in advertising, and so on. The emphasis was mainly on the corporation, an institution to which was attributed social and moral duties as well as strictly economic ones. The 'social audit' was held to be as important as the financial one.[4]

Of particular importance was the moral status of the corporation itself. The animus against business (both in the USA and Britain) was not so much against free enterprise, but against 'Big Business'; the giant corporation (to be considered in detail below), with its legal features of limited liability, perpetual life, separation between management and owners, and so on, was itself held to be a threat to the (not unacceptable) market order. Its alleged power to exempt itself from competition, to collude with its 'competitors', fix prices and exploit individuals, to harm communities through morally arbitrary plant relocations and to attenuate market disciplines through its dealing with government, became the target of intellectuals, such as John Kenneth Galbraith[5] and political activists, such as Ralph Nader.[6]

In fact, if anything the defence (what little there has been) of capitalist behaviour since the Second World War has taken a rather different form from one which might identify it as a special kind of virtue. This defence represents commerce and business as somehow separate from morality (although of course not outside the rules of civil and criminal law); that it is simply inappropriate to impose on participants in capitalist processes moral duties that are distinct from the conventional ethical obligations that apply to everyone as citizens. Thus to expect business people and corporate executives to display virtue by going beyond what the law requires in the way of fair employment practices or protection of the environment, would be to disrupt the genuine rules of business relationships, most notably the contractual arrangement between the management of a corporation and its stockholders. Indeed, its most articulate spokesperson, Milton Friedman, claims that the attribution of social responsibilities to business people, if successful, would allow them to arrogate the political function.[7] The assimilation of special virtues to business enterprise would also, Friedman claims, lead to the attenuation of the property rights of the owners of corporations (that is, the shareholders). However, many critics have mistakenly interpreted this view to mean that business is outside the realm of ordinary morality, that virtue and commerce do not mix, and that the phrase 'business ethics' is an oxymoron. But what Friedman was objecting to was the extra morality that apparently applied only to business agents and also the violation of owners' rights should managements spend shareholders' money on causes that they deemed to be worthy.

THE ORIGINS OF 'AMORAL' BUSINESS

The 'myth of amoral business' perhaps originates in the infamous *Fable of the Bees*[8] by the eighteenth-century writer, Bernard Mandeville. In his parable, Mandeville posited a dichotomy between virtue and commerce and claimed that the adoption of traditional Christian standards of self-restraint and charity makes everyone worse off, as well as running counter to the universal mainsprings of human action. The encouragement of the baser motives would lead to an extension of the division of labour, the widening of the market and the growth of international trade, all of which would make everyone better off. But this encouragement, he claimed, could not make us virtuous. Hence his observation of the beehive in its *non-moral* state: 'Every part was full of vice/Yet the whole mass an earthly paradise.' Greed was admirable because it released energies for productive activity. Conventional virtue, which admired self-sacrifice, was an impediment to progress. Mandeville also regarded it as hypocritical, since in his view human behaviour was always governed by self-interest, whatever moralists might say.

This attitude, if applied, perhaps does not quite eliminate morality from business, since the whole activity is given an overall utilitarian justification. A society requires conventions and artificial rules to guide human conduct, for without them there would be no security. But these devices have no moral value beyond their contribution to the process of the co-ordination of actions of dispersed individuals. However, the application of 'Mandevillianism' to capitalism seems to confirm the argument that successful business requires a suspension of at least some virtues. Contemporary business ethicists are, in effect, either validating Mandeville's argument by suggesting that capitalism and virtue are not naturally compatible so that ethical standards have to be imposed on business people by the artifice of law, or trying to refute him with the argument that ethics is, in fact, 'good for business': that is, moral restraint is ultimately profitable. Of course, the cynic might suggest that even the latter view is a subtle manifestation of the Mandevillian spirit, since it sees the observation of moral rules as instrumentally rather than intrinsically valuable.

Adam Smith had a much more plausible explanation of commercial morality in his *The Theory of Moral Sentiments.*[9] In an explicit critique of Mandeville, he insisted that the values of justice, probity and prudence traditionally associated with commerce were perfectly acceptable, and essential, moral virtues. Only if morality was interpreted exclusively as altruism and self-sacrifice was it antithetical to business. As he famously put it, in *The Wealth of Nations*, it is not from the benevolence of the butcher, baker and brewer that we get our dinner, but from their regard to their interest. Benevolence is a most implausible motivation for the creation of prosperity. It is true that he also said that the 'wise and virtuous man is at all times willing that his own private interest should be sacrificed to the public interest'[10] but this is only his way of saying that commerce (and its virtues) was only one aspect of social life, it did not mean that the practice of business itself should be governed by a morality alien to it. He would have been the first to condemn those modern business ethicists who would impose on commercial agents principles drawn from general social philosophy that go beyond minimalist justice and social convention. The basic rules of justice were all that commerce required; and although Smith would have been the first to claim that a truly virtuous social order required more than this, he would not have expected it from merchants (about the morality of whom he had some well-known doubts).

It is doubtful whether even the most extreme opponents of the 'social responsibility of business' thesis are really Mandevillians. After all, the rigid dichotomy between virtue and commerce would permit certain business practices – for example, bribery (itself a complex issue) – yet the most vociferous free market advocates contend that business must not only be conducted within the law but also be consistent with general morality. Milton Friedman, for example, claims that, although the only responsibility of business is to maximise profits, this activity must be pursued in conformity to the 'basic rules of the society, both embodied in law and those embodied in ethical custom'.[11] The problem is to determine what the customary ethical rules are and what they imply for the practice of business. A generous interpretation of them would narrow the gap between the proponents of business freedom and its critics. At least, it is doubtful whether any would claim that business need necessarily be 'amoral'. What is important here is a distinction between the attribution of normal moral responsibility to business agents and the imposition of *additional* social duties. Whilst the distinction is clear enough in theory, in practice there may well be serious problems.

In fact, what is probably behind the case for free markets is a much older argument; that commerce has positive moral advantages even apart from the utilitarian considerations that tell in its favour. It is the claim that the business relationship, so far from being destructive of moral values, actually advances them; that peaceable co-operation and exchange between individuals in search of gain will improve their character. This was certainly the argument of the eighteenth-century and nineteenth-century celebrants of commercial society, Montesquieu, David Hume, Adam Smith (with some qualifications) and Benjamin Constant. Of course, the virtues of the market seemed obvious enough to these writers, since the contrast that they drew was between trade and war; self-advancement through markets was more enlightened morally than national glory through global conflict. In their eyes, the very anonymity of market society, with its opening up of the possibility of peaceful relationships between strangers held together only by simple rules and the cash nexus, was itself a moral achievement. In the nineteenth century, socialists assumed that global conflict between nations would be replaced by conflict between classes. It is no accident that Herbert Spencer,[12] in lamenting the decline of the commercial order, complained that its replacement by socialism was not a progressive move but a recrudescence of an older, 'militant' form of society.

It is perhaps regrettable that historically this aspect of the justification for business proved to be short-lived, vulnerable as it then was to Marxist historicism and to the overtly moral criticism of commerce. The latter was directed more at the emergence of industrial and corporate forms of business society than to the simple commercial order described by Adam Smith. However, contemporary apologists for capitalism are implicitly drawing upon this tradition when they contrast the market and the state; the former being the realm of spontaneous co-ordination of otherwise disparate individuals while the latter is often depicted as a coercive institution that exists for the imposition of plans upon them. A large part of the defence of capitalism rests on the assumption that market-generated income which comes from the free choices of individuals is more concordant with morality than that which derives from the exercise of the state's monopoly power to tax and redistribute resources.

Indeed, the corporation itself is seen by some writers[13] as having a moral purpose, forming a locus of identity for individuals who would otherwise be either soulless inhabitants of an anonymous market or subservient to an all-powerful state (as in communist regimes). The moral value of the 'personality' of the corporation then holds independently of the overtly utilitarian value of this form of economic organization. The corporation could not exist in a fully-collectivized society because that economic order does not permit rivals to the state. Even the much-maligned multinational corporations have great moral value from this perspective. After all, they bring employment and the prospects of wealth to the Third World in the way that government never has. And if they pay employees lower incomes than those earned by workers in the developed world, that is simply a response to the laws of the market. A company cannot pay workers more than their marginal product and remain in business for very long.

All this suggests that throughout its history commercial activity has been to a limited extent a moral enterprise; an activity that required the recognition of constraints on human action and the submission of individuals to rules of just conduct, be they explicit, as in the criminal and civil law, or tacit, as in the 'rules of the game' that have traditionally governed financial and asset markets. Business is historically a part of Western civilization, yet it is that part which has failed to receive the approbation of the moralists of the twentieth century. The virtues of the commercial age looked real enough to Adam Smith when contrasted with the bellicosity of former times, but in the contemporary world business has been set more exacting tasks by the whole panoply of moral philosophy, including the promotion of social justice, equality, rights and the public interest.

It has been hampered mainly by the fact that the traditional business values seem to be at odds with some of the dominant themes of contemporary social philosophy. Conformity to rules and procedures seems to be too minimal an ethic to justify the values of the business enterprise; such minimalism might permit actions which, although lawful, run counter to current moral standards. Since these standards have included, from the end of the Second World War at least, a commitment to social or redistributive justice, the enterprise society has been especially vulnerable. The allocative mechanisms of the market necessarily involve inequality of factor reward, and this phenomenon bears only the faintest resemblance to conventional distributive criteria, such as desert or need. Thus the fact that Michael Milken earned $550 million in 1987 on Wall Street was as decisive in the moral condemnation of him as the wrongs or harmful acts for which he was eventually prosecuted (see below, Chapter 6). It seems to be the conventional wisdom that a person cannot earn that kind of money without harming someone (though economic theory would have it otherwise). The modern business moralist, in condemning profit, is echoing Aristotle's comment that trade is 'justly censored because the gain in which it results, is not naturally made, but is made at the expense of other men'. Ever since Aristotle the common complaint against commerce has been that it is a zero-sum game, that the success of one person is always bought at the failure of another. It is true that competition does sometimes gives this impression but this, as we shall see, conceals the spirit of co-operation that underlies business enterprise.

THE MEANING OF THE MARKET

The reason why the business community has been subjected to moral criticism, the explanation of its vulnerability to extra-economic ethical imperatives, derives partly from the fact that the environment in which it necessarily operates, the market, does not, and rarely has, operated in the way that the economics textbooks imply. The business ethics school misunderstands the market and much of the criticism of capitalism emanates from this misunderstanding: it is important to indicate at this stage the source of the confusion. In the textbooks, competition tends to be represented in a static form, a state of perfect co-ordination between individual transactors in which full efficiency has been achieved. Prices exactly reflect marginal cost and there are no opportunities for enterprising individuals to make excess profits. But most exchange systems are not like this. There are opportunities to be exploited and extra-market gains to be made by astute individuals. Business agents operate in a world of uncertainty – which offers chances for success and failure.

Business ethics tends to respond to the phenomenon of imperfect markets in two ways. Some regard them as curiously welcome; their existence indicates that individuals are not driven by the 'iron laws' of economics, that they do not always have to act in efficiency-maximizing ways or face ruin and can therefore use the slack in the market for morally-pleasing activities.[14] Thus someone who captures a market position that to an extent protects him from competition would appear to be under some kind of moral duty to indulge current ethical ideals. His advantages enable him to pursue worthy goals that would be quite unrealistic under the full rigour of the market. Perhaps he ought to act virtuously as some kind of payment for his extra-market privilege.

Although this approach has a certain appeal, it has odd consequences. For example, it would imply that the monopolist who gave a large portion of his 'unjust' profits to charity would be something of a moral hero. But, given our normal assumptions about human nature, it is difficult to imagine that economic agents would act in the morally-prescribed manner. A more feasible approach for the moral critic would be to attack monopoly, and other market imperfections, rather than attempt to moralize market agents. We can assume that human behaviour is more or less unchanging and the attempt to moralize business agents may produce unintended consequences, as when managements of companies take on wide ethical functions and undermine the property rights of owners.

The second way to approach imperfect markets from an ethical standpoint is to point to the value of perfect competition. Its existence precludes cheating or other manipulation and it eliminates the 'excess' profit that goes to successful entrepreneurs; they may gain their rewards by exploiting other people's ignorance. One crucially important point is that the morality which is produced by perfect competition is not a function of each agent being moralized, by propaganda or ethical education, but is produced automatically by institutional arrangements. Human nature does not change but the incentive structures individuals face do the closer we move to perfect competition.

It is true that, as it is described in microeconomics texts, the ideal of a perfectly competitive market is a quasi-scientific concept: it is not thought to express anything of moral value. It is accurately described as ethically neutral and solely concerned with efficient realization of whatever values the participants may have. The theory merely tells us how individuals' choices, which could be for quite immoral things, may be realized in the least-cost way. There is a perfectly-efficient market for the supply of heroin, cocaine or sex. Still, some of the features of perfect competition are potentially interesting for the moralist.

In a world of many firms, none of which can influence price, and where there is costless entry, an absence of externalities and perfect information on the part of all participants, some of the problems of business ethics would be definitionally absent. For example, perfect information would preclude the possibility of insider dealers in securities taking an 'unfair' advantage of other people's ignorance, competition would have whittled factor earnings down to the minimum required for efficient production so that there would be no entrepreneurial 'profit', and the ability of free agents to make highly specific employment contracts would exclude those problems of 'civil rights' and 'authority' in the workplace which arise from the highly general contracts that are made in the modern business enterprise. Perhaps the most important feature is that the firm or corporation does not exist in perfect competition (or static equilibrium). Each individual is a rational contractor who instantly negotiates the best terms. She does not obey the corporate hierarchy (there is none) but negotiates with others on a purely individualistic basis. Of course there are costs to all this and that is why corporations and firms have developed.

Of course, none of this is meant to imply that there cannot be legitimate moral criticisms of the features of competitive markets (leaving aside the question about the values that are produced in them) even if exchange tended to work in the way the textbooks describe it. The psychological foundation upon which they rest may be said to be not a universal attribute of humans but a contingent feature of a pre-existing set of capitalist institutions; the theory says nothing about initial resource endowments, which may be condemnable from the perspective of social justice; 'welfare' is limited to the satisfaction of individual desires, whereas there may be other actions that may be plausibly advanced as welfare-enhancing; and the market, by treating individuals as anonymous maximizers, separates them from their communal bonds and attenuates the altruistic sentiment. These, and many other, objections have been raised against even well-functioning markets.

However, the intuitive appeal of the theory and practice of the market is now great enough to attract socialists formerly wedded to central planning. This is no doubt due to the market's freedom-enhancing properties and, surprisingly, to the fact that its distributive mechanisms seem often to produce results that are broadly 'just' (though it was not the intention of the founders of the theory to praise it for this reason). There is, then, a potential harmony between payments to factors and the moralists' notion of desert. If each factor of production is paid its marginal product, then the inequality that emerges is linked to efficiency rather than to exploitation or greed. It is the way in which capitalist economies have developed that has provoked the demand for a broader notion of business ethics (which includes social justice) rather than the idea of exchange itself.

The problem, however, is that to the business moralist, success in the market often looks like exploitation. It is not merely that people start from unequal positions in the market, it is that competition itself seems sometimes to involve a breach of the principle of reciprocity; the principle of the mutual assumption of benefits and burdens that is implicit in Adam Smith's moral defence of the market. For this principle seems to be breached when one or more persons seem to get a lot more out of commercial deals than do others. Often the inequality of reward seems not to be validated by any conventional moral principle, such as desert or effort. Profit may be the result of sheer luck or the ruthless taking advantage of people's vulnerability and ignorance. The way imperfect markets operate suggests to critics that there is no reciprocal assumption of burdens or fair enjoyment of benefits. Imperfect markets are as often the venue for questionable ethics as they are the stage for virtuous and socially responsible behaviour. This is why it would be unwise to rely too much on them to provide business agents with the opportunity of altruistic behaviour, for once they have been relieved from the pressures of the iron laws of competition self-interest may produce less than benign results.

Profit is the main target of the moralist because it appears to be payment above that required to draw a factor, for example, labour, into productive activity. Because markets are normally imperfect there are opportunities for entrepreneurs to make money by noticing what others have not noticed, for example, the value a particular good might have on the market. Sometimes it is the result of simple arbitrage, the exploitation of the fact that the same good sells for different prices in different markets.[15] This rarely accords with conventional ideas of desert.

Is someone who buys a Rembrandt for a few pounds from a completely ignorant seller merely getting a return on his knowledge of old masters, or is he exploiting someone else's weakness? What if the seller were his grandmother? Is the deal legitimate because the vendor was too indolent to find out the true value of the object? Reciprocity could be said to be satisfied because there was no cheating, yet the fact of vastly disproportionate rewards casts doubt on this. For most moralists there is a difference between the formal propriety of the arrangement (which is clearly satisfied in this case) and the moral features of the phenomenon that emerges. The fact that in Western economies much of business is transacted between strangers tends to highlight the differences between formal propriety and substantive morality. In deals like the one just cited, there could be 'unfairness' but it is difficult to define them as exploitative, in the way that a monopoly seller of a desperately-wanted good is exploiting people's vulnerability. All moralists would object to such a deal being conducted with one's grandmother but apologists for market capitalism would deny that family ethics had anything to do with business. However, there are grey areas between pure market ethics and that morality associated with friendship and family affections.

Of course, entrepreneurial profit is acquired in less spectacular ways than the above hypothetical example. It normally consists in reorganizing the factors of production in novel ways, correctly anticipating future consumer demand, or in any other of the myriad ways in which ever-changing markets offer alert people opportunities for profit. Theoretically it requires no capital, that can always be borrowed, or even the conventionally valued meritorious skills and efforts, but rather the uncanny ability to spot gaps in the market. To many people entrepreneurship is the driving force of capitalism and the source of that creativity that market systems display.

Although most socialist critics now concede that markets do co-ordinate human actions better than central planning, they still believe that a market can operate without entrepreneurship, that some other method than the profit motive can be used to draw factors into their most productive uses. They still prefer reward to accord with long-run production costs (a proposition of perfect equilibrium theory), largely because this excludes entrepreneurial discovery, which may look suspiciously like good fortune. But what creativity could there be if reward were limited to that determined by simple production costs? I shall later indicate how a moral case can be constructed for profit, in addition to its utilitarian value in the incentive structure of a free enterprise economy, and show how its economic necessity and moral value can be detected in superficially unpromising areas of capitalist economies – for example, takeovers, buyouts and corporate restructuring.

It is important to note also that entrepreneurship is behind the structure of the large-scale corporation; an economic institution whose personnel *appear* to behave differently from the swash-buckling innovators of economic history. However, entrepreneurship is a feature of big businesses, indeed many of them were the result of organizational flair, and the ethical problems of capitalism occur in whatever form the system manifests itself. Equity owners provide the capital for a corporation (or firm; I shall use the terms interchangeably except where the context indicates otherwise) and they are therefore residual claimants on any profit; that is, income earned above the normal rate of return. They are ultimately responsible for the choice of the board of directors and the management, even if their role may appear to be passive. The morality of profit is applicable here just as much as it is to the individualistic entrepreneur who makes discoveries in the marketplace and is entitled to the rewards they generate. Employees do create extra value by their innovative behaviour and are therefore entitled to rewards that exceed normal salary. However, moral problems in relation to the corporation flow from the possibility that the managements may exploit the owners, siphoning off returns (that should go to the owners) in the form of high salaries and perks. They may exploit *specific* human capital: that is, labour which has been invested in the acquisition of skills which have little transfer value. Although underestimated, these moral issues are probably as important as the question of the social and moral responsibilities of the corporation, which is (unfortunately) the major concern of orthodox business moralists.

It is crucial to stress that it is the presence of the corporation that generates the problems adumbrated above; and it is the rationale of this institution, and the ethical justification for some of its behaviour, that are relevant to the moral evaluation of business enterprises. For the corporation is absent from the neoclassical model of perfect competition and it was scarcely present in the 'virtuous' commerce of the late eighteenth century described by the early apologists of market capitalism. It is its great power, and perhaps more importantly, that of its management, and its (alleged) relative immunity to moral and political constraint, that has generated most of the problems located by business ethicists.

It should be apparent that the defender of business enterprise, and its attendant culture, cannot make simple appeals to the ideal of a perfectly competitive market alluded to above. For one thing, not only has this never obtained in practice but a variant of it, the commercial society of the eighteenth century, and its attendant virtue described by early writers, is no longer with us. The presence of the large corporation, or conglomerate, in the contemporary world has made a moral difference. For another, the world of perfect competition is very much the ideal of market socialism;[16] and this means the defender of capitalism has not only to show that the 'perfect' competition model is an inadequate explanation of the way that markets work, but also that the phenomena that it excludes, especially profit, are not only functionally necessary but ethically desirable (or, at least, not condemnable).

CRITICAL BUSINESS ETHICS

The ethics of business encompass two major areas; they may be termed the macro and the micro. The macro is about the validation of the enterprise culture, especially in its corporate manifestation. This involves such questions as the nature and justification of the market and the role of profit within it, the 'social responsibility' or otherwise of business, the regulation of commerce and the rule of law. The micro issues are about ethical problems that arise in the day-to-day activities of the business corporation and private agents. Should ethical constraints be allowed to override profit-maximization in plant relocation? Does the employment contract deprive the employee of his or her 'rights' to criticize the firm publicly ('whistle-blowing')? Does insider dealing necessitate unfairness in the securities market? Is a corporation under a moral duty to go beyond legal requirements in order to aid disadvantaged minorities? Should a profit-seeking business agent refrain from despoiling the environment in the absence of prohibition when he knows that his competitors will not be so virtuous, even if he is? These phenomena comprise the basic features of the doctrine of the 'social responsibility of the corporation'.

The principles that are used in the evaluation of business activity are likely to be the same whether they are used in macro-level or micro-level problems. Thus an ethicist who regards the market and the profit system as justifiable on utilitarian grounds is likely to be highly sceptical of restraints on business activity – for example, the imposition of wide social obligations on business corporations; they are condemned as destructive of market mechanisms. On the other hand, a sceptic of these mechanisms would welcome such restraints as necessary consequences of the application of morally superior principles to economic organization. Thus, if the doctrine of justice implies that there should be a 'level playing field' for business activity, then the enforcement of insider trading rules in the stock market is legitimate, even if such a policy coagulates the flow of information on which the successful co-ordination of activities depends, as some critics maintain.

However, the difficult and interesting problems of business ethics arise because there is usually a plurality of principles at work in the evaluation of commercial activity. Few apologists for business would claim that restraint on its actions should be limited to that provided by the law; indeed the idea of commerce as a civilizing influence would be incoherent in the absence of certain ethical conventions. Again, few writers on the Left, apart from unreconstructed opponents of capitalism and the market order, maintain a complete indifference to the effect on productivity that a rigorous commitment to certain abstract moral principles might have.

In fact, most moralists pay an unwitting tribute to the commercial ethic by arguing that morality is 'good for business'. This might be the case in the aggregate, but surely the problems arise precisely in those situations where morality is costly for a particular enterprise, and where, for reasons alluded to above, individual corporate agents cannot be expected (or predicted) to shoulder the burdens imposed by the necessity of maintaining a morality that favours business in the aggregate but which may not benefit them individually. Business dilemmas largely arise out of the competing claims made on agents by utility, justice, rights and, indeed, the whole range of morality. However, all this requires an understanding of the meaning, and substantive implications, of these ethical concepts.

2 Value Systems

In ethical theory there are, to simplify matters, two competing approaches to the evaluation of conduct, whether it is the behaviour of politicians, ordinary people in their daily lives, or business (either the appraisal of the whole system or actions of individual agents operating under its rules); they are the *teleological* and the *deontological*.[1] These apparently irreconcilable value systems colour, in one form or other, all of our moral judgements. Briefly, teleological judgements are based upon some desirable state of affairs, either for an individual or a group, which some action brings about; and the action is evaluated in accordance with its conduciveness to this wanted outcome. It is states of affairs themselves that are intrinsically valuable rather than the moral quality of the actions that bring them about. In contrast, deontological principles relate to those moral duties that restrain us from performing certain actions irrespective of the value of consequences. The duties themselves are intrinsically compelling.

This perhaps crude dichotomy conceals a host of complexities and subtleties but it, nevertheless, encapsulates well enough the ethical context within which business is conducted. Moral theory reflects in important ways the ethics of ordinary life for which competing theories try to account. Business ethics should be about the ethics which most people are familiar with through practice and experience. The special circumstances of business may produce moral conundrums that people are unlikely to come across in ordinary life but the values and principles that are used for the resolution are not substantially different from conventional ethics.

It is a somewhat misleading view of business ethics to see it as a simple application of one or the other of these moral philosophies, deontology and teleology, to particular problems. The practice of business, like any other social activity, generates rules which are not easily described in the conventional language of moral philosophy. The important point here is that business ethics involves economics and although that discipline may claim to be value-free, it has much to offer moral discussions of business. Business undeniably is about worldly success, normally measured in monetary terms. The usefulness of economics is that it describes coherently the constraints to which human action is subject. As we shall see, some of the unrealism, indeed, otherworldliness, of some versions of business ethics is in need of the reminders from economics about

17

scarcity, the almost infinite range of human wants and the more or less immutable 'laws' that govern human behaviour.

The teleological theory most relevant here is utilitarianism: that ethical doctrine which evaluates states of affairs in terms of happiness, welfare, well-being or some other phenomenon that relates to identifiable satisfactions.[2] There are teleological doctrines that locate intrinsic value in other things than sensuous experience – for example, self-realization or some Aristotelian notion of virtue – but they make only fleeting appearances in the literature of business ethics.

Deontological doctrines are best represented by justice: there are certain moral rules of fairness which are so compelling that our adherence to them overrides all other considerations. They are necessary side-constraints on action. Although utilitarians always try to incorporate the rules of justice (fair dealing, giving each person his due, the obligatory nature of promises, and so on) into a comprehensive moral calculus by arguing that they are conducive to overall utility, it is not difficult to see how conflicts can arise between the demands of justice and the dictates of utility. Perhaps it was immoral to trade with apartheid South Africa (because it was an unjust regime) but if it could be shown that everyone was made worse off by a ban, the blacks suffering worst of all, then such a prohibition would be unacceptable by the principle of utility. Many people quite plausibly argued just that. In contrast, the deontologist discounts consequences (although it is a rare theorist who discounts them entirely) in her evaluations and therefore she will have good reasons for condemning such trade. She would argue that it is simply unethical to trade with a regime which denies a fundamental equality, irrespective of the utility gains that might result from such commerce.

Deontological ethics comes into play in business when questions of the entitlement to particular rewards from business activity arise. Is the insider dealer morally entitled to his profits, even though his actions push the capital market towards equilibrium and bring about a correct valuation of assets? Obviously problems of ownership arise here and these cannot be settled conclusively, if at all, by utilitarian considerations alone. The market may make everybody better off, but is its distribution of wealth fair? Do the demands for a 'level playing field' in the securities market exemplify equality of opportunity or do they smuggle in the much more contestable moral notion of equality of outcome?

It should be clear that utilitarianism is not the only ethics relevant to business activity, that commerce is not merely to be evaluated in terms of a calculus of pleasures and pains. Yet it is its most plausible rationale. Since commerce is an activity that responds to people's desires, it seems the ideal candidate for favourable evaluation by a moral doctrine that exclusively understands good and bad in terms of want-satisfaction. However, utilitarianism is itself a complex doctrine, the meaning of which is constantly in dispute, and its prescriptions are not always determinate. It sometimes seems to offend against deeply-held moral beliefs.

It bears a superficial similarity to the Mandevillian doctrine mentioned earlier: that business does not rest upon virtue but on self-interest and that the latter motivation is validated morally (if at all) by the fact that it generates beneficial outcomes. Although there is more than a trace of Mandevillianism in 'Invisible Hand' versions of utilitarianism, Mandevillianism itself has not secured a respectable niche in business ethics: utilitarianism proper, however, has. It is a comprehensive ethical doctrine and (unlike the 'amoral business' view) has implications at the macro and micro levels of business activity which can and do run counter to the egoism and amoralism implied in *The Fable of the Bees*. Business may be said to generate practical rules which, although they may have an ultimate utilitarian justification, are inconsistent with, and would condemn, egoism. The rules for the self-regulation of business activities would be of this type. These rules, which are designed to restrain immediate gratification, are nevertheless in the long-run interests of transactors, for if they do not restrain themselves, government regulation, and the opprobrium of the public, are more likely to occur. It is not clear how Mandevillianism (or any 'greed is good' business doctrine) could explain the utilitarian necessity for self-restraint. Pure egoism is self-destructive, a properly-understood consequentialism or utilitarianism is not. The only question is: how such restraint can be generated given the motivations that must govern successful business?

Utilitarianism supposes that actions are to be evaluated solely in terms of how much they contribute to the well-being or happiness of a community: rules, conventions and orthodox moral principles have a provisional value only, and are subordinate to the compelling imperative to maximize happiness. In the work of the doctrine's founders, notably Jeremy Bentham (1748–1832),[3] happiness could be calibrated in discrete units of pleasure, the pursuit of which, it was alleged, was the sole purpose of human endeavour. Pleasure was assumed to be as tangible as heat and cold, and a 'hedonic' calculus was proposed for evaluating actions which would be as accurate in the measurement of pleasure as a thermometer is for recording temperature. Two further assumptions are made by Benthamite utilitarians: every person is the best judge of his or her own interest, and each person's interests must be taken into account in the overall calculation of utility. The former requirement rules out paternalism and the latter is a vague and ambiguous commitment to a notion of equality of consideration. It should be noted that there is only a contingent (though some would say, easily demonstrable) connection between the maximization of social utility and the existence of the private enterprise, commercial order.

Because of the requirement to take everyone's interests into account, and to perform intricate (and some would say, impossible) calculations as to the social effects of alternative courses of action, utilitarianism imposes controversial and almost always conflicting duties upon agents. Thus a utilitarian-minded management of a corporation would, in plant relocation decisions, have to take into account the interests of a community whose residents had 'invested' in the firm, the interests of the shareholders who would benefit from efficiency, those in another community who might be badly in need of employment, and so on. These are extraordinarily difficult calculations; great enough, critics of an business ethics would say, to negate the very possibility of a 'social audit' for business derived from utilitarian considerations alone.

A special difficulty is the requirement of making interpersonal comparisons of utility. This necessitates the observer saying by how much an action affects particular persons. Can great gains for some outweigh the minor losses of (perhaps) a minority? Of course, we make rough and ready judgements of this type in our everyday lives, and the morally-minded business agent does so constantly, but the credibility of such judgements has always been questioned. They are ruled out by a strict deontology.

Because of the difficulty of measuring pleasure, and of the making of interpersonal comparisons of utility, contemporary economists tend to limit their welfare judgements to that implied in the 'Pareto principle' (named after the Italian economist and social theorist, Vilfredo Pareto): this holds that it is only possible to speak of a welfare improvement when an action (for example, a two-person exchange) makes (at least) one person better off without making anybody else worse off.[4] Although it rests on a similar view of human motivation to utilitarianism, it is in theory much weaker. Since it precludes interpersonal comparisons of utilities, it must remain silent on actions that although generally beneficial, harm at least one person, however minutely. Almost all business decisions adversely affect some people to a degree.

Unfortunately, the Pareto principle is not much help in the typical business problems. Operating on a restricted notion of harm, a Paretian could maintain that untrammelled markets, in the absence of externalities, do maximize social welfare in the sense described. But the operation of market forces, which generate never-ending change and uncertainty, leaves many people who can claim to be 'harmed'. A successful innovator may drive rivals out of business but can they be said to be harmed and therefore deserving of compensation? This may seem implausible but some business ethics writers have implied as much. But the Pareto principle itself is too weak ethically to give any firm guidance in this vexed area. It has little use in the texts of business ethics: except perhaps at the macro level, in the overall justification of the market system. At the micro level, in the justification of particular business decisions, harm itself appears to be a contestable concept. Also, a more generous interpretation of the Pareto principle might require each transactor to be fully informed of all possible facts and circumstances of economic life. But this could rule out as 'inefficient' (or exploitative) many otherwise acceptable exchanges.

Thus despite the problems inherent in the notion of pleasure, and the possibly insuperable difficulties of aggregation, the major elements of utilitarianism have survived. Whether it is pleasure that ought to be maximized, or the superficially more tractable notion of preferences,[5] it is always to the consequences of action that moral appeal is made, and the restraints imposed by moral and conventional rules are acceptable only if they are conducive to good outcomes, however these are understood. Utilitarianism does not necessarily justify the capitalist system: indeed, it might well validate constant interventions in search of improvements in cases where suffering might appear to be avoidable. Such a superficially benign doctrine, one exclusively addressed to human well-being and unencumbered by possibly archaic rules, has not surprisingly appealed to governments and the owners and managers of business enterprises. The doctrine is given a greater appeal when compensation is paid to losers in the competitive process or to those who are victims of technological progress or changes in the terms of trade. Farmers throughout history have managed successfully to persuade governments that they should be immune from the adverse effects of economics. Victims of necessary industrial change have used a similar strategy; and owners of enterprises that generate change are often expected to pay compensation to the losers.

Utilitarian considerations are sometimes present in decision-making in business when cost–benefit analysis is used. It is especially relevant to product safety. A corporation will often take a controversial decision on the basis of a measure of the benefits of the product, taking into account the interests of consumers, stockholders and employees, compared to the costs of safety requirements. Safety considerations alone cannot be decisive, it is claimed, since no product can be perfectly safe and utility gains will be forgone because of the probably excessive costs involved in the pursuit of an unattainable ideal of a perfectly harmless product.[6] Often the costs of potential litigation in civil actions will be included in the final calculations, and it is this factor that can make corporations vulnerable to the charge of cynicism. As will be shown in the next chapter, the Ford Motor Company was involved in a famous case that involved the morally dubious use of cost–benefit analysis.

Deontological theories therefore claim that there should be constraints on human action that defeat all claims derived from utility. In fact, it is maintained that the moral autonomy of the individual is attenuated to the extent that his or her judgements are tainted by the thought of any consideration of satisfactions or beneficial consequences. In the history of moral philosophy there has been a variety of foundations for the apparent austerity of deontological ethics but for our purposes a brief indication of this style of thinking is all that is required.

In principle, deontological ethics rests on the claim that the right is prior to the good; that certain rules and practices, normally those that honour the integrity of the individual and encapsulate universal notions of justice, truth-telling and promise-keeping and so on, take precedence over well-being. In fact, the rules of the French stock market (the Bourse), are called '*les principes des deontologies*'. It is these considerations that are brought to bear most heavily on businessmen engaged in the pursuit of profit.

At the heart of deontological ethics is an argument about the sanctity of the person: that no amount of goodness generated by an action can justify any violation of individual rights. This moral axiom (the Categorical Imperative) is expressed in a famous sentence by Immanuel Kant: 'Act so that you treat humanity, whether in your own person or in that of another, always as an end and never as a means only.'[7] This should not be misunderstood. It does not prohibit individuals using each other as a means to certain ends; almost all human interactions involve just this. The business system, which is a complex network of individuals relationships that permit the using of some people's skills and endowments for other people's ends, would be impossible if the Kantian principle were interpreted in the restrictive way. What the injunction does forbid, however, is people being used *merely* as a means for the gratification of others: as the breach of a promise would, or the failure to disclose vital information prior to a purchase or an agreement. These actions involve deception and possibly fraud. A proper interpretation of the Kantian principle encourages reciprocity and forbids exploitation. Controversy arises, however, over what the doctrine requires in particular cases. Should advertisers tell the *whole* truth about a product? Surely not. Do securities markets require perfect information on the part of all transactors? An impossible demand which if seriously followed would make such markets redundant. Successful business is ethical when it observes the morality of everyday life which often includes rules that are not strictly utilitarian; but they are not the rules of a monastery. The rules of everyday life are a better guide to conduct in business than the speculations of abstract philosophers; though the latter can provide some sort of order and coherence to the whole system.

It might superficially seem that deontological ethics would be hostile to business; that an activity driven by the profit motive and concerned primarily with the gratification of desires would fall short of the standards of the right. But this is not necessarily so, for deontological ethics is concerned only with the constraints that should obtain in whatever activity human beings engage in. A properly conducted business arrangement indeed exemplifies much of the deontological argument, especially in its emphasis on the obligatory nature of contracts and its recognition of the fact that each party is the author of his or her own actions. Indeed, many of those conventional rules that govern business, although they are often given a rule-utilitarian justification in the claim that business could not work without them, could just as easily be interpreted as constraints on action which have an intrinsic moral value. But it has to be conceded that deontological rules occupy a small (though important) place in the moral vocabulary of business and the nature of the activity makes the constraints they impose vulnerable to rule-breakers and opportunists.

JUST BUSINESS

It is on the question of justice that many questions in the ethics of business turn; and the competing appraisals of both the business system and the behaviour of agents within it turn on widely divergent accounts of this crucial concept. It is important to remember that when people talk of the justice or injustice of business, profit and so on they have different exemplars of the concept in mind so that it rarely functions as a kind of Archimedean point against which competing claims can be evaluated. Nevertheless, it is true that the appeal to *social* justice which is often made by anti-business philosophers is an appeal to the most contested of moral concepts, and one which often bears only a remote resemblance to the original meaning of justice.[8] It is also important to note that principles of social or distributive justice have little connection with business ethics: they are properly the concern of social philosophy. But unfortunately they are implicitly alluded to when complaints are made about some of the vast earnings that are occasionally made in business and when employers are censured for pursuing allegedly 'unjust' hiring policies at the workplace in relation to women and racial minorities.

The concept of justice that is most conducive to the business enterprise is one that is limited to the rules of fairness that ought to govern all human relationships: honouring promises, respecting the rights of justly acquired property (either through labour, exchange or gifts) and giving each person his or her due. It might be more accurately called procedural justice. It is not concerned with the 'outcome' of an economic process – that is, the particular distribution of income and wealth that is generated by trade – but with the rules that govern it and the behaviour of individuals under those rules. Claims of injustice relate only to the intentional actions of persons under fair rules. It would be illegitimate, therefore, to condemn inegalitarian distributions of income and wealth that emanate from the following of fair rules as 'unjust'. Adam Smith argued that: 'Mere justice is, our upon most occasions but a negative virtue, and only hinders us from hurting our neighbour.'[9] Contemporary proponents of capitalism, such as Hayek,[10] Friedman[11] and Nozick,[12] have added only sophistication to this fundamental proposition. Smith, and others, may have thought that these rules were morally sparse, and not descriptive of the 'good' society, but they were all that commerce required. They are often likened to the 'rules of grammar', the following of which may not generate beautiful prose but it is essential for communication.

It is a position that can have either a utilitarian or a deontological rationale. The utilitarian argues that to operate at maximum efficiency a market requires inequality of factor reward and that to sanction interference with this process by the invocation of abstract, external principles based on, for example (moral) desert or need, simply leads to the misallocation of resources. The rules of negative justice are simply those basic procedural devices that are required to make the market work efficiently, to guarantee security for property and contract and to provide a framework of predictability for transactors.

However, this rather simplistic utilitarianism is vulnerable to criticism when it is used to validate existing business practices. It is not entirely clear that the (sometimes) vast profits that are achieved in business, especially in the securities market, are required for the efficient working of the system. Market socialists have claimed, in a variety of complex schemes, that the efficiency properties of free-exchange systems, and the liberty that markets grant to individual agents, can be reproduced without the excess profits and other imperfections that are said to characterize capitalist economies. They claim that a market system could work efficiently with a wider conception of justice than that used by Adam Smith and his modern epigones.

However, it is not solely utilitarianism that sustains the theory of negative rules of justice: most writers in the free-market tradition implicitly allude to the intrinsic value of fair rules. Hayek,[13] for example, argues that socialism cannot be implemented without disrupting the rules of justice. The imposition of a rational plan can, he claims, come about only by the issuing of particular commands which will undermine the universality of just rules. Furthermore, no matter how inegalitarian the outcomes of a market may be, they cannot be regarded as unjust because, in his view, injustice can only be the result of the intentional acts of responsible agents: the market, of course, is an impersonal, anonymous process. Again, Nozick, in a famous argument,[14] argued that the maintenance of a preconceived pattern of distribution, even if its morality could be agreed upon, would involve an unacceptable interference with people's choices, the undermining of the rule of law, and the use of individuals on behalf of collective purposes. However, what makes these views vulnerable to moral condemnation is that they exclude reference to desert or worth in the understanding of economic justice; in fact inheritances or sheer luck are sources of just entitlement as long as the rewards are achieved within the rules.

The critics of the capitalist system who use arguments derived from justice have a much more substantive concept in mind; they are less concerned about questions of efficiency anyway. Much of their argument derives from the deontological claim that the exchange system (and its associated framework of law and private property) exploits workers: their autonomy to pursue their own ends is badly compromised by the wage-relationship, the existence of profit means that they do not receive the full value created by their labour, and the private owner makes little or no contribution to output (since he merely allows his capital to be used, his role is replaceable by the state). Thus concepts such as desert and need become highly relevant to the distributional questions that are repeatedly asked of capitalist orders.

Although most questions of justice in relation to business are raised at the macro level, problems can arise at the level of the individual enterprise. To what extent is a corporation under an obligation to practise 'affirmative action' in its hiring policies? Does not this lead to a conflict between efficiency and justice? Indeed, is not such a policy itself unjust? In most cases there is also the problem of a conflict between the duties that a management owes to its shareholders and the demands of social justice that are prescribed in much of business ethics. As I shall show, these problems are exacerbated when the rules of negative justice are expanded into a more substantive social doctrine. The injunctions of the protean doctrine of social justice are too vague, multifarious and incoherent to offer a precise guidance for individuals, even if it could be agreed that the corporation and other business enterprises were under some obligation to act justly in the wider sense. None of this, of course, implies that the business imperative for management to safeguard the interests of shareholders, employees and consumers releases it from the obligation that everyone has to observe rules of fair play. But there is a difference between an enterprise being under a moral duty and its being under a social duty.

ARM'S LENGTH MORALITY AND MINIMALIST ETHICS

It is because of the difficulty of the direct application of moral principles to commercial life that an approach to business ethics has to take account of the circumstances of business enterprise. Commerce cannot require saint-like behaviour because we are not all saints (and if we were, to whom would we be saintly and what are the duties that saintliness implies?). The whole tradition of market economics, which maintains that good, utilitarian consequences occur through spontaneous processes irrespective of the moral motives of the agents, is still an important starting point for business ethics. It is a kind of utility qualified by deontological rules: indeed Smith's *The Theory of Moral Sentiments* is not so much a celebration of utilitarian ethics as a description of those rules of conduct that we apply to everyday conduct because they are felt to be 'right'. The structure of business ethics must not be about the foundations of 'rightness' but about the role of rules as restraints on egoistic actions in basically anonymous market orders. I shall later call this 'arms's-length morality'. It may today have more resonance in Anglo-American economies than other capitalist regimes but its value will be more appreciated as trade becomes globalized.

It is somewhat far-fetched to imagine that the actions of business agents should be directly guided by the kind of philosophical principles outlined above. These principles are best understood as criteria by which the actions of individuals are evaluated retrospectively by external observers. They are, if anything, ways of appraising the whole of business, and their application to particular cases may be hard to discern. Indeed, the disputes in business ethics themselves are not normally about whether, for example, utility is the only sustainable ethic but whether a particular action would enhance the well-being of the business enterprise. Again, the relevance of justice to commerce is not, surely, because some new distributive criteria may be discovered there but to understand if some particular action was fair or unfair by conventionally accepted standards of right conduct. The difficulty is that these standards have been made infinitely contestable by ethics and political philosophy. Thus in the securities market the sometimes vast earnings that occur are condemnable as unjust, irrespective of the fact that these may have been achieved fairly, because they do not appear to be the outcomes of productive effort, or because some have an unfair (normally informational) advantage over others. Business ethics is special only in the sense that particular commercial practices and organizations (especially the corporation) may make some moral decisions significantly different from everyday ones; although the rules that govern them are not so far removed from conventional ethics.

In many areas of business life, the standards and values of the market, which are broadly utilitarian, conflict with public morality. The latter has strong deontological elements: some actions are just not 'right', whatever the 'goodness' of the consequences that they bring about. This problem is compounded by the fact that public standards of morality are not only disputable in their application to particular cases but also they are relative to particular communities. For example, 'bribery' in business is condemnable in Western capitalist economies but may be an integral part of social and business life in some communities. Can the deontologically-based prohibition of it be applied incontrovertibly to international trade? The Lockheed bribery scandal of the mid-1970s is the *locus classicus* here.[15] The executives of the corporation bribed Japanese officials to secure a contract that (allegedly) 'saved' the investment of the stockholders and the jobs of the employees. However, some people would say that the bribery was simply wrong, despite the utility gains it produced. The problem is that in Japanese society such action is not thought to be morally wrong (or even as 'bribery'). What are companies to do in such circumstances? Abstract moral philosophy is not much help, though an ethics more closely related to the practice of business may be.

The reason for the failure of abstract ethics to give definitive answers is that the morality of business is comprised of a plurality of potentially

conflicting principles, an unstable amalgam of possibly competing practices and maxims. But business itself does not seem the type of activity
appropriate for evaluation by rationalistic ethics. It is at best the ethics
of self-interest, sanitized by the utilitarian claim that decentralized economic action does on the whole lead to better results for the anonymous
public, and tempered by the restraints that deontological principles (im-
precise though they are) impose on egoism. The notions of trust and
honesty are relevant here: although a short-term gain could be achieved
by their breach they are essential for the activity of business in the aggregate.

In an important sense, business morality does differ from the morality
of the family or that of small, closely knit communities. In these phenomena, ordinary egoistic action is restrained by principles of solidarity
which are clearly understood and which can secure almost unanimous
agreement: they are reinforced by the close proximity of the human
agents involved. But Anglo-American business morality is not like this,
although some business ethicists would seem to want to make it so.

The obligations of family members are not 'self-assumed' (they are
for the most part involuntary) while in business they clearly are: they
are the voluntary obligations created primarily by contractual arrangements between strangers to advance their interests. There is no escaping
this and a business ethics that underestimates it will (if 'legislated',
as it frequently tends to become) systematically undermine the commercial enterprise. Of course, the formal agreements between individuals in basically anonymous markets have to be underwritten by
moral rules and conventions which are not 'assumed' by agents, otherwise business would be uncertain. But they are of a minimalist kind,
and in many ways are self-enforcing. What this approach does imply
is that extreme caution, if not outright scepticism, should be exercised in the face of demands that business agents should be encouraged or compelled to conform to values that emanate from outside the
business relationship. Normally these extra-business values come from
highly contestable social and political philosophies. Business is a moral
enterprise that depends upon trust and honesty for its validity rather
than the pursuit of all-embracing social goals, about which there
can be little agreement. Indeed it would be hubristic for business
agents to suppose that they know what these are; that they can know
what is good for the community. It is also a mistake to suppose that
business practices and mores can be easily transported across cultural boundaries. Critics of Anglo-American business all too often
assume that the intimacy of communitarian business cultures can be

costlessly adopted for the more impersonal worlds of Wall Street and the City of London.

Business relationships in Western societies are therefore conducted at arm's length; the participants do not in the main know each other and therefore can have no other duty than to respect their interests and the rules under which they exchange. Using this elementary model I shall cast doubt upon the possibility of 'contracts' between business and society[16] since this presupposes that society can be represented as a determinate agent with a well-ordered and consistent hierarchy of values suitable for the exchange relationship. Again, attempts to mimic the business practices of more intimate, communal societies such as Japan's may not only be detrimental to Western business, but also fatal to its morality. In fact, Western society consists of a multiplicity of conflicting values to be realized and demands which press for satisfaction. I shall show that a properly structured set of legal and moral rules, emanating the business enterprise itself, may very well be the only means for 'solving' problems raised by a more activist business ethics.

Western morality has an advantage over its rivals that derives from its *universalism*. The rules which apply to it are indifferent to race, religion, nationality and any other feature that is merely contingent. The pursuit of profit is a great solvent of cultural differences and reconciler of divergent ways of life. Business agents are held together by rules that enable them to pursue their self-chosen goals and each actor has the right to choose whatever business method he likes as long as he remains within these constraints. In more intimate business relationships, outsiders seem not to enjoy the same protection of rules. This is why there are probably more serious business scandals in Japan than on Wall Street.[17] Those that come from outside the groups are treated very differently from insiders. There are few restraints that operate on the members of intimate organizations and groups when they deal with strangers.

It should also be noted that the more successful a business becomes in its fundamental aim, to provide cheap and reliable products through competition for the consumer (surely a moral enterprise in itself), the less 'fat' there will be for other activities, for example, charitable donations to worthy causes. Ironically: only monopolies, because of their 'immoral' and socially inefficient rents, will be able to comply with the more ambitious demands made by some business ethicists.

This suggested restriction of business ethics to the conduct of agents under rules appropriate to the commercial order, and expressed doubt about the wider social obligations of business that have been urged by business ethicists, nevertheless leaves a host of ethical problems. In

Britain and the USA the complaints and scandals that occur in commerce are precisely about breaches of what I have called minimalist rules. It is also the case that these rules do not apply solely to large-scale conglomerates. For although the moral indiscretions there are, for obvious reasons, likely to attract publicity, unethical conduct can occur in any relationship between strangers that is powered by self-interest. As the prominent US business ethicists Robert Soloman and Karen Hansen once pointed out: 'There is no reason to suppose that Mom and Pop's grocery store is any more moral than IBM.'[18]

A dominating principle inherent in this approach is the concept of *harm*. The most compelling of the negative obligations applicable to business is the injunction to refrain from damaging the interests of the trading partner: the crucial moral feature of the commercial order is voluntariness and it can be safely assumed that individuals do not voluntarily submit to actions that harm their interests. This is not to say that harm is the only consideration in the evaluation of business. An action may be adjudged right or wrong even if no one is harmed by it; for example, sometimes all people may gain in the long run from an action which was originally fraudulent. But business could not go on without this minimum condition of non-harm being met. The strict prohibition of harm is the most important of the side-constraints on self-interested action and it is this that must constitute the primary element in a viable business ethics.

The difficulties with the notion of harm are exemplified in the debate about 'victimless crimes'; for many critics of the over-moralization of business maintain that the current legal and moral persecution of insider trading in the stock market invokes precisely that. As we shall see, straightforward utilitarian and efficiency principles might well sanction insider trading, yet people feel uneasy about it: largely, I suspect, because they are distressed by the particular distribution of rewards that comes from it. However, as we shall see, (Chapter 5) the question of harm in insider dealing is an extremely complex one. The minimalist conception of justice in the sense of fair rules (in which the 'no harm' principle occupies pride of place) clashes with certain deeply held and probably communally-based values of desert and merit. Even within the minimalist view, there may be disputes about what is or is not a fair contest, irrespective of the question of harm. The difficulty of identifying victims of alleged immoral practice has led some business ethicists to claim that, irrespective of the absence of injured individuals, the business community as a whole has been harmed, though this is disputable. It is an example of the intrusion of collectivist notions in what is basically an individualistic activity. The assumption of these ideas for the evaluation of business practice ends to corrode the concept of individual responsibility for action which is integral to the Western moral tradition. I shall deal with this problem more fully in the next chapter.

There are other equally important problems relating to the harm principle. Just as there are problems of identifying the victims of actions commonly held to be wrong, there are disputes about the perpetrators of the wrong. Since business largely takes place through corporations which have a technical legal personality, and since commerce has strong features of a collaborative enterprise, it is often difficult to locate exactly who is responsible for a wrong. The minimalist wants to locate moral responsibility for action in individual biological persons: they are the only agents, it is claimed, who can act with intent, an essential condition for legal and moral responsibility. Yet there has been a tendency, in the USA especially, to make corporations legally liable for criminal wrongs, as if a corporate agency were capable of a *mens rea* (guilty mind). The process began with the famous (but ultimately unsuccessful) prosecution of the Ford Motor Corporation for reckless homicide because of its failure to correct known faults in the Pinto car. The nearest example in Britain was the prosecution of the P&O company for corporate manslaughter over the Zeebrugge ferry disaster. What was theoretically significant about this last case was the fact that the prosecution was allowed to go ahead: not the final result, which was an acquittal of the corporation, as represented by its directors, by the judge.

The moral problem raised by these cases is not so much the possibility that the prosecution of corporate bodies for criminal acts may be used to shield individuals from legal liability (in cases of corporate crimes the common law requires that culpable individuals are prosecuted as well) but the meaningfulness of the claim that corporations can be treated as if they were moral persons. Arm's-length business morality requires that praise and blame be attributed to identifiable, biological persons who are the only agents who can be said to be causally responsible for actions. A corporation is formally identified through its owners, the shareholders. Although they are in normal circumstances remote from the alleged wrong, it is they who have to pay the costs flowing from the wrong if the corporation is convicted of a crime.

I shall point out later the disturbing implications for business ethics that this growing legal phenomenon has. At this stage it is sufficient to say that it represents a dramatic departure from the individualism associated with arm's-length morality: it substitutes collective for individual responsibility and hence blurs lines of moral accountability. It may even

be said to replace justice with vengeance. From a strictly utilitarian position, corporations might be deterred from economically worthwhile
activity if their owners knew that they were to be liable for every action of
individual employees. It would make the 'monitoring' of agents by company owners extremely costly. Hence, many of the obvious economic
advantages of the corporate form of organization would be forgone.

Arm's-length morality is concerned with agents exchanging properties for their well-being, and exploiting whatever assets they might have
in a rule-governed context in which rights are clearly specified. Ethical
problems normally arise in those grey areas where property rights are in
dispute and where the effects of business on third parties are neither
clear nor quantifiable. This becomes especially important in the corporate form of organization where the right to exclusive use of assets, especially knowledge, is indeterminate. Much of the dispute over insider
trading arises from the doubt as to whether a company employee has the
'right' to use information for her own share purchases and sales: it is always knowledge which she has not disclosed to the company's owners
(the stockholders). Is this a form of theft?

A most important feature of arm's-length morality is the emphasis it
places upon individuals as responsible, independent and autonomous
agents; whether they are consumers, traders or other transactors in voluntary market relationships. It makes the somewhat ambitious claim
that the market and the conventional legal system 'filter out' many of
the problems identified by the more critical business ethicists. Hence
arm's-length morality contains a moral bias toward *caveat emptor* in all
of its manifestations, and a distrust of paternalism. Since much of business ethics consists of injunctions to government to provide protective
services to persons whom, it is maintain, would be helpless against,
among others, corporations and advertisers, it is often in conflict with
the arm's-length tradition. It is *ipso facto* dissatisfied with the effectiveness of market mechanisms as a corrective to perceived moral wrongs
committed by business personnel. It wishes to provide other remedies
than those contained within civil and criminal law and the exchange
system itself. It is, of course, true that we must have some regulations in
the business world, especially in product safety, in financial markets and
in the environment, precisely because the slowness of common law and
the market in correcting wrongs in these areas means that many people
would be harmed unnecessarily. The need for such regulations would be
reduced, however, if business could effectively regulate itself. It would
also be less required if a traditional liberal notion of personal responsibility for action were to be revived. No consumer, or any other economic

agent, can be protected against the vicissitudes of economic life but the desire to hold corporations responsible for every misfortune has become a feature of some business ethics.

THE DIFFICULTIES OF SELF-RESTRAINT

The possibility of business regulating itself independently of government, in the way that other professions, such as law and medicine, have through established and enforced codes of ethics, seems (superficially at least) to be remote. This is so, despite the fact that, as suggested above, it would be in the business community's self-interest to do so. The reason is that such co-operative activity comes up against a familiar problem in social theory – the 'public good' trap (or, in the technical literature, the 'Prisoner's Dilemma').[19] Put simply, this means that cooperative activity, which would be to the benefit of rational, self-interested agents, is unlikely to be forthcoming through the voluntary action of the same agents, since however well-motivated each person might be he cannot be sure that the others will be so reliable.

The existence of this phenomenon creates real dilemmas for business. A familiar example is the problem of pollution. The business community has been assailed by ethicists for not taking account of the environment in its profit-maximizing activities: a proper audit would therefore include the costs imposed on third parties. Yet pollution cannot be wholly bad, for the activity that generates it is productive of jobs and lower prices for consumers. It cannot be assumed that the efficiency solutions imposed by the state produce an appropriate balance between, on the one hand, productivity, employment and lower costs, and on the other, environmental protection. Yet if possibly counter-productive regulation is to be forestalled, business would have to behave in a more co-operative manner. Is this precluded by the omnipresence of self-interest? The problems of co-operation in business can be explicated by a brief discussion of game theory.

In the Prisoner's Dilemma 'game' two suspects, Smith and Jones, are questioned separately by an interrogator about a robbery they have committed. If they both remain silent they will face a less serious charge carrying a short prison sentence of three years; if they both confess to the serious offence they will get 10 years each; if one, for example, Smith, confesses and implicates Jones (who remains silent) in the serious offence, Smith will get off scot free but Jones will receive a punitive sentence of 12 years. The best co-operative outcome, that is the outcome which involves the minimum combined prison sentence (a total of six years), would require both prisoners to remain silent. However, since they cannot trust one another, rationality dictates that they confess, hoping to implicate the other in order to get the reduced sentence. The interrogator has so arranged the 'payoffs' that whatever strategy is selected by Jones, it is better for Smith to confess, and vice versa. Confession is the 'dominant' strategy for both. The problem is shown in the accompanying table, which illustrates all possible outcomes. Even if the prisoners could communicate, each could not be sure the other would co-operate. There is no possibility of the build-up of trust.

		Smith's choices	
		Silence	*Confession*
	Silence	Cell 1 3, 3	Cell 4 12, 0
Jones's choices	*Confession*	Cell 1 0, 12	Cell 3 10, 10

Figure 2.1   The Prisoner's Dilemma

The application of this arcane argument to business is actually quite straightforward. Business agents are normally driven by self-interest and this according to conventional market theory is socially beneficial. However, on some occasions it may be harmful to the agents themselves; a measure of co-operation is therefore required and this might be impossible under the conventional assumptions of market theory. Business agents would clearly gain if they could agree to observe common moral standards, and behave 'responsibly', since this would reduce or even eliminate heavy and profit-reducing government regulation. However, in the anonymous world of Western commerce can agents be relied upon to keep to voluntary agreements? All may be well-motivated but they lack the assurance which is required for co-operation to occur. What is needed here is, of course, that elusive quality of *trust*.

An example is the recent Clean Air Act passed by the US Congress in 1990. It is conceded that this will impose heavy costs on industry, costs that will ultimately be passed on to the public in the form of higher prices, fewer jobs (temporarily) and lower returns to stockholders. What cannot be known is whether the gains the community secures in the way of environmental protection exceed the costs measured in orthodox business terms. Many observers think that they will not but, however that may be, is it likely that the business community could behave with the kind of self-restraint which is required for it to resist such legislation? There have been other examples of environmental legislation that involve the same problem. It is certainly the fact of 'large numbers' that makes co-operation between business agents unlikely.

Again, it is possible that the self-enforced 'rules of the game' in the financial world would have been sufficient to restrain those practices – insider dealing, the fixing of share prices and so on – which seem to be an affront to widely-held conceptions of justice? People think not, hence the rise of excessive regulation, which has in fact hampered the efficiency of these markets and, as we shall see below, brought threats to the rule of law. In Britain, even with the Financial Services Act of 1986, the City of London is to some extent self-regulating. However, the code of rules under which it operates is regarded as inadequate by critics, who recommend that it should be replaced by something akin to the more coercive US model. The presence of self-interest in business makes its agents appear morally feeble and hence vulnerable to intervention. Business self-restraint, which would benefit all agents, is perhaps a type of public good which it is in no one person's interest to generate.

However, it should not be assumed that rules of restraint for business could not develop spontaneously and hence preclude the need for often heavy-handed state intervention. Although the rules of commerce require everyone to observe them if they are to be effective, they are not quite like the conventional public goods. They are co-ordination rules which make transactions smooth and efficient over an extended period of time. Violators of rules can be identified and punished through the 'tit-for-tat' strategy,[20] and the success in co-ordinating commercial activities which rules achieve leads to their spread from small to large groups. Unlike the classic Prisoner's Dilemma, where the game is played only once and self-interested agents have an incentive to defect from agreements, commerce is an 'iterated' (or repeated) game which, despite being competitive, still depends on a certain amount of voluntary co-operation. It is because the business game is played almost endlessly that agents have an incentive to co-operate voluntarily under informal rules. An evolutionary process[21] can gradually weed out non-cooperators: nobody will trade with rule-breakers.

In fact, the rules of commerce developed out of medieval fairs in precisely this voluntary manner.[22] That such rules have developed is a tribute to the fecundity of the concept of 'economic man', for the adoption of them does not depend on a change from self-interest to altruism but on the promotion of an enlightened self-interest; it is an historical fact that the rules of commerce developed in advance of the state. Indeed, in the chaotic world of post-Soviet Russia, where the state's law is unreliable, and often unenforceable, business agents are developing their own rules of conduct.[23] Of course, things may get so bad that a genuine Prisoner's Dilemma comes about which requires an all-powerful sovereign for its solution.

In certain areas business agents may be confronted with what look like genuine Prisoner's Dilemmas, where there is little incentive to co-operate. As already mentioned, the environment is an obvious example because normally no one agent is specifically responsible for adverse effects on society; it is the *additional* polluter who causes the problem, and he cannot be readily identified. Although business agents would undoubtedly gain in the long run if they exercised restraint, there are circumstances where self-interest and moral or social duty do not coincide. But even here, as we shall see, the solution to the problem is not always state control. As has often been demonstrated, moral restraints, when strengthened by a property rights system that encourages socially responsible behaviour (for example, the issuing of pollution 'permits', see below, Chapter 7), may obviate the need for what is almost certainly efficiency-reducing state regulation.

Apart from in obvious examples of 'one-shot' Prisoner's Dilemmas (a game that is played only once so that trust cannot be built up), the business community can develop rules of self-restraint which are in its long-term interest. Indeed, historically it did. The rules of the City of London were quite effective in regulating the securities market before the rash of legislation that has emerged in the last 20 years. There is no real evidence that the latter has reduced the number of scandals. The interesting question is: why has such excessive regulation occurred in all aspects of business life? It does partly reflect a failure of self-regulation on the part of business, or the reluctance by politicians to allow it to develop, but it is also a response to the distrust which many people still feel for commerce (at least in comparison to the conventional professions): scepticism which has been powered by certain intellectual developments in the Western world. We shall explore some of these problems in relation to the corporation in the next two chapters.

3 The Corporation

In its economic manifestation at least, the concept of the corporation leads a shadowy existence and has to some writers a morally ambiguous biography. It is treated as an object of opprobrium by those opposed to a free economy who can exploit and have exploited a superficial tension between its existence and the moral premises on which that system is conventionally founded, and it is looked on with some scepticism even by some who are predisposed to defend capitalism.

To those favourably inclined towards individualism, private property and the rule of law, it appears as a complex phenomenon whose rationale has been difficult to explain. Certainly it is at least plausible to maintain that the contemporary capitalist order, characterized as it is by large conglomerations of wealth and economic power that appear to stand in a curious midway position between the individual and the state, and to whom it is difficult to apply the conventional liberal notion of personal responsibility for action, seems some way removed from the world of decentralized traders described in Adam Smith's *The Wealth of Nations.*

The realm of the corporation, with its diversified activities and 'plan-like' behaviour, seems far removed from *catallactics*,[1] that spontaneous activity in which decentralized individuals co-ordinate their activities in some ignorance of any data that lie beyond their *immediate* concern. Again, in pure catallactics, these very same individuals exchange their rights and property without the protection of that carapace of limited liability (and other legal 'privileges') that are said to shield the modern corporation from those vicissitudes of economic fortune that affect others. It is claimed, furthermore, that the obvious feature of the modern large corporation, the disjuncture between ownership and control, places its management beyond the control of stockholders in a way not envisaged by the early apologists of market capitalism. To modern critics, the corporation is invulnerable both to the correcting mechanisms of the market and to democracy.

I do not wish to suggest that these and other cognate 'facts' are necessarily true, or that the adverse normative conclusions that are drawn from them by critics of the corporation hold, but only to imply that certain developments in capitalist economies have lent credence to the argument that traditional justifications of liberal capitalism require some

37

revision, if not outright rejection. As the US writer Irving Kristol re-marked:

> one must concede that both the Founding Fathers and Adam Smith would have been perplexed by the kind of capitalism that we have [to-day]. They could not have interpreted the domination of economic activity by large corporations as representing, in any sense, the work-ing of the system of 'natural liberty'. Entrepreneurial capitalism, as they understood it, was mainly an individual – or, at most, a family – affair.[2]

It is perhaps because of the alleged absence in the corporate world of self-correcting mechanisms to individual economic and moral actions, emphasized by Adam Smith in both *The Wealth of Nations* and *The Theory of Moral Sentiments*, that has powered the ethical critique of business. The attempt to impose exogenous restraints on corporations derives from an implicit acceptance of the proposition that decen-tralized exchange systems do not spontaneously generate those ethical rules and conventions necessary for their moral integrity. Individualistic utility-maximization is explicitly repudiated as a mechanism for ethical well-being and even for the pursuit of economic satisfactions. It is claimed that the development of corporate capitalism has systematically undermined those restraints that at one time tamed self-interest. It was until quite recently argued that the great power of the corporation would eventually lead to its downfall as people would resent, and eventually reject, its apparent immunity from competition and law. The large-scale corporation seems, superficially, to be the least desirable of the products of economic man.

However, the contemporary business ethicist has no more succeeded in elucidating that mechanism, if there is one, outside the market and the organization of business, for co-ordinating the best efforts of non-self-interested persons than did earlier writers in this critical tradition. Attempts to replace economic man by a more desirable agent have regu-larly produced something far worse. Nevertheless, there is a continu-ing attraction to forms of economic organization different from the traditional, exclusively profit-maximizing corporation. Hence the rise of stakeholder theory and the allure of the ideal of 'corporate citizenship'. These, and other commercial devices, are attempts to moralize the corporation; endeavours which are supposed to be to its long-term advantage.

THE GENESIS OF THE CORPORATION

A cursory glance at the implications of general equilibrium theory in neo-classical economics reveals how the problems of the corporation in particular, and business ethics in general, arise. For in that model there is no place for the corporation, and therefore the ethical problems that are said to flow from its existence. I should add here that I use the term 'corporation' here when most economists talk of the 'firm'; but this makes little or no substantive difference. It is true that not all firms are corporations but, in their economic manifestation, all corporations are firms. It is also true that there are corporations, churches for example, that do not have an economic purpose yet which have historically evinced, superficially at least, those features of corporate 'personality' that have always intrigued statist and organic political philosophers. Their existence gives further support to the claim that the corporate form is not fully consistent with individualism.

Since the equilibrium world of neo-classical economics is inhabited by atomized individuals, motivated by self-interest, possessed of perfect knowledge of present and future states and capable of making (instantly) those calculations that are necessary for the achievement of their goals, there would be no need for intermediary institutions, such as corporations and firms, to co-ordinate their actions and to cope with those problems of ignorance and uncertainty that are features of any social state short of this imaginary nirvana. Again, such individuals are unencumbered by any of those social feelings of obligation of a non-contractual kind that might find expression in corporate entities which are irreducible to individual choice. The equilibrium model is purely contractual; but the contracts in it are of a special kind. They are multilateral and *specific*: each person engaged in an enterprise contracts with others in terms that eliminate (theoretically) any 'waste' that would occur in loosely-formulated arrangements; and, of course, the agent can better protect her interests the more specific the contract is.

While this ideal construction might appear to be a theoretical delight to some individualists, it is clearly not the world with which we are familiar. The latter is characterized by radical uncertainty and incomplete information to which institutions, such as firms, corporations and money are a response; a response which has an obvious utilitarian justification. Yet however abstract the equilibrium model is, its derivation from certain features of the human condition and its grounding in the liberal idea of free contract, makes for a complex of social and economic arrangements eminently suitable as a normative standard for the evaluation of actual economies. Against this heady ideal the claims of the 'corporate economy' look, at a cursory glance, to be unsustainable.

The morally relevant fact here might be: the apparent prevalence of *bilateral* contracts in firms and corporations. These agreements are not specific and they bind each individual to a single contractual agent in a way that has a least the potential to reduce his liberty. In a sense, firms and corporations are non-market phenomena, since they reduce the range of contracting and establish hierarchies which have a kind of power over individuals. Furthermore, the plethora of legal 'privileges' – for example, limited liability, perpetual life, 'entity' status, and so on – seems to differentiate corporations from the owner-managed enterprises in the typical Smithian *catallaxy*. Giant corporations, it is claimed, do not exchange, they dominate and the relationship between them and their employees and consumers is not that of 'consenting adults' but of, almost, sovereign and subject. Thus Berle and Means write, in reference to the disjuncture of ownership and control, that the:

> Concentration of economic power separate from ownership has, in fact, created economic empires, and has delivered these empires into the hands of a new form of absolutism, relegating the 'owners' to the position of those who supply the means whereby the princes may exercise their power.[3]

Even those favourable toward the structure of capitalism have, perhaps unwittingly, fuelled such criticisms with their descriptions of the modern business enterprise. It was Ronald Coase[4] who, in a significant departure from equilibrium theory, first located the main features of firms, and his description of them and his account of their rationale (they are formed and survive as an institutional response to transactions costs, in this case the immense expense of contracting in pure market forms) was formulated in terms almost deliberately inviting a comparison with the benign anarchy of freely contracting individuals. Bilateral contracts produce an enduring master and servant relationship rather than the desirable phenomenon of the infinite and costless exchangeability of roles. The much-vaunted freedom of capitalist society looks less persuasive in the context of individuals being bound to companies and subject to the whim of owners and managers. In economic terms, because the market involves costs, notably the expense of arranging a myriad individual contracts, the firm is more efficient than pure exchange. From a moral perspective the existence of the firm produces a certain kind of authoritarianism.

The problem of 'whistle-blowing' is explicable in this context. For a person may genuinely feel that the actions of her employers (the corporation) are wrong but the terms of her contract (which is likely to be general) expose her to serious risk should she reveal to the public all that she knows. Her contractual obligations, which can be onerous, may conflict with her more general moral duties.

The fact that one is free to leave one firm and join another is thought to be an inadequate compensation for the loss of liberty the corporate form apparently produces. Of course, Coase had very good reasons to explain the emergence of the firm, all of which turn on the immense transactions costs that are involved in multilateral contracting, but this economic rationale has not satisfied the moral critics of the corporation. Coase was, however, explaining the logic of the firm, not justifying it morally.

Again, as Sir Dennis Robertson and Stanley Dennison pointed out, the firm and especially its large-scale corporate manifestation, introduces *planning*: not, of course, anything like that of a centrally-planned economy, but enough to generate 'islands of conscious *power* [my emphasis] in an ocean of unconscious co-operation'.[5] The implicit reference to spontaneity in the second clause of this quotation is inadequate to disarm even the moderate critic of the modern corporation, let alone radical socialists. By joining corporations individuals give up some vital liberties, even if they are free to choose for which firms to work. Also, they may sacrifice some security, since their skills may only be appropriate for a particular organization. Human capital becomes vulnerable to economic change. It may be specific to one activity so that when demand falls off and market conditions change it ceases to have much economic value. In the purely economic view of the corporation, the owners have no moral duties to the 'victims' of economic change. Although contracts could be designed which protect vulnerable human capital, it is still felt that corporations have moral duties to personnel who might become redundant. They might be especially at risk to corporate raiders.

It is not surprising then that there is a desire to attribute responsibilities to the managements of corporations that exceed their normal economic and financial obligations. It is not quite enough, critics claim, to say, as Milton Friedman did in a famous essay, that the social obligations of the corporation are to increase the returns to its stockholders, limited only by the need to conform to the basic rules of society, both those embodied in law and basic ethical custom.[6] Whatever utilitarian justification there may be in this, and however persuasive is Friedman's objection that the assumption of social responsibilities usurps government's legislative and taxation powers, it begs the question as to what exactly these rules of the game are, and side-steps the issue of the nature and evolution of the corporation itself. Efficiency-generating processes are not always legitimating processes. Economics operates through impersonal laws and an exclusive commitment to them is thought to ignore the human element in business.

Germane to this issue is the question of whether the corporation emerges in a spontaneous manner or whether its existence, and the special legal structure that it represents, is a product of some governmental act exogenous to the exchange process. For if it is the case that the corporation is the product of the state, this would obviously give some purchase to the argument that the state has a claim to regulate it, and impose duties on it (presumably of a social kind) that may not be in the direct interests of its managers and owners. Thus, it is claimed that, however persuasive the utilitarian arguments for the corporation are in an economic sense, its autonomy and independence must always be provisional, depending on whatever conceptions of the public good happens to prevail at a given moment.

Irrespective of the rationale of its origin there is the further question of the *identity* of the corporation as it is presently understood; rival interpretations of this identity can make a difference to an understanding of the claims that are made for and against corporate activity. This consideration relates to a rather familiar debate in social and political theory; between methodological individualism and holism. For it is true that methodological individualists regard the corporation as an artifice (or perhaps a 'fiction') and interpret its actions as metaphorical expressions of the actions of individuals. Any attribution of moral responsibility to business must depend therefore on the tracing out of those discrete steps by individual agents which led, causally, to the occurrence of certain events. The actions of the corporation are ultimately reducible to the actions of identifiable persons.

Using a combination of causal and moral argument the holist claims, in contrast, that the explanation of corporate action is not exhausted by an account of the intentional actions of individuals, and that not only can a corporation act independently of its identifiable agents but these actions can also be evaluated as emanating from a corporate will that has similar features to the will of a biological person. It has then an existence and purpose that transcends the apparently transitory and ephemeral desires of biological persons. The actions of individuals that occupy corporate positions are defined by the existence of the corporate entity itself. The differences between the individualistic and holist interpretations of the corporation obviously are relevant to such notions of 'corporate social responsibility' and corporate liability for crime.

A further complication within those modes of thought concerns an important difference in attitude towards the morality of the corporation displayed by those who claim that it has a supra-individualistic existence and hence can be morally accountable and those who deny that it can be anything more than an aggregate of individual agents. For some this is a reason to condemn it, normally because it constitutes a source of power potentially and actually resistant to political regulation, while to others it is a source of morality, an institution without which the identification of the person would be impossible. According to the latter, more Hegelian view, in the absence of a corporate life, the person remains the fragmented and alienated self of abstract individualism and hence incapable of that moral unity on which civil society depends. The business corporation is, of course, only one of such intermediary institutions and has only recently come to be valued in anything but economic terms, but the origin of the corporate form lies in non-business enterprises, such as charitable organizations and churches. It is a moralized conception of the business corporation, derived from non-business enterprises, that is reflected in contemporary demands for corporate responsibility.[7]

THE STATE AND THE CORPORATION

The classic statement of the dependence of the corporation on the state in the USA is to be found in Chief Justice Marshall's observation that:

> A corporation is an artificial being, invisible, intangible and existing only in contemplation of law. Being the mere creation of law, it possesses only those properties which the charter of its creation confers upon it, either expressly or as incidental to its existence.[8]

Here, Marshall would appear to be saying that the law does not merely *recognize* voluntary agreements to create the corporate form but that law is the only source of its validity, whether that law is statutory or not. In fact, the particular case involved a charitable foundation, Dartmouth College, but Marshall's argument is typically used to explain the rationale of business corporations. In fact, in the USA corporations were originally founded for specific *public* purposes and were chartered accordingly.

In Britain, non-business corporations had existed since medieval times and their legal status was not the outcome of spontaneous evolution. They were the result of specific grants of power from the state (the Crown) and were the recipients of monopoly and other privileges. However, this is by no means the only way corporations could have been generated; if it could be shown that their development was possible *without* statute law, or the grant of Crown privilege, then a part of the case for their public regulation would fall away. Indeed, business corporations or joint stock companies did emerge spontaneously. They were banned (except in special circumstances) in 1720 as a consequence of the famous 'South Sea Bubble' financial scandal. At this time there were about 150 joint stock companies that were quoted on the rapidly developing London Stock Exchange. The prohibition was not repealed until 1875 and ever since then the business corporation has been subject to extensive regulation by statute law. Many writers have argued that statutory regulation was not needed and that it led to some unnecessary 'privileges' which later were used in arguments against corporate business.

What emerged from legislative history was the 'legal creation' theory of the corporation; the conjecture that since its identity and structure are validated by the state it has no other grounding for its liberties (or claim to moral autonomy) than that provided by *positive* (statutory) law. If this were true, then the corporation would indeed lead a precarious existence, permanently vulnerable to the potential invasions of the state. In fact Marshall's statement rests upon a confusion between law and state. For it is surely possible to say that the corporation is in some sense the 'creature' of law, those rules and conventions that have historically constituted the common law, without conceding that it is the offspring of the state and *its* law. Implicit in Marshall's claim is a typical piece of Benthamite (and ultimately Hobbesian) jurisprudence; the clear implication of these doctrines is that all liberties, individual or corporate, depend upon the permission of the sovereign. This inference can be made even though Marshall was dealing with a case arising out of common law, and in a legal system that does not have a formal sovereign. Still, it is the acceptance of this jurisprudence in *economic* matters that has done most to undermine the autonomy of the corporation in this century. In Britain and the USA it is assumed that the corporation depends upon the state and positive law for its existence. But it is not surprising that this confusion arose because the early corporations in Britain and the USA were non-commercial entitles with public purposes. When they were commercial enterprises they were usually given monopoly powers, as was, for example, the East India Company. At first

glance, legal history does appear to validate the claim that the corporation depends on the state for its existence.

However, this is not the whole story, for by the middle of the nineteenth century business corporation were already being recognized at
common law in the USA. In a crucially important Supreme Court case,
Louisville, Cincinnati and Charleston Railroad Co. v. *Letson* (1844), the
corporation was regarded as an artificial person, with the rights and
privileges of full citizenship.[9] However, this decision did not imply that
the entity was granted any special powers or privileges by the state, it
simply meant that certain voluntary acts of individuals produced corporate entities, the powers of which derived solely from those of consenting
individuals. The law simply recognized corporations, it did not create
them. The business corporation emerges when private agents pool their
resources, make contracts and create a kind of collective institution; it is
a body that has rights, but these are no more extensive than those rights
that are attributable to individuals.

The fact that corporations today operate under a myriad of statutory
rules and regulations, which confirm and specify its various rights and
'privileges', does not mean that these positive rules are logically required for the existence of the corporate form. After all, the fact that
monetary instruments today are created by the state does not mean that
money could not exist without the state: it clearly did at one time. If those
typical features of the corporate form, for example, entity status, perpetual life and limited liability, could be shown satisfactorily to have arisen,
or could arise, without the imprimatur of the state, then this would
strengthen considerably the individualist's argument for the compatibil-
ity of the corporation and the market economy, and go some way to answer Kristol's argument that modern capitalism is theoretically deficient
in this respect.

There are two significant ways in which the corporation may legitimately be said to arise independently of the permission granted by posit-
ive/statute law. Neither would require the invocation of a holistic entity
or corporate personality existing apart from individuals, or the attribution of responsibility to anything other than biological persons. Although the policy implications of the two explanations may amount to
much the same thing, especially in connection with the question of corporate social responsibility, their foundations are significantly different.
One derives the idea of a corporation solely from a theory of individual
rights, the other understands it as developing in a spontaneous manner as
a response to individual needs and interests, in precisely the same way that
the rules of morality, the common law, money and other institutions

have developed. Though in both cases the corporation is a *convention*, in the former it is derived from a morality that is explicitly not conventional but rational, while in the latter it is a convention that emerges from rules that are themselves customary and not dependent on a rationalistic notion of natural law. Since the second explanation is a distant relative of utilitarianism, at least when it is used normatively, it is slightly more receptive to the idea of some public regulation of corporations than is the pure rights approach.

Roger Pilon's[10] theory of the morality of the corporation is couched entirely in terms of rights as infinitely weighty side-constraints. They are vetoes that defeat all claims to the regulation of corporations that might be derived from a notion of the public interest that is not reducible to the unanimous agreement of individuals. Thus the rights and obligations of the corporation are expressive of the rights of individuals; and these in turn are limited to negative rights – that is, rights to forbearance from invasive action on the part of others. Any action which is permitted to an individual, no matter how condemnable it might be on *other* moral grounds, is permitted to a rightfully-constituted corporation. The moral justification for the corporation is derived entirely from the moral rights and duties that are ascribed to individuals in free societies. By the same reasoning the duties of the corporation are no more than those ascribed to individuals: they must refrain from violating the rights of others.

A legitimately constituted corporation is one that is created by individuals through the exercise of their rights. Thus it would be possible to explain its conventional features as a product of the rights of contracting agents. Any group of people could pool their resources, delegate their legal powers to others and alienate their property. Limited financial liability could be constructed by contract without violating rights precisely because it would depend on the consent of the creditors. Since continuity or perpetual life depends on the continuing consent of later individuals then this, too, is morally permissible and can happen quite spontaneously. In fact, the implication of this analysis is that the distinction between the corporation and other forms of co-operative activity, such as partnerships and trusts, is by no means clear-cut. It only appears to be so because of legislative and judicial interventions which have tended to strengthen the contentious view that the corporation is some special kind of entity, an organization that would not emerge by natural processes. One example would be the creation of legal liability rules that shift attention *away* from the tortious or criminal acts of identifiable individuals within the corporation toward the corporation itself (that is, the tendency to treat is as a separate agency for the purpose of law). Indeed, it arguable that this is a privilege the corporation does not actually need. It could still function if these liabilities were attributed to its individual members.

However, if the case for the legitimacy of the corporation were to rest entirely on the doctrine of natural rights, with no justificatory role for efficiency or utility (for Pilon, these are merely welcome side-effects), the argument becomes *exclusively* one about the viability of the theory of rights itself. That there are such rights has yet to be irrefutably demonstrated, so that someone who rejected them could then go on to reject the claims made on behalf of the corporation. Furthermore, the plethora of rights that have been invented in the past few decades by philosophers, and indeed courts, has led some writers to doubt that an unambiguous theory of rights can be constructed. As has been suggested the intrusion of 'rights talk' in business, except where they are specifically linked to property and contract, has had a deleterious effect on normative argument in this area. It is probably much safer to use rights to describe the genuine moral claims that derive from traditional common law rather than refer to them as universally valid and indefeasible demands that arise from natural law.

Furthermore, it is difficult to see how all the perplexities that emerge from the actions of the corporation could be resolved by the application of rights-based solutions, even if the moral validity of rights theory were acceptable. It is certainly true that the familiar accusations made against corporations for their alleged production of negative external effects is rebuttable by a property rights theory that would allocate responsibility to individuals and firms for rights-violation. But in many cases that cannot be done uncontroversially so that *public* criteria, resting necessarily on vague conventions and agreements, have to be invoked to buttress considerations that might derive from rights. Thus to *know* what is or is not a rights-violation in some important human activities is a matter that involves a large subjective element. Many activities of corporations, especially in relation to the environment, have an irreducibly *public* aspect so that it is sometimes impossible to conduct the argument entirely in terms of absolutely compelling and individualistic natural rights. Furthermore, many of the arguments against the corporation are now conducted in rights terms, even with regard to the environment. Given the seemingly inexorable expansion of rights claims, it is probably unwise to defend the corporation exclusively in terms of moral rights. The whole approach has brought an intractability in contemporary ethical and economic argument; an intractability which is encouraged by the deontological nature of rights claims: they are immune to empirical counter arguments. Yet the theory does have purchase when some of the more contentious claims for corporate personality are made, especially in relation to corporate crime. Corporations are not persons capable of bearing rights and shouldering duties, except in very special circumstances.

Yet, the main features of the individualistic corporation are also explicable in terms that do not invoke inviolable 'natural' rights. It could (and did) emerge from the exercise of Smith's 'natural liberty': it is a market phenomenon no less significant than money. Again there is a whole range of economic phenomena, from the limited partnership through to the giant multinational corporation, all of which are 'validated' by the same reasoning that explains other spontaneous social institutions. More specifically, their rationale lies in their success in coping with the problem of the co-ordination of *knowledge* that confronts all economic systems beyond the most primitive and repetitive production processes. It is interesting, but not relevant to the main issue, that Adam Smith thought that efficiency would always favour the small, owner-managed enterprise. He wrote that 'negligence and profusion ... must always prevail, more or less, in the management of the affairs of a joint stock company'.[11] The rationale for the corporation would lie not so much in its derivability from absolute rights but from evolution, and its moral validity would derive from the moral conventions that are a feature of societies based on natural liberty. His doubts about the joint-stock company occurred because he failed, not surprisingly, to anticipate checking mechanisms, such as the takeover device, on managements which the free market has developed. But despite Smith's scepticism, the corporate form developed through the activities of freely-contracting agents. Its emergence may not inaccurately be described as another product of the Invisible Hand.

There is much to be said for Robert Hessen's claim that 'at every stage of its growth the corporation is a voluntary association based exclusively on contract'.[12] The rationale from the corporation derives from the convention of contracting through the exercise of natural liberty rather than from come contestable and indeterminate notion of natural rights. The only problem might appear to be limited liability for torts. It is true that limited liability for financial obligations is a consequence of spontaneity, since no one is compelled to trade under such circumstance, but the aforementioned statutory protection for the private assets of corporate owners against tort actions does superficially appear to be a legal device or privilege which would not emerge spontaneously. But is it essential? It is true that large corporations probably do not need this, but it surely has efficiency advantages for smaller, especially start-up, companies. But as Hessen[13] points out, the solution is to require insurance against tort liability as a condition of corporate recognition. The grant of limited liability for torts by the state certainly gives the impression that corporations only exist by permission of that institution. Furthermore, it provides a rationale for state regulation of corporations which is not required. But it is by no means clear that it is necessary for the existence of the corporation. All that is needed is the state to recognize corporate forms that have evolved spontaneously.

OWNERSHIP AND CONTROL

The historically suspect argument that, because the corporation is a creature of the state, and owes its existence to positive, statute law, is not simply an arcane, academic hypothesis; it has a resonance to public policy debates today. In a speech in February 1996,[14] the Secretary for Labor in Clinton's first Administration, Robert Reich, said: 'The corporation is ... a creation of law. It does not exist in nature.' He went on to say that in return for their special privileges it is 'only reasonable to ask corporations to be more accountable for the social costs and benefits of economic change'. He proposed that corporations which fulfilled government-promoted social goals should be rewarded with favourable tax and regulatory treatment. It is just this type of relationship between government and business which is damaging to efficiency, for it tempts commercial agents to invest time and money in seeking favours from politicians. Anyway, how can government know what the appropriate social goals are? It is also a threat to the rule of law, since the legal arrangements under which corporations operate become a matter of unpredictable political negotiation. If it were widely recognized that corporations are natural developments in a market society, Reich's argument would have no force.

The separation between ownership and control in a corporation does not present any specific moral problems. The corporation, although it is derived from the morality of freedom, exists primarily for efficiency reasons. The owners of capital (shareholders) hire managements to handle their assets productively: in theory the latter act at the behest of the former. Indeed, it may not always be the case that the owners want to make profit-maximization their overriding goal. They might prefer to let social considerations, on occasion, modify the desire for financial gain. But it would be a breach of the relationship between owners and employees if managements decided for themselves the respective priorities. The owners are residual claimants to any surplus after all the expenses involved in corporate activity have been paid. Whether one calls this surplus 'profit', in the pure entrepreneurial sense, or a rate of return on the investment, does not matter from an ethical perspective. Its receipt still depends on ownership rights.

It is often claimed that the owners of a corporation are not the shareholders. They merely own the shares, which is not the same thing as full ownership of the company.[15] If by this is meant that there are limits to ownership rights, it is perfectly true. All property owners are limited by law in what they can do with their assets. The owners of a company are limited in what they can do with their property by criminal and civil law. They are forbidden from commanding the company employees to pollute the atmosphere in the pursuit of profit and turning the headquarters into a brothel. Again, no individual shareholder has the right to trade on advance information about the company's plans. His ownership rights are severely restricted in important respects. But these points are not relevant to matters of ultimate control exercised within the law. We know who the owners of the company are in a takeover battle – they are the people who sell out to the raider. Ownership changes hands. Doubts about ownership are created by those who wish to regulate the corporation or to persuade (or coerce) it to act on behalf of the community or some favoured group which has not actually invested in it.

In fact, the major problems for owners is ensuring that their assets are used efficiently and that managements do not shirk their duties. While in business ethics one often reads of exploitation by corporations of employees, or of the consumers and the community, it is just as important to point to the possibility of managements exploiting owners: they may capture the quasi-rents,[16] earned legitimately in business operations, through excessive pay rises, unjustifiable perks and other examples of opportunism. In any successful business enterprise economic rent will be created. Formally, rent is the income paid to a factor in excess of that necessary to bring it into production. Although it was originally derived from land ownership, we now speak of writers, musicians and other people of natural talent whose fortunate possession of valued skills leads to great rewards, or rent.

In any successful enterprise, economic rent (extra value) will be created by innovative individuals. It is important for business efficiency (and, indeed, fairness) that this economic rent goes to the appropriate persons, to those who contribute to its creation. 'Rent-seeking', or the attempt to capture this extra value, can take place in any organization. It is a special feature of politics, where individuals and groups lobby political leaders to help them (through things like tariffs and the grant of monopoly privileges) appropriate rents that properly belong to others. And it goes on within corporations.

What is relevant to the modern Western business system is the claim that aggregate phenomena such as corporations are, *pace* contemporary critics, grounded in individualism; not least in the fact that they reflect the various ways in which decentralized agents adjust their actions to the ever-changing facts of complex societies. Thus the criticism that the separation of ownership and control makes a mockery of the original claims of economic individualism is beside the point. For the absence of immediate supervision of an enterprise does not, of course, mean that control over the management by owners is lost; it is simply exercised in more efficient ways, especially in the stock market. It is the ultimate method by which owners can control rent-seeking by the employees.

In the Anglo-American, loosely-held corporation the takeover threat is the major instrument that owners have to discipline managements (I leave aside the question as to whether this is an efficient mechanism in the long run, though it probably is in the absence of close, face-to-face business relationships). Hence, contemporary policies (ironically sometimes made on behalf of moral and economic individualism) to 'democratize' the corporation would, to the extent that they replaced financial sanctions by a 'Rousseauistic' system of constant participation in management by shareholders, plus 'outside' directors (who are sometimes quasi-political appointments) actually reduce control by owners: especially if their rights to dispose of their property (shares) as they think fit were attenuated.

The morality of the corporation is quasi-utilitarian and is a special feature of the morality of the market. It embodies rights only to the extent that they are generated and created (via contract, property, and private law in general) by the system of natural liberty. Against this, the morality of the market and the corporation it generates is often understood and justified in terms of a set of absolute rights, and morality and efficiency are said to be satisfied if the market expresses some perfect equilibrium, in which there is little room for the corporation at all. Both the latter approaches exhibit a certain kind of 'perfectionism' and therefore neglect the many ways in which new forms of economic organization are generated by enterprising individuals through the market system. The fact that the corporation has certain non-market features, and that managements can appear dominant, are not reasons for abandoning the corrective processes of the market.

Descriptively, the market has much to do with the opportunities it offers for *autonomy*: the emergence of the corporation (and other forms of co-operative activity) is therefore explicable as a product of spontaneous individual action. That it is accompanied by the authority relationships described in the Coasian theory of the firm does not require a re-writing of the ethics of business life. For the obligations, however onerous, that arise out of the bilateral contract are still self-assumed, voluntary assumptions of burdens consistent with the major tenets of the theory of natural liberty. Anyway, the bilateral contract described by Coase masks the great variety of contracts that may be made by individual transactors.

Furthermore, post-Coasian descriptions of business behaviour suggest that the master–servant relationship is not necessarily an accurate account of relationships within the firm. The development of co-operative devices and complex incentive structures have mitigated the potentially authoritarian features Coase described, while falling short of the benign anarchy of the theoretical world of specific, person to person contracts. Although, the large-scale corporation is a type of 'planning', exercises in catallactics may take place within it. Those ideal employer–employee relationships suggested by business ethics may happen spontaneously. Indeed, the presence of entrepreneurship within the firm, and the rewards that accrue to this activity, is itself a significant qualification to its superficially authoritarian structure. None of this proves that Coase's original analysis was mistaken: it is just that transactions costs change through time so that differing forms of commercial organization become viable which were hitherto infeasible. The corporation is not rigid and immutable but develops in unpredictable ways. The fecundity of the market in producing new forms is likely to be superior to the state in both economic and moral terms.

This quasi-utilitarian justification of the corporation must be distinguished from any kind of *activist* utilitarianism. The fact that its spontaneous development is a response to the problem of dispersed knowledge immediately suggests the inappropriateness of an omniscient legislator for social and economic life. More important, the circumstance of its natural emergence from conventional rules means precisely that it does not exist through the permission of a legislator. If law precedes the state, then so does the corporation. The moral properties of the corporation arise precisely out of the moral features of freedom. However, whether the constraints that apply to corporations are logically equivalent to those that apply to individuals remains a controversial question in business ethics.

Furthermore, spontaneous developments in commerce and the accompanying employment practices, mean that attempts by business ethics to 'moralize' the corporation and to introduce quasi-political notions of citizenship are no longer necessary. The old Coasian concept of the firm or corporation as a rigid power structure different from the spontaneity of the free market is becoming dated in the face of modern technology. Transaction costs are changing and they are making possible more decentralized employment relationships. Increasing numbers of people work on temporary contracts. They work from home and are free to organize their lives independently of any power exercised by an employer: in fact, they do not have an 'employer' in the traditional sense. The emergence of benign and freedom-enhancing forms of employment will be in response to such phenomena, not as a consequence of legislated business ethics. Self-interest will generate pleasing business relationships. Of course, it is unlikely that the large-scale corporation will disappear but its pre-eminence as a commercial form is diminishing and its quasi-political power (if it ever had any) is being eliminated by various forms of competition.

SELF-REGULATION, THE CORPORATION AND BUSINESS CODES

The corporation will remain for some time and certain problems will persist. The explanation of the existence of aggregate phenomena is of no direct help in those areas where there are public good problems. The corporation may emerge spontaneously through individual interaction but there is no guarantee that its development and behaviour is always in the interests of those same individuals. The tracing out of the corporation through an Invisible Hand mechanism is vulnerable to precisely those same objections that plague other manifestations of the same phenomena; rational self-interested action does not always produce benign outcomes. Restraints on corporate activity may be in the long-term interests of corporations themselves; yet since self-restraint is superficially an unlikely occurrence, given the nature of business enterprise, the corporation is vulnerable to the kind of political regulation that may be destructive of its long-term interests. But is self-restraint an impossibility?

It might be possible for a business ethics to emerge that is not based on a naïve altruism (which runs counter to the major rationale of the business enterprise), but which, nevertheless, generates certain feelings and attitudes favourable to a notion of moral duty that extends beyond the observance of basic, protective laws. What modern commerce requires is a set of conventions which, although they require the suppression of *immediate* self-interest, are consistent with the long-term maximization of utility. There is a need for conventions that impose restraint on business agents; even if the ultimate rationale of such constraints is their contribution to profit-maximization. It is in this restricted sense that moral conduct in business 'pays'. As has been noted, even such a modern Mandevillian as Milton Friedman stresses the importance of observing social conventions, including ethical custom, in addition to the binding obligations of positive law, in the conduct of business. What he does not explain is how these conventions come about, the precise nature of their obligations and most important of all, their stability. The last point is crucial, since the very nature of business activity, and the omnipresence of the profit motive, renders it an unpromising form of human endeavour for the spontaneous evolution of extra-legal rules of restraint; at least in comparison to the established professions, such as medicine.

One possibility frequently suggested is the development of business codes.[17] These are rules spontaneously generated by corporations which lay down standards of conduct for their employees. They cover the marketing practices, relationships with consumers and competitors: indeed, anything that affects the long-term viability of the enterprise. The most important effect is to counter the problem of ignorance that afflicts all business agents. Employees are utility-maximizers and are subject to the same temptations as other economic transactors in the pursuit of their careers. However, in the absence of rules of conduct they may not know what is appropriate conduct. It is noticeable that in the controversy[18] involving British Airways and the Virgin airline, in which the former was accused of spreading libellous stories about Virgin and interfering with its passenger schedules, that the erring company did not have a code. It was not clear to the employees of British Airways what their duties were in relation to company activities. Most publicly quoted British and US companies do have formal guidelines for their employees. Obviously such codes should not be limited to compliance with criminal and civil law but must extend to those conventional ethics which go beyond these formal constraints. They may perhaps be useful instruments for the development of a 'corporate culture' which encourages respect for law and everyday morality.

Much of the effectiveness of codes will depend on the existence of an appropriate corporate culture. Any collaborative activity will be conducted in the context of an ongoing set of standards and typical employees will find themselves obligated to comply with rules and practices which they had no part in creating. While it is highly unlikely that a corporate culture will encourage deliberate wrongdoing (people do not normally set up corporations to commit crimes) business enterprises will vary in their attitude to conventional moral standards. In certain activities, especially those that involve the possible exploitation of consumer ignorance, corporate cultures may develop which encourage a certain kind of laxity (to put it mildly). Again, it would be in the interest of business to develop codes, and to encourage compliance, for it is almost certain that government regulation will be much more severe. It is also likely to be an over-reaction to a spectacular, and untypical, scandal.

Perhaps the securities industry in the 1980s is an example of all this. Sophisticated financial practitioners had a clear advantage over a relatively ignorant public, especially in Britain, where, because of deregulation and privatization, many individuals were entering the securities markets for the first time. In such circumstances the defence of *caveat emptor* may be thought unsatisfactory. But it should not be dismissed. Most of the scandals of the 1980s involved straightforward crime. The consumers of financial services were engaged in the same activity as the suppliers – that is, making money – and it is absurd to demand that they should be protected from the vicissitudes of the market. In a market economy each transactor faces risk, though it will not be equally distributed.

There is, however, a disturbing phenomenon which is developing in the Anglo-American economies. It is the strange idea that investors should be protected from all risk. Both in the USA and Britain there is regulatory action to compensate people from bad advice. There have been court actions and suggested legislative reform (in the USA) which would make it possible for any investor to sue if a company's share price failed to reach some arbitrary standard. All this is quite different from protecting people against fraud and deception: if taken seriously it would have very serious consequences for a market economy and deleterious effects on personal responsibility.

A complex issue is whether there should be *industry-wide* business codes to which individual enterprises should conform. Certainly medical ethics is a more tractable subject than business ethics because the nature of medicine is specific, and compliance to its prescriptions is relatively easy since the profession is more or less monopolistically organized. It is possible, however, that business could develop similar informal sanctions to enforce compliance to rules in the manner suggested in Chapter 2. The public good that would be promoted by this is that of fending off unwelcome regulation. It could be generated by economic agents refusing to deal with those who took actions, for short-term profit reasons, which are ultimately harmful to the industry.

While the idea of industry-wide codes has a superficial plausibility, it is subject to the serious objection that such codes are quite likely to be anti-competitive. Dominant producers may form alliances which prevent outsiders, who can offer a good or service at a lower cost, entering the activity. It is quite likely in the USA that successful industry-wide codes would fall foul of anti-trust laws. Indeed, there is one spectacular example from economic history which shows that such industrial agreements can have disastrous results. I refer here to the development of cartelization in the German economy in the early part of this century.[19] German industries became dominated by groups of producers which, operating under quasi-legal rules, kept out competitors. There, freedom of contract was used to generate voluntary agreements which suppressed competition. Tragically, the existence of cartels enabled Hitler to operate a more or less command economy without formal socialization.

Of course, those who recommend industrial codes have nothing like the German cartelization experience in mind. Indeed, the existence of international competition may well wipe out anti-competitive practices that might occur in normal market economies which develop milder forms of industry-wide collaboration. But the potential misuse of codes should alert us to the fact that competition is itself a public good which individual transactors have no immediate interest in promoting. Industrial codes might develop into devices to avoid its rigours. Furthermore, the existence of business codes might actually retard the development of business morality. Personnel might feel relieved of their moral duties once they have adhered to the code. Yet moral problems might well arise which are not catered for in the code. No book of rules can account for every circumstance. Indeed, it is not possible to codify, or encapsulate in precise rules, all the appropriate moral responses to unpredictable events. It is surely just as important to develop a corporate culture which encourages right conduct in business personnel and enables them to act in a morally autonomous manner rather than to follow unthinkingly the rules of a code. Education in conventional morality rather than the learning of formal rules of an ethical system concerned exclusively with business might be advisable too. It is doubtful whether business scandals can be correlated with the absence of a code, despite the British Airways example.

CORPORATE MORAL WRONGS AND RIGHTS

The development of business codes may well be a method for ensuring compliance with moral standards, a conformity that would be in the long-term interests of commercial agents. However, because of the nature of business activity opportunities for the exploitation of ignorance will always exist. Furthermore, doubts about what is required of business personnel will remain. It is highly unlikely that codes could be devised which would resolve such doubts. If we look at three controversial US business stories we can see the difficulties. They are the Ford Pinto case, the Nestlé infant formula saga and the Tylenol story. In fact, these three cover a range of evaluations: from the general agreement of immorality in Pinto (though there are dissenters from the conventional line even in this case[20]) to serious doubts about right and wrong in Nestlé and an apparently general acclaim for the virtuous behaviour of Johnson & Johnson in the Tylenol case.

The Ford Pinto case

In the late 1970s the Ford Motor Corporation, in fierce competition in the small car market, manufactured the Pinto which, critics claimed, the company knew to be an unsafe vehicle.[21] Its rear-mounted petrol tank exploded on collision with vehicles at not particularly high speeds. A number of accidents occurred which led to some deaths. Quite apart from the question of Ford's moral responsibility, another ethical problem emerged: the company (as a collective entity) was charged with reckless homicide. This was the first time a corporation had been charged with a crime hitherto thought to be only capable of commission by *individual* agents. The question of corporate criminal responsibility will be considered below.

The original moral question turned on knowledge and the potential for the exploitation of consumer ignorance in free markets. It seemed to be the case that Ford knew of the dangers but calculated the likely cost in civil damages, compared that to the expense of redesigning the petrol tank and, since the former was less than the latter, decided to go ahead with production. Indeed, the company was in the forefront of the campaign against a proposed tightening up of federal regulations. Did Ford knowingly choose recklessness (to secure profit) over safety?

The general consensus is that they did, especially in view of the fact that consumers were not given the right to purchase the same car with an extra safety device. Still, the company could, and did, mount some sort of an argument. After all, they had conformed to existing safety standards for petrol tanks. Ford also challenged the number of casualties that could be directly attributed to the design of the Pinto. It is indeed true that there is no such thing as a perfectly-safe product, and the pursuit of it would price important goods out of the reach of most consumers. The type of cost–benefit analysis undertaken by Ford is not that different from similar calculations that government and business pursue as a matter of routine. It is, indeed, prescribed by utilitarian ethics. Furthermore, the kind of 'regulatory rights' recommended by zealots, which are designed to give consumers absolute protection at whatever costs, would preclude almost any cost–benefit analysis. As Wildavsky[22] pointed out, we actually improve safety over-all by encouraging a certain amount of risk-taking. That is how knowledge is built up. To concentrate exclusively on eliminating all potential risks would waste resources and not increase overall safety.

Still, few of these considerations seemed to apply in the Pinto case. The culpability of Ford is surely traceable to its knowledge of the potential and avoidable risks and to its concealment (originally) of pertinent facts. The difficulty is the anonymity of modern markets; the maker of unsafe products does not know the potential victims and those restraints that are effective in face-to-face and family relationships are absent in mass consumption (although some Ford executives did claim that their relatives actually purchased Pintos). It appears that Ford did use consumers *merely* as means to the end of their profits. It is true that the market and the law do provide protection for consumers in the long run but there clearly can be harms committed before their curative effects are decisive. Business ethics tends to deal with particular phenomena, and readily identifiable victims of specific actions are always available. Economics is concerned with large impersonal processes which submerge individual identities in the superficially benign language of efficiency. It was Ford's manipulation of knowledge that made its action unethical. Economics tends to be about what is unseen[23] – that is, unobserved co-ordination and error-correction – while ethics is concerned with what is seen, normally spectacular examples of wrongdoing which obviously occur before error-correction takes place.

The Nestlé case

A similar, and only slightly less controversial example, was Nestlé's sale of 'infant formula' to Third World mothers.[24] This was a highly useful product, especially to these customers, but it required careful use (it should not be mixed with contaminated water). Uneducated mothers used it incorrectly and some deaths resulted. What was worse, the company continued to market the product after the health dangers were well-publicized. However, the example is not straightforward. It is certainly plausible to mount a defence of Nestlé from a straightforward utilitarian perspective; this is indeed what the corporation did in the face of organized protests and boycotts. The company argued that the social benefits outweighed the costs. Furthermore, Nestlé could not be held responsible for the misuse of their product, as there was no deception in its marketing and advertising. Were they not treating the consumers as autonomous agents capable of making rational choices?

However, certainly a broadened utilitarianism would have taken account of the possible harmful effects on a minority in its use of the formula. It would be a morally crass form of cost–benefit analysis that permitted, in an unqualified manner, the gains (however massive) of the majority to outweigh completely the harms caused to a minority (however small). Furthermore, it would certainly not be inconsistent with utilitarianism to take account of the informational disparities between various sets of consumers.

It would therefore be possible to regard Nestlé's action as condemnable from that version of arm's-length morality which is primarily utilitarian in emphasis. But the argument would not be conclusive. However, the major criticism of Nestlé was grounded in a much more controversial deontological framework. The corporation was actually accused of violating the rights of mothers in the Third World by continuing to market the product in the face of mounting unfavourable evidence. Apparently the competitive impulse and the desire for profit had been decisive over all other considerations. The consumers had been used only as a means to the end of corporate commercial success. This seems a much more contentious case; for there was nothing in Nestlé's actions that specifically violated the rights of individuals and, indeed, a genuine deontological ethic would not turn upon the material interests of individuals (as perceived by outsiders) but upon the recognition of their personal autonomy. It is rather odd to describe restraints, either voluntary ones exercised by the corporation or compulsory regulation by the state, as rights-enhancing, since a market transaction which leaves the consumer to make up his or her own mind is an expression of individual choice and autonomy.

The Tylenol case

It is true that normal business practice (rather than high-flown moral philosophy) is sufficient to guide companies in such cases, and in the long run such action often pays off. In the famous Tylenol[25] case, packets of the medication had been poisoned by someone and then planted in a very small number of shops. Though the company, Johnson & Johnson, was in no way responsible for this (and there was only a slight danger) it immediately withdrew all of the product, incurring a considerable loss. As it turned out, it earned moral plaudits for this action and eventually regained market share. Cynics have suggested that there was no real moral merit in what Johnson & Johnson did; that it was actually good marketing strategy. Still, when the action was taken the company was not to know that it would be successful. It was taking a risk, since there was no real evidence that there would have been a drop in public confidence if it had not withdrawn the product. In fact, it could be, and was, suggested that Johnson & Johnson was rather craven in its action, too anxious to assume responsibility when no blame could be attributed to it.

Most of the famous corporate scandals are not as clear cut as many critics suggest. These days large companies are extraordinarily careful to avoid the kind of opprobrium to which they were once subjected. This is not so much a response to business ethics (though some of the practitioners of this discipline have done much to publicize even quite trivial wrongdoing) as an example of prudence. This was one of the virtues stressed by Adam Smith. Also, the continued pressure from the media to which companies are exposed is likely to be more effective in ensuring normal prudence than is the moralizing of some writers on business ethics.

CORPORATE CRIME

The moral and legal constraints that have been imposed on business behaviour have been added to recently by the development of the theory of corporate criminal responsibility. Given that corporations do sometimes act wrongly, there is the ethical question: who exactly is responsible for corporate misbehaviour? The corporation is a legal personality liable for civil wrongs committed in the course of its operations. There is nothing controversial in the arrangement whereby individuals, through pooling their resources in order to pursue commercial gain, make themselves liable in civil law for the possible costs that might be incurred in business. The fact that the owners (as the principal) and possibly the board of directors (the agent) ultimately bear the costs of civil action is neither inconducive to efficiency nor offensive to morality. The separation of ownership and control theoretically makes no difference; for the entrustment of corporate assets to management necessarily involves risk. The joint-stock company emerged precisely for efficiency reasons; authority is delegated by owners to managers. Indeed, the possibility of civil action is an incentive for shareholders to take a more active interest in the affairs of companies that they formally own.

In theory, the rights and duties of the corporation derive from the rights and duties of individuals. In practice, however, the development of the modern corporation, and its alleged social and economic power and falsely proclaimed immunity from corrective competitive processes, has led to the demand for a greater control over its activities than that provided by civil law and the market. Hence the growth in the past few years of criminal prosecutions of corporations (for which managements take the 'blame' but shareholders pay the costs if the result is a heavy fine). Undoubtedly, the theory that corporations are the creatures of positive law, with its strong implication that the corporation is something more than a legal entity constructed solely out of the legal rights of concrete individuals, has been influential. A corporation could be treated as more than a legal artifice. It is perhaps a 'real' person of whom one could predicate actions independently of the actions of its individual members (for example, its board members and employees). Superficially, it sounds bizarre to speak of a corporation as an entity capable of performing actions normally thought to be only possible of biological persons, but there is some philosophical literature on the subject of corporate personality.[26] This has some relevance to the questions of whether it is legitimate to prosecute corporations for manslaughter, theft or any other serious criminal offence.

In neither law nor morality has the question of corporate criminal responsibility been solved, though the issue has been given a much more thorough airing by lawyers and philosophers in the USA than in Britain. The first important example of alleged corporate responsibility for serious crime was the prosecution of the Ford Motor Corporation (in the Pinto case) for reckless homicide in 1980. Of course, criminal responsibility had previously been attributed to corporations, both in Britain and the USA, but this had been for less serious (and less obviously personal) offences: normally those which lie on the borderline between torts and crimes. Although Ford's original defence to the charge of reckless homicide, that a corporation is not a person and cannot commit homicide, was rejected, it was eventually acquitted at the trial. Nevertheless, there have been some successful prosecutions of corporations for criminal offences, including corporate manslaughter. Recently, fines and restitution totalling $5m were imposed on the Boeing Corporation for a two-count felony of corporate theft. The Exxon Corporation was fined $1bn over the Alaskan oil spill (even though they had already paid the clean-up costs) because they had apparently breached an obscure criminal statute. The example of the unsuccessful prosecution (1990) of the P&O Company for corporate manslaughter over the deaths involved in the Zeebrugge tragedy is close to the US models. In English law it has been established that corporations can be charged with crimes which were once thought possible only of biological agents, but as yet the conditions for success are extraordinarily difficult to satisfy.

Irrespective of how the law develops, the question of corporate liability for serious crime raises fundamental ethical (not to mention philosophical) issues. Can the notions of intention and *mens rea* (a guilty mind) seriously be attributed to non-human agencies? Who are the people to be considered as representative of the corporation in such actions? What kind of penalty is appropriate if and when the offence has been proved? Should shareholders, who normally have nothing to do with criminal action, have to pay the heavy fines that result from convictions? Is it likely that an increase in, and extension of, corporate criminal liability will make it easier for culpable individuals to hide behind the 'corporate veil'? Finally, and of growing importance, does the criminal prosecution of the corporation reflect a desire for 'vengeance' in response to horrific accidents rather than a concern for justice?

The claim that corporations can act intentionally and have a guilty mind arises out of a proposed distinction made by Peter French,[27] between an 'aggregate' and a 'conglomerate'. An aggregate is merely a set of individuals who may do things together which they could not do separately; but it does not constitute a permanent, ongoing entity capable of being identified independently of these discrete individuals. However, a conglomerate has the feature of permanence and it exists irrespective of the changing composition of its membership. It is identified not by the attitudes of particular individuals, but in its collective biography or record of its aims and purposes, successes and failures. American business ethicists tend to locate the separate identity of the corporation with the Corporate Internal Decision Structure or CIDS (which contains basically its fundamental *telos*, or state at which it aims). This identification enables us to say that the corporation can 'act' and hence exhibit intention and responsibility. Nevertheless all writers who take this position do say that it still requires some individual endeavour to activate the CIDS.

Now it is true that many organizations (and not only firms) have a life that transcends the lives of individual members, and we do often speak metaphorically of collective minds. It is also true that individuals can do things in concert, both good and bad, which they cannot do as individuals. The whole nature of the corporation presupposes that part of its essence is that it has a life beyond the lives of its individual members. The identity of corporations cannot simply be established by knowledge of the identities of its individual, and possibly transitory, members.

Indeed, philosophers favourable to free enterprise, such as Michael Novak,[28] have been anxious to distinguish the corporate for of business organization from *laissez-faire* individualism. The corporation is a collective institution, it does have a kind of life qualitatively different from the lives of its individual members and the most successful enterprises develop a kind of corporate culture which imposes restraints on individual egoism. Of course, it is logically possible for a corporation to develop an immoral, or even criminal culture. It would be difficult to describe this culture in purely methodological individualist terms. Furthermore, apologists for capitalism often claim that the development of corporations constitutes a valuable protection for individuals against the state, and it is true that a socialist economy would abolish the corporate form because that can only exist in conditions of liberty, private property and the rule of law. Its survival is an important protection for individuals against excessive state power.

However, none of these features, or all taken together, is sufficient to justify the claim that corporations can act intentionally in the way that humans can, or that they can experience shame, regret, remorse and so on. In fact, philosophers systematically misunderstand the nature of the business enterprise. It is a means to an end, not an end in itself; a legal contrivance which individuals have discovered to advance their interests in a world of uncertainty. Indeed, its purpose in most important respects can only be established by reference to the purposes of those who manage and own it. Since, as I suggested earlier, the corporation only exists because of the absence of perfect competition, it must be understood primarily, but not exclusively, in economic terms. In a world of uncertainty the success of the corporation depends upon the skill and ingenuity of its individual members in exploiting profitable opportunities.

Only if corporations behaved in a regular and predictable manner, and every agent fulfilled a specified and unchanging function, could it be plausibly said that it displayed a group cohesiveness equivalent to biological personhood (and even then this description would be little more than a metaphor). But in fact a great deal of entrepreneurship goes on in corporations, and this is the phenomenon of identifiable individuals responding to changes in the environment and displaying that alertness to new opportunities in the inevitable flux of economic life. If these known individuals are to be rewarded for their contributions to the success of the enterprise then surely they are equally responsible for its moral (and other) failings. There is a compelling moral symmetry here. Sometimes it may be difficult to disentangle individual efforts in necessarily collaborative activities, but the exposure of a practical problem is not the same thing as demonstrating some metaphysical truth, that collective responsibility can exist which is irreducible to the actions of separate individuals.

From this it follows that guilt for criminal wrongdoing should properly be attributed to the individuals directly concerned. French's point would only have plausibility if the CIDS itself was criminal in inspiration, or at least grossly immoral. And even then its criminal genesis would be individualistic. Indeed, those business ethicists who insist on corporate criminal liability also claim that both individuals and the corporation should be prosecuted for crimes. In fact, the issue was confused in the Ford Pinto case because none of the culpable executives was put in the dock. This has not happened since (in the Boeing case, a separate charge of theft was brought against the person who had actually committed the offence). But in complex fraud cases in the USA, companies can be convicted without the identification and prosecution of individuals. If companies are to be charged with serious criminal offences, without particular individuals being arraigned, then certain problems of corporate identity come to the fore because companies do change ownership over time. Which corporate agent is deemed to be responsible for a criminal act? It is the case in English law that the 'directing mind(s)' of the corporation have to be identified before the criminal charge against the company can succeed. The conviction of the corporation depends on the conviction(s) of individual employers or employees.

The desire to go beyond individual actions in the kinds of horrific events that lead to corporate manslaughter charges is understandable. Civil actions, no matter how costly they may turn out to be, seem superficially inadequate an expression of the revulsion that people obviously feel at these, sometimes avoidable, distressing events. It is because criminal law has an 'expressive function', that is, it indicates strongly society's disapproval of certain actions, that the desire to 'punish' corporations should be so prevalent. Nevertheless, the imposition of punitive civil damages may well be a solution to this problem, although the generosity with which the courts in the USA award them creates other difficulties.

None of these observations justifies the claim that a corporation is a 'person' which exists, for moral purposes and for the punishment of the criminal law, apart from the actions of individuals. Of course, corporate executives may often find themselves in difficult positions, circumstances in which 'loyalty' to the company might compete with the constraints of ordinary common sense morality, but such dilemmas are not solved by shifting responsibility to, or sharing it with, an artificial (if not quite 'fictitious') agency. Surely those Ford executives should have resigned and 'blown the whistle' on the company for the manufacture of the Pinto. Indeed, evidence was readily available of the morally crude calculations that were made of the costs of civil actions if crashes were to occur compared to the production losses if the fault were to be corrected. These calculations were made by individuals and the decision not to correct the fault was taken by individuals.

Presumably, the logical implication of the argument that corporations can be liable for serious criminal offences is that boards of directors should be imprisoned, even if they were not immediately involved in the reckless or other behaviour that caused the catastrophe. This would be plausible if individual board members could be shown to be responsible by the normal processes of criminal law. But in the Zeebrugge case, for example, the catastrophe was caused by the irresponsible action (actually, inaction) of the bosun and his immediate supervisor, who both failed to comply with company procedures. It may be the case that, in this and other similar tragedies, the procedures were inadequate. Again, is this not a problem of locating responsibility in particular officers, difficult though that may be? If the corporation is to be charged in addition to identifiable individual wrongdoers, then the consequences can logically only be massive fines. These are ultimately paid by the owners (shareholders) who had nothing to do with the original offence.

It is also important to note that in the Zeebrugge case the judge specifically refused to allow the range of individual wrongs and irresponsible actions to be aggregated so as to constitute a corporate wrong.[29] It was impossible to show that senior executives of the company were *directly* responsible for the catastrophe. Only in one case has a prosecution for corporate manslaughter succeeded in Britain, but in it the company was a one-man corporation. The legal requirements in Britain make the crime of corporate manslaughter extraordinarily difficult to prove in law. What is the point of bringing this type of charge against a corporation if it really is the case that only an individual can commit it?

Despite the failure of the prosecution of the P&O Company in the Zeebrugge case (it could not be proved that its procedures constituted 'obvious' risk) the possibility of corporate liability for serious criminal action was accepted in principle and this runs counter to the principal–agent theory of the corporation. For while that theory can accommodate the idea that the principals (the owners) should shoulder the burdens of civil liability (indeed, it may encourage investors to be more active in the monitoring of the companies they own) it is difficult to see what kind of theory could convincingly establish the guilt of a collective institution which is required for cases involving criminal intent.

The argument that without the invocation of a corporate mind (embodied in the board of directors) crimes would go unpunished because of the difficulty of establishing individual responsibility is unpersuasive on two grounds. If that were the argument then particular persons (board members taken collectively) would be 'used' as means to advance some particular end. The end (safety) itself is obviously good, but it is at least plausible to suggest that this could be advanced without the potentiality for injustice that the invocation of corporate criminal liability involves. Perhaps the judge in the Zeebrugge case had this in mind when he refused to allow individual wrongful acts to be 'aggregated' so as to produce a collective wrong. Also, he did not dismiss the case against the culpable individuals involved in the tragedy (although the prosecution did not proceed against them).

Secondly, it may be questioned how difficult it really is to establish individual responsibility? In most of the standard cases in the USA, and all of them in Britain, individuals are charged along with the company. Most theorists of corporate criminal liability admit that the actions of a corporate person have to be activated by biological persons. If this is so, then it is surely in principle possible to identify individual agents in human tragedies.

The morality of corporate responsibility for crime is as confused and indeterminate as is the law. Sometimes it consists of a certain kind of utilitarianism; that the threat of criminal sanctions is the only way of ensuring that the constant monitoring of activities, which is required for the avoidance of tragedies, actually takes place. It is assumed here that civil actions for damages, to which nobody could object, are inadequate. Yet utilitarian considerations could point in a different direction; it is plausible to suppose that corporate enterprise would be seriously deterred if the organization were criminally and collectively responsible for every wrongful action committed by subordinates. In advance of more convincing moral argument, it is tempting to assume that current pressure for the criminal prosecution of corporations for actions normally thought possible only of biological persons is motivated by 'vengeance' rather than by justice.

It is an attitude no doubt strengthened by the low esteem in which the corporation is held, especially in US society. Some such view was implied by the judge in the Exxon case.[30] In rejecting the company's original plea bargain he said that the fine would not sufficiently affect its profitability. Thus he was not concerned simply with the wrong committed (which would be required by justice) but with raiding the 'deep pockets' of Exxon. In such cases, the full costs are borne by those very remote from the incident, the shareholders. Ultimately, perhaps those furthest away have to pay – that is, consumers faced with higher prices. Also, it is noticeable that Exxon's hitherto good moral record, and the fact that it had a corporate code, were not much help in what might be described as an oppressive prosecution.

4 Corporate Social Responsibility

The attempts to moralize corporations are by no means limited to enforcing very strict rules of behaviour on their activities, rules which might not be thought applicable to private individuals. Business ethics now seems to be imposing positive moral duties on commercial enterprises. They are now required to perform duties which private persons are not expected to perform: that is, actions which go beyond the observance of basic and conventional rules, respect for property, contract and conventionally established rights. They are not merely to refrain from wrongdoing but are to act positively for the public good. The rationale for the imposition of such duties on corporations derives largely from the claim that their existence depends solely upon a grant of privileges from the state. It would seem that they owe something to society in return for this (in addition to supplying wanted consumer goods and creating employment). If this idea were taken to some of the extremes suggested, corporations would have fewer rights than private persons.

Corporations must not only act morally, in the conventional sense, they must also act socially – for example, they must pursue *social* justice even if that means the sacrifice of profit. Indeed, in some bizarre versions of US business ethics[1] the moral credibility of the corporation can only be established when it forgoes opportunities for profit by its pursuit of some supposedly compelling moral goal. The language of contemporary moral philosophy, encompassing communitarianism, egalitarianism and social justice, is now enthusiastically used to endorse, or more likely condemn, corporate behaviour.

But does capitalism not depend on self-interest and the elimination of the more ethically pleasing altruistic motive? As we have noted, it was Bernard Mandeville in *The Fable of the Bees* who first clearly posited a sharp dichotomy between virtue and commerce, and asked questions which are still relevant today. However, one does not have to resort to Mandevillianism to cast doubt on the corporate agendas of modern business ethics. These agendas are quite inconsistent with the aims and purposes of business, which are reducible to the major goal of enhancing owners' profits, interpreted as either a return on capital or the value created by original acts of entrepreneurship. There are other opportunities and venues for advancing desirable social goals, the political sphere being one. Indeed, it could be plausibly said that the imposition of social responsibilities on business is a substitute for that political action which has failed to attract electoral support. The demand for social responsibility does seem to have coincided with the rejection of conventional socialism. As has often been observed, the promotion of social responsibility is not unwelcome to business employees. Though no doubt a wider spread of share ownership to employees would dampen their enthusiasm for the more extreme versions of the social responsibility thesis.

THE SOCIAL RESPONSIBILITY OF THE CORPORATION

The corporate social responsibility thesis covers a wide range of social issues; from the organization of the firm itself through to the relationships between it and the community. But all of these matters are approached from a particular moral perspective – one that claims that the minimalist morality of the free market, with its stress on personal responsibility for action, on the sanctity of contract and on the moral and economic significance of private property, is an inadequate ethical validation for the existence of the business system. Profit is not understood as a reward for entrepreneurship (the ability to spot a difference between resource costs and final product price), a creative act which benefits everybody, but is condemned as an unjustifiable exploitation of the ignorance of others; workers are not recognized as willing contractors into mutually beneficial arrangements but are pitied as helpless victims of the (alleged) monopoly power of corporations. In these and a myriad other examples it is contended that business must be checked and corrected by moral principles not intrinsic to the activity of commerce itself.

In conventional political economy the assumption is that the corporation exists to make money for its owners, the shareholders, and not deliberately to do 'good' for society. This occurs automatically in a well-functioning market system. Of course, under the rules and rights of property, owners are at liberty to do what they like with their assets, and this logically may include the desire to engage in non-profit, charitable activities. However, from a behavioural point of view, this is less likely the more competitive an industry becomes, because then there is simply less profit available for distribution to non-business activities. It seems odd to award moral praise to those agents who are in a position to act morally, at no great cost to themselves, because of favourable economic circumstances. Ironically, the nearer a monopoly is approached, the more opportunity there is for benevolent activity. This produces a paradox for business ethics, for altruism appears to be possible only in a context, monopoly, which is (superficially at least) unethical. Perhaps monopolists ought to be benevolent as a payment to society for its grant of their extra-competitive privileges; although monopoly profits can be the reward for superior foresight and risky activity.[2]

It might be the case that the above description of the profit-maximizing corporation applies exclusively to the Anglo-American corporate form: other types of enterprise may not stress so much returns to owners (though this has ultimately to be important) as other social goals which might, in an elusive way, contribute to economic stability. Perhaps the ideals of the German 'social market economy',[3] which encompass co-operation and social solidarity rather than competitive individualism, are ethically superior to Anglo-American capitalism, as the Japanese notion of 'trust', which leads to corporations retaining unproductive labour, is somehow morally pleasing in comparison to the more insensitive methods of employers in the USA. Certainly the anti-takeover mentality of both those countries is highly suggestive of socially-responsible ethic.

However, it is by no means clear that the Anglo-American version of capitalism is ethically inferior; certainly if that is measured by the prevalence of business scandals. Furthermore, the openness and freedom of the Anglo-American corporate form produces a flexibility which has contributed vastly to its success in an efficiency sense. Those who would attempt to transplant the German or the Japanese systems of corporate governance to the unpropitious environments of the USA and Britain should be aware of the unwelcome side-effects that such operations might produce. The Anglo-American economies are simply less solidaristic, but they are also more inclusive: their moral and legal rules provide protection and fairness for all-comers, not just group members or the inhabitants of some community.

The problem about corporate social responsibility in the Anglo-American economy has largely arisen because of the separation of ownership from control in large-scale modern corporate enterprises. This necessarily reduces the direct control the owners have over enterprises which are nominally their property. The discretion which is granted to managements now means that they, not the owners, are thought of as the prime instruments of social responsibility. Thus the contemporary theory of the corporation presents us with a contradiction. On the one hand, according to capitalist economics, the managers of a company should use what discretion they have on behalf of its owners (this is implied by the principal–agent relationship), yet on the other hand, because of the alleged legal privileges of the organization, they should use it to advance the interests of society. But is there not something intrinsically immoral in entrusting managers with the task of fulfilling highly controversial social obligations? Are they not in breach of their fiduciary duties? Are not ownership (property) rights seriously attenuated when managers pursue non-profit-making activities? Is this not an opportunity for managers to become rent-seekers?

What are these social responsibilities and what is the relationship between them and those conventional efficiency principles which are supposed to guide corporate activity? This brings us to the heart of business ethics and it is helpful to make use of a familiar distinction in moral philosophy – between rules of strict obligation and supererogatory duties. The former are those moral rules which impose strict duties; they encompass obligations which morality dictates that we perform. No special merit is accorded to those who comply with them, although the breach of them is a reason for serious criticism. The rules of justice are the best examples of such obligatory rules. The difficulty here is that the meaning of justice has been distorted. What were once strict rules of perfect obligation have been confused with what are basically welfare demands. The latter properly belong to a quite different sphere of morality.

Supererogatory principles prescribe actions that might in themselves be valuable but which lack compelling force. Great moral credit accrues to those who fulfil them but no opprobrium is attached to people who do not observe them. Adam Smith's distinction between justice and benevolence is relevant here. Justice is a negative principle that prohibits harm and rights-violation. Benevolence, however, requires positive action for the realization of an intrinsically desirable goal, the well-being of others. Smith thought that commercial society required only the traditional rules of justice for it to function effectively. He maintained that benevolence was the highest of the moral virtues, but he also argued that it would be foolish to rely on this to motivate individuals to generate the public good. He was fully aware of the fact that the incentive for benevolent action weakened as the circle of people to be affected by it widened. Benevolence could only flourish in the narrow circle of the family and in intimate communities. As Smith observed: 'Nobody but a beggar chooses to depend chiefly on the benevolence of his fellow citizens.'[4] In the large, more or less anonymous, commercial societies of the contemporary world it is highly unlikely that benevolence will flourish out-side the family and the small community. Yet modern theorists of corpor-ate social responsibility expect it of the business enterprise.

Corporations which are urged to refrain from 'downsizing', (laying off workers to boost the share price) are, in effect, expected to act out of be-nevolence, to the detriment of profits. Such recommendations look like the importation of values appropriate to the family into the business en-terprise. This corporate altruism might work for Japan, where much less concern is shown for shareholder value, but it is inappropriate for indi-vidualistic economic cultures. Still, downsizing may not always be in the interests of the corporation. A time may come when it is advantageous to retain workers who are less than fully productive. It might think they will be needed in the near future, or it may want to encourage company loyalty. But whether a company does this or not will depend on economic circumstances, not on some contestable prescription from a super-erogatory business ethics. The appropriateness of downsizing does not depend on morality.

Paradoxically, business ethicists wish to make the supererogatory du-ties strictly enforceable, either by law or public opinion. But does this not drain them of genuine supererogatory morality, which is surely about the voluntary assumption of burdens? There is also the important qualifi-cation that various incentives, of a negative and positive kind, are offered to corporations to pursue the kind of virtue that is favoured by business moralists. It is said, for example, that it will ultimately increase profitabi-lity, it will make government regulation of business less likely, or that it will secure business agents high status in their communities. Even those anxious to make business genuinely moral tend to rely on the familiar incentives.

Critics of the social responsibility thesis have a point when they sug-gest that there is some hypocrisy at work here because a genuine moral-ity (except those ethical rules and conventions required to service a commercial order) normally involves a choice between adherence to a principle and the pursuit of self-interest (in the business world, profit). In most cases, the pursuit of the supererogatory duties involves cost. No doubt Mandeville, with cynical amusement, would have thought that the current claim that 'morality pays' is simply a slightly more complex affirma-tion of his basic egoistic principle. There is little doubt that the obser-vation of minimalist moral rules in business is not normally costly, but this is not what the social responsibility advocates have in mind. They recommend supererogatory principles for business, as if the com-mercial system were some kind of family or small, intimate community characterized by agreement over goals and purposes. Anglo-American economies are not often like this and require the sometimes ruthless application of the price mechanism to settle economic differences.

The type of corporate social responsibility that is usually suggested involves such things as the diversion of a certain portion of profits to community purposes, the protection of jobs and established working conditions in such things as takeovers and plant relocation, the enforcement of affirmative action in hiring policy, zealous protection of the environment and the inclusion of non-owners in important decision-making. Social responsibility is supposed to be exercised both in the way a corporation treats its employees and in the manner in which it behaves in society. Good 'corporate citizenship' is the phrase frequently used to describe this behaviour.

The question of affirmative action and quotas privileging certain minorities and ensuring equality by gender (sometimes called promoting 'diversity') has now become crucially important in the USA. For just as some court decisions (and prospective legislation) have reduced the effect of such policies in the public sector, they are even more significant (and diverse) in the private sector.[5] Ironically, it is probably the case that corporations are now more socially-responsible in relation to affirmative action policies than is the public sector. It might be that managements fear legal action if they do not guarantee diversity, although this is becoming less likely; or it might even be true that owners actually want this, though they would not be involved in day-to-day decisions. However, it might not be too cynical to suggest that the expansion of such programmes is an example of opportunism by managements. The promotion of social agendas is probably easier than working to maximize shareholder value. Indeed, the problem of opportunism is endemic to all principal–agent relationships: it is likely to be exacerbated by the desire for corporations to be socially responsible.

The potential range of the social responsibility thesis is clearly indicated in the language that is currently used to describe the types of relationships that are now thought to characterize an ideal modern economic society: at least for moralists. The company does not merely comprise owners, directors, managers and workers, all bound together in various sorts of individualistic contractual relationships, but is envisaged as an entity, the members of which are connected by other and vaguer social bonds. The ties that bind the participants in such organizations are moral rather than strictly economic and legal. They can be summarized by the claim that elevated social and moral duties are of equal importance to commerce as are contractual ones. If the company is interpreted in this way there are few limits on its social responsibility – except bankruptcy.

THE STAKEHOLDER IDEA

The dominant theme in the social responsibility thesis is the 'stakeholder' theory of the corporation. This is an unsubtle play on the word 'stockholder' but it has considerable emotional appeal. It is, of course, true that all the participants in a business, even one driven exclusively by the profit motive, are stakeholders in some sense. No successful organization treats its members in *purely* contractual terms, though the instrument of a binding contract is a crucially important feature of modern commerce. Workers and suppliers, for example, who contribute to long-term value, are not normally treated as merely means to an end, agents that can be easily disposed of in the pursuit of short-term profits. Quite apart from any substantial moral objection to heartless treatment of valued employees whose skills might temporarily be redundant, or a cavalier attitude to an established supplier who is suddenly undercut by a (perhaps) ruthless competitor, it is likely that such relentless short-termism does not contribute to long-term owner value. Reciprocity is a feature of good business. Firms will find it commercially advantageous to establish a good *reputation* in its dealings with employees and others. But this is more accurately described as prudence than the pursuit of an extra-commercial morality.

Indeed, critics of Western capitalism often point to the fact that economic organizations that build on long-term relationships of *trust*[6] actually do better than those which make immediate profit their goal. One reason for this is that participants in Western commerce tend to rely on *law* as a protective device in the face of the vicissitudes of economic fortune. A purely contract-based economy undoubtedly incurs significant legal costs.[7] The development of trust between business agents reduces transactions costs and therefore increases long-term value. Still, the moral significance of all this should not be exaggerated. All these apparently virtuous constraints on immediate gratification are sanctioned by a concern for economic value. It may not be the value revealed by the share price, which might possibly be influenced by short-term factors, but it is a concern for ultimate profitability that determines business behaviour.

It is highly unlikely that any owner would find it in his or her interests to deal in *completely* arm's-length terms. However, to refrain from so doing is not an example of that altruism or benevolence which many business ethicists recommend, but is to be interpreted as the kind of ethical behaviour which is necessary for good (in both its economic and moral sense) business. It is, in fact, a normal feature of sensible commerce. Since Adam Smith, writers on business have noticed how self-imposed constraints on egoism contribute to long-term well-being.

But all this is a long way from the kind of stakeholder theory that is recommended by contemporary business moralists.[8] For what they demand is a significant modification of the original minimalist rules and a reduction in the powers of owners. They should no longer have the familiar rights of ultimate decision-making; these must be located in the whole network of groups and interests that compromise the firm or corporation. And the decisions that emerge here must not be solely dictated by the need to create long-term owner value but must honour the claims that particular stakeholder groups may make. Thus the contemporary stakeholder theorists of the corporation, Evan and Freeman, write: 'The reason for paying returns to owners is not that they "own" the firm, but that their support is necessary for the survival of the firm, and that they have a legitimate claim on the firm.'[9] What we have here is the elimination of any coherent idea of ownership: for if anyone who has some vague connection with an enterprise has some claim on it, then no one properly owns it. If no one properly owns something, then nobody will preserve, let alone enhance, its value.

It turns out then that the owners' returns are not a necessary reward for their investment but merely payment for their contingent, although necessary, role in the success of the enterprise. The owners' position is on a par with that of any other stakeholder. By definition, all stakeholders are essential for an enterprise's success, but this is a long way from saying that each stakeholder's contribution is of *equal* value (which is what Evan and Freeman are saying). As the authors recognize, what is at work here is an explicitly Kantian conception of the corporation: a notion that sees the fulfilment of certain duties taking precedence over the maximization of any kind of want-satisfaction, especially that of the owners. What is not recognized in such theories is the obvious fact that shareholders are being used merely as means to the ends of other stakeholders, or at least to the ends of a shadowy collective entity – a decidedly unKantian idea. These ends consist of whatever social duties the theorists of business ethics have in mind. But is easy to demonstrate that

Business Ethics

this stakeholder theory is clearly incompatible with any meaningful theory of the firm.

STAKEHOLDERS AND THE ORGANIZATION OF THE FIRM

In the conventional structure of the firm, the nexus of rights comprise residual rights, control rights and decision rights.[10] The residual rights are held by the shareholders and these entitle them to the surplus (or profits) that remain after all operating costs have been paid. Control rights are the rights to appoint managers and these rights are normally delegated to directors by the shareholders. Decision rights are exercised in the day-to-day activities of management. Now it is true that because of the separation between ownership and control in the large-scale corporation, the owners will not exercise decision rights, although ultimately they can withdraw the control rights (and appoint new directors) from which the operational arrangements derive. It is clear that in the hierarchical structure of the firm, the various personnel have differential rights according to the positions they occupy. There will, of course, be considerable *inequality* in terms of decision-making power (and income earned) in the firm.

The determining factor in all this is property. If the purpose of the corporation is to maximize owner value, the owners will normally want their property to be used in the most productive (in an economic sense) ways. They *might* wish that property to be used for other purpose. They might forgo profitable opportunities to advance some social goal, or to grant the employees some privilege, for example, paying them more than the market value of their labour. They might want to adopt certain hiring policies that advantage particular deprived groups. But if they do so, they are simply recognising supererogatory, not compelling, duties. Such obligations are not at all implied by the theory of the corporation. Indeed, it may be improper to describe corporations that behave in this way as genuine business enterprises. If any do exist, they are better described as charities. But what theorists of corporate responsibility want to do is to impose these duties on managers of business enterprises. It is likely that they will be more receptive to these blandishments than owners proper.

However, if non-owners act in ways that are antithetical to the interest of owners, they are in breach of their contractual duties. The fact that employees have considerable control and decision rights delegated to them does not mean that they have unfettered discretion, for they are bound economically, legally and morally to the terms of their contracts.

Because of the dispersed nature of ownership in modern corporations it might be difficult to enforce contracts rigorously all the time but eventually they will have to be honoured and the market will develop appropriate methods of enforcement.

Now what is not realized by the theorists of corporate responsibility is that managerial discretion is just as likely to be used to advance the private interests of managers as it is to promote the apparently compelling non-economic duties of the corporation. In practice managements are likely to use their discretion in an opportunistic manner. This is always a danger because of the absence of direct control by owners. This was, of course, why Adam Smith distrusted the joint-stock company. For both economic and ethical reasons he preferred owner-managers. It is realistic to suggest that the assumption of social responsibilities by managements will quickly degenerate into opportunistic, purely self-interested behaviour.

Indeed, the really serious problem in the corporate form arises out of the difficulty of monitoring managements to ensure that they perform their contractual duties. This looks as if it is simply an efficiency problem, but it is partly moral, at least in the sense in which that word is used in market economics. For in the complete absence of trust, short-term gratification may result in long-term disadvantage for all participants in the system. If owners cannot trust managers, all sorts of costly monitoring devices will have to be used to guarantee compliance. It is a fact that in the USA shareholders do not trust their managers, and that is why the takeover mechanism is essential. But the heavy costs involved here could be avoided if managers always behaved ethically, and honoured their contractual duties. But this is not at all what business ethics has in mind when it talks of corporate responsibility. Still, the famed lack of trust between owners and managers in the USA has not harmed that country's economic prospects.

In fact, the greatest opportunistic and selfish behaviour by managers occurs in non-profit organizations, because here there are no identifiable 'owners'. Adam Smith noticed this in his short sojourn at Oxford University, where the dons were responsible to no one and behaved in a purely selfish manner.[11] The problem with non-profit organizations is that the donors have no guarantee that their funds will be used for the purposes for which they were intended. There is nothing especially virtuous about non-profit organizations; their personnel are likely to be governed by the same motivations as agents in conventional markets. Since the property is not 'owned' by identifiable persons it can easily be effectively appropriated by insiders. A number of important, and well-funded, US charitable foundations have been shifted by their personnel to directions far from the intentions of the original donors.

It is ironic that the duties of social responsibility should be left largely to managements of corporations, since all the behavioural evidence is that in the absence of direct ownership and control they will act in an opportunistic manner. The claim that they are advancing stakeholder, and general community-wide, interests can be an excellent cover for this. The long-run effect of stakeholder theory would be to turn commercial enterprises into *de facto* non-profit organizations, vulnerable to capture by managers. Yet this form of immorality is rarely noticed in the conventional business ethics literature. Apparently, the much-maligned 'imperialists' of earlier critical literature on the corporation[12] are now to be entrusted with the task of encouraging moral behaviour.

STAKEHOLDERS AND EFFICIENT BUSINESS

The stakeholder theory of the corporation subverts completely the conventional account of the firm, for it assumes that decisions should be made in the organization according to moral and social considerations (perhaps even political ones), and not solely for financial reasons. The management does not have to act so as to maximize shareholder value but is apparently under a duty to balance the possibly conflicting interests within an organization. This is openly admitted by Evan and Freeman when they claim that: 'The very purpose of the firm is to serve as a vehicle for stakeholder interests.'[13] The overtly political nature of the exercise is revealed by the use of the term 'constituencies' by some writers to describe subsections of an organization that press for consideration in its decision-making.[14] For them ultimate profitability, least of all that reflected in the share price, can never be an adequate test of corporate well-being.

It is, of course, true that the daily verdict of the stock market may not be an infallible guide to long-term owner value. Managements will often take decisions that seem to be in defiance of it, and there may be an economic rationale for this. It is also true that they are likely to be influenced by the opinions of the constituencies, and the effects that such decisions will have on significant interests. Indeed, it would be part of the rational long-term strategy of the firm to reach accommodations with those constituencies that have an effect on profitability. But this does not mean that members of constituencies have 'moral rights' to favourable treatment.

These considerations, however, are fully consistent with the economic theory of the firm and with business strategy. But they are much less than what the stakeholder theorists have in mind. What they wish to do is to make supererogatory duties, which attenuate profitability and the rights of ownership, obligatory by positive law, or at least by the force of public opinion. These duties are not likely to have anything to do with the interests of the firm: they will reflect the *social* concerns of business ethics. A good example in the USA has been the long campaign by anti-business activists to enforce the federal chartering of corporations.[15] At present they can be chartered (that is, secure legal recognition of their articles of association) in any state. For historical reasons, and because of the tradition in corporate law that it has developed, Delaware is the favoured location for large corporations. Still, the possibility of jurisdictional competition for corporate chartering remains. But it would be ended were federal chartering to be enacted. Then corporations would be vulnerable to whatever restrictions the Congress might wish to impose on them. Corporations could then more easily be captured by non-owner interests precisely because competition for corporate chartering would be eliminated.

So far the campaign for federal chartering has failed but it is important to know what its proponents have in mind. The most important feature would be a change in boards of directors (those who exercise control rights) of publicly-held companies. The suggestion is that up to a majority should be 'outsiders' – that is, those not directly connected with the management or ownership of the company – and that they should represent constituencies that would presumably not to be adequately promoted by the normal operation of the market economy. Indeed, the outsiders may not even be stakeholders in a direct sense, let alone shareholders. Can these outsiders really be expected to behave morally – in accordance with the tenets of the dictates of the corporate social responsibility thesis?

Under such circumstances it is difficult even to imagine how the corporation could function efficiently. In heavily-politicized conditions, economic rationality could not survive. For if the corporation is a nexus of contracts, the imposition of externally-imposed (political) requirements on the parties to those agreements would atrophy that creativity which is a crucially important feature of the market. New forms of contracting, which emerge in order to maximize shareholder value, would be forever vulnerable to outside pressures. Equally important is the fact that if a majority of outsiders were empowered by law to make corporate decisions, then it is certain that those decisions would not be in the interests of the owners. Indeed, who would entrust their assets to a company under such circumstances? Ironically, the proposals would *artificially* complete the separation between ownership and control which had developed spontaneously from at least the early part of this century. The nominal owners really would have little influence at all and the returns they earn would almost certainly decline.

As has been noted, this disjuncture between ownership and control presents opportunities for managements to shirk their responsibilities. Corporate owners develop methods for policing managements, and there is always the final sanction of selling shares to a raider who will then replace existing inefficient personnel, but the problem is a more or less permanent feature of the corporate form. However, it would be immense if some of the reformers' recommendations were implemented, since these would virtually deprive ownership of all its traditional and essential rights. Even in the German economy, which is often presented as the model of a stakeholder society (trade unions are represented on the supervisory boards of companies and social factors are apparently taken into account in decision-making), the owners exercise ultimate control. Recently, they have been using that power by investing overseas, where the returns to capital are higher than at home. The laws of economics, if they are allowed to operate, will quickly defeat the injunctions of business ethics. They will do so eventually anyway, whether they are formally allowed to or not, although at a slower pace. Economies that attempt to resist them will eventually decline.

Fortunately, the campaign for federal chartering in the USA seems to have abated in recent years. Most observers, including even J.K. Galbraith,[16] now concede that competition is an effective constraint on corporate imperialism. Indeed, the observed tension in the USA between shareholders and managements is quite productive since it reduces opportunism. In fact, in an efficient market economy, corporate governance should be mainly about ensuring responsibility of managers to owners, although in Britain, notions of community responsibility and the alleged necessity of outside representation on boards are entering the debate. Non-executive directors are sometimes recommended to represent community interests on the board. But this could have an adverse effect on internal entrepreneurship; non-executive directors might allow social values to subvert economic logic and impede innovation which offends the interests of a particular constituency.

In the stakeholders' economy of Japan, stockholders earn very low returns and have very little influence on the companies they nominally own. Any gains they made were only possible through the increase in the capital value of their holdings. But even this prospect was shattered by the meltdown of the Tokyo stock market that began in the early 1990s. The great influence of the banks on business in Japan and the overweaning power of managements do not make her system a model of the stakeholder society which is suitable for imitation by Anglo-American companies. Furthermore, the closed nature of Japanese business has made it susceptible to infiltration by criminals.[17]

STAKEHOLDER THEORY AND CONVENTIONAL ETHICS

The aim of stakeholder theory is to establish some sort of equality between the groups that make up an enterprise. But this is surely an impossible project (short of the socialization of all productive assets, including labour). While they are nested in the context of legal equality, commercial arrangements will generate inequality according to the value that the various participants add to enterprise. In fact, the value of shareholders' contributions is undermined to the extent that the freedom to dispose of assets is limited by statute law. The best example of this is in the limitations on takeover activity that have been placed by state legislatures in the USA since the 1980s. This has resulted in the further entrenchment of managements, who are stakeholders themselves. The statutory limitations on takeovers were no doubt introduced to protect stakeholders from the adverse effects of industrial restructuring. But it is difficult to see how such interventions advance a meaningful notion of equality; they simply result in one group being advantaged at the expense of others.

Even if it were possible to sustain an enterprise economy in the circumstances described (or prescribed) by stakeholder theory, either by statute or the voluntary actions of corporations, it is unlikely that the aims of fairness could be achieved in practice. The point here is that the interests of stakeholders conflict, and the possibility of irreconcilable differences increases, the wider the range of stakeholders becomes. And it has become successively wider. Now it includes not just employees, suppliers and others intimately connected with the business itself, but also the local communities in which a particular enterprise is located. Some corporations even claim that their purpose is to serve the customer (the ultimate stakeholder?) not the shareholder, though why there should be a conflict between these two groups is hard to imagine. In fact, this claim is merely a piece of commercial rhetoric.

Conflicts between various stakeholder interests are certain to occur over things such as a plant relocation. In this example, economic logic, and therefore the maximization of shareholder value, might indicate that an enterprise should move to a new site some distance from its original location. Though this will be good news for the inhabitants of the new site, it will reduce the well-being of the original employees. Is there any definitive solution to this conflict between two rival stakeholders? One group must inevitably lose in this and similar economic processes. Of course, the market is not 'fair' to everybody in its allocative function, but the alternative, a heavily democratized and politicized system of corporate management, would surely be even less fair.

It might be objected that the use of shareholder interests (and the share price) as the criterion of value is no less arbitrary than the accommodation of competing groups that stakeholder theory implies. This is, of course, logically true, but to point it out merely asks us to differentiate between rival general economic systems: one based on individualism and free choice and the other dedicated to the promotion of collective purposes. And this is surely a problem for economic philosophy. But who today could deny that the market is superior, not just to completely planned systems, but also to those mixed economies which are often favoured by writers on business ethics? It is true that capitalism can flourish in a variety of social systems but profitability and economic value are tests that are common to them all. The verdict of the market is preferable to the opinions of coalitions of stakeholders. The difficulty of these combinations reaching coherent decisions is compounded by the fact that individuals are likely to belong to more than one stakeholder group.

Furthermore, it must be stressed that shareholder interests are not simply those of millionaire investors: they overwhelmingly encompass the savings of ordinary people in insurance policies, pension schemes and so on. What is clear is that the Western market capitalist system would be unsustainable if some of the claims of stakeholder theory were accepted and incorporated into law, or carried out informally by opportunistic managements.

Of the many problems associated with stakeholder theory the most serious is the potentially conflicting nature of the demands that the various groups make on the organization. The most adventurous of the stakeholder ideologues, Evan and Freeman, recognize that there is a problem with their own case. To counter the argument that there is likely to be an absence of agreement between stakeholder groups they recommend that the corporation should have a 'metaphysical director'[18] who would reconcile and balance the competing claims that are made on the firm. But who would make the appointment to such an exalted position, and why should not that decision itself be subject to the opinions of all stakeholder groups? Apart from the somewhat bizarre nature of the idea, which sounds like rent-seeking by philosophers, it is clear that it is vitiated by the absence of a common scale of values by which the claims can be assessed and out of which some definitive solution can be reached. One can only assume that should a 'metaphysical director' be appointed, the first thing he or she would do would be to reject the exclusive claims of the market in decision-making. An acceptance of them would, of course, make the metaphysical director redundant.

In Western pluralistic societies there is an absence of common purposes, beyond a commitment to general, impartial rules of just conduct. This pluralism is undoubtedly reflected in economic arrangements which are characterized by considerable fluidity and labour mobility. Things are different in more communal social orders where there is an agreement about purposes and in which the individualistic impulse is subordinated to a collective endeavour. Indeed, the Japanese industrial system, with its tradition of lifetime employment and its pronounced distaste for the takeover mechanism, is looked upon by some Western business ethicists as a more morally pleasing commercial model than the conventional Anglo-American variety. However, it should be remembered that the typical Japanese corporate structure only applies to a portion (about 40 per cent) of the country's economy and that the *de facto* prohibition against takeovers is (from an efficiency point of view) productive of considerable rigidity. A long period of recession (since about 1990) is compelling even Japanese companies to rethink their corporate strategy. Economically and ethically they appear inward-looking and insular and their much-vaunted non-individualistic values function as barriers to outsiders.

What would happen if the ideas embodied in stakeholder theory were taken seriously as a model for corporate governance is that the strategy of the firm would be virtually paralysed by the incessant bargaining that would have to take place between interested parties. It would be a kind of industrial reflection of the often self-destructive activities of pressure groups in parliamentary politics. Both phenomena arise out of the pluralism that is ineluctably a feature of Western societies. In the absence of a common scale of social values which can authoritatively order the competing claims that are made on the organization, there really is no alternative to using profitability as the criterion of value. After all, the purpose of a business enterprise is to increase owner-value. The people most likely to promote owner-value are those most closely associated with the

business and those who face an incentive structure which encourages innovation and internal entrepreneurship. The influence of outside directors representing the community can only be detrimental to this.

The claim that an economy organized under market principles maxi-
mizes social utility is part of the *overall* justification of private enterprise
(which is actually well-founded) but it is not *logically* a part of the rationale
of the prevailing corporate form in the West. Free societies may generate
competing commercial systems, of which the largely shareholder-driven
Anglo-American type is only one. Thus the objection to the application
of stakeholder theory to the West is moral as well as economic: it under-
mines property rights and would convert a free enterprise individualist
order to a collectivist system in more subtle ways than communism
ever did. Whether or not the Western form of capitalism is the most efficient is simply an empirical question which economic history will one
day answer.

Interestingly, the empirical tests are now beginning to support the
Anglo-American style of economic organization and corporate governance. The rigidities that stakeholder capitalism produces are now undermining the efficiency of the German economy and there are increasing
demands for a more American style of stock market-driven enterprise
system. Furthermore, a fundamental law of economics that business
ethics thought was not universal – the theory which says that capital
flows to where the returns are highest – is now proving to be inexorable:
German capital is now being invested more heavily overseas than at
home.[19] This is partly due to the excessive non-wage labour costs imposed
by the prevailing version of the 'social market economy', but it is also
a consequence of the rigidity of German corporate organization and its
relative lack of concern for shareholder value. There is evidence that the
takeover device is being looked on more favourably in that country and
it is likely to produce something the diverse stakeholder groups can
agree on – opposition to the necessary change and reorganization which
corporate raiders threaten to bring about.[20] But such an agreement can
only harm the economy.

CORPORATE VIRTUES AND VICES

The most common way in which ownership rights are subtly undermined by business ethics is in the demand that corporations should be
charitable; they should not be concerned solely with maximizing shareholder value, but must devote part of their resources to the community.

It is rare that the observation of conventional moral rules is inconsistent with profitability but it is obvious that the following of supererogatory duties (of which corporate giving is one example) often is. It might be the case that corporations do it so as to gain a favourable public image, the activity is then related to long-term profitability, but if that is the reason for such action its genuine supererogatory morality is highly questionable. No one could possibly claim that corporate sponsorship of sporting events is anything other than an advertising strategy (whatever companies might say about the need to promote the nation's health or its international athletic stature). What, then, is the logic of corporate giving and what part does it play in the morality of business enterprise?

In orthodox market theory, the owners of an enterprise are residual claimants, they have a legal title to the surplus generated once all operating costs have been paid. As has been shown, the reason why we have corporations, as well as owner-managed firms, arises out of efficiency: it is simply more efficient in many circumstances for the owners of capital to entrust the management of their assets to others. It is also better to organize production in the corporate form than to use the *direct* market. This, of course, does not in any way reduce their property rights in a formal sense but the existence of the corporation does make a difference to the arguments about corporate giving. It is not always clear to whom the demand that corporations be charitable is addressed – the owners or the managers?

It might be thought that it is obviously the owners. But this is not clear from business ethics. Many of the writers in this field do not accept that the major purpose of a corporation is to maximize shareholder value, they do not recognize property ownership as decisive in the control of the firm (as we have seen from stakeholder theory) and they claim that private enterprise exists only by permission of society. From this perspective it does not matter who approves, and chooses, corporate charitable giving, since the conventional authority structure of capitalist institutions has been rejected. Yet a sensible argument about corporate charity has to focus on owners and managers.

There are reasons to doubt the sincerity of the moral motivations of both groups. We have already noticed that there is no objection in principle to owners forgoing profit on behalf of a cause. But it could be argued that in most cases the owners are simply using the corporate form to secure a tax advantage. We would hardly call charitable giving to secure a tax break a good example of genuine altruism. Although the opportunities are somewhat limited in the USA, and significantly less in other capitalist countries, the very fact of their existence is sufficient to

Business Ethics

doubt the sincerity of much corporate giving. In a fully competitive economy there is little opportunity for it anyway.

If managements take the decisions on corporate donations, which they often do given the discretionary authority which the corporate form gives them, then this can hardly be called charitable at all. They, of course, welcome this activity, since it affords them an apparently legitimate opportunity to evade their primary responsibility of working for the shareholders. It seems rather odd to assign to managers the roles of moral agents, as we have noticed they are the most likely persons in an organization to behave opportunistically. If they require monitoring to ensure that they perform their normal commercial duties (as defined by the principal–agent relationship) then they should be subject to similar supervision when playing the charitable role.

But even if they are appropriately motivated there is still the problem of moral knowledge. To whom are corporations to be charitable? Just as in the case of stakeholder representation, there are many interests that press on the charitable actions of the corporation and the decision to reward one group with special benefits and not others must ultimately be discretionary, if not arbitrary. This does not matter in cases of genuine charity; the donor is at liberty to give to whatever cause he or she likes since it is his or her assets that are being disbursed. But is surely significant when managements are distributing other people's money on behalf of 'society'. Are there any objective standards by which rival claims to corporate largesse can be evaluated?

One of the reasons why corporations, either through their managements or their owners, are eager to be seen to be acting charitably is that the beneficiaries of such activity are visible. Owners may have a self-interest in performing such acts because their very visibility may be useful in their attempts to ward off threatened excessive regulation by government. One of the reasons for the only modest popularity of the market with the general public is that its benefits are invisible.[21] The increase in productivity and general prosperity that the private property system brings are enjoyed by essentially anonymous people. But the 'victims' of the incessant change generated by the market are highly visible and easy to identify by those anxious to modify the behaviour of the participants in the exchange system.

But the undermining of the property rights of owners is not the only consequence of managements taking on the role of corporate benefactors. In fact, it is probably minor. Of greater importance is the fact that very often what look like acts of corporate virtue have consequences (presumably unintended) which are not at all beneficial. Using the above distinction between visible and invisible effects, and an actual example from Henry Manne,[22] it can be shown how alleged cases of corporate social responsibility had malign results. In the late 1960s Coca-Cola introduced a private welfare scheme for its employees who were working in somewhat undesirable conditions in Florida, although these workers were immigrants from the Third World where conditions were far worse. However, this virtuous action significantly raised Coca-Cola's costs so that they were forced to hire fewer workers. What was noticed were the improved conditions of those who remained employed, but no one was aware of the unknown people who were deprived of jobs. It was another example of the difference between economics and ethics. The co-ordinating processes of the former rarely attract publicity, no matter how beneficial they are. The latter, whether they involve good or bad behaviour by business agents, are a constant source of fascination for observers. This Coca-Cola example has been repeated elsewhere in the world of business charity.

Few of these problems would arise if social responsibility, in the expanded sense, were displayed by *private* companies. Here there are no public shareholders to worry about and the owners are personally putting their capital at stake and can (presumably) afford to sacrifice profit in the pursuit of supererogatory moral goals. It is interesting to note that perhaps the most virtuous of British companies, Body Shop plc, did once consider going private so as to be free of shareholder pressure in order to pursue its goals of environmentalism, the rejection of animal-tested products and concern for inhabitants of the Third World.[23] However, it soon reasoned that the burden of bank debt, which would be required if it were to go private, would produce the same irksomeness of pressure for value as shareholders do. In a later public statement the company actually said that it would include shareholder interests among its goals. Ethics always runs up against economics.

In fact, the market does offer opportunities for moral action, for there are publicly-quoted companies that advertise their socially responsible behaviour and financial trusts that pick and choose their investments according to ethical criteria. The evidence so far on the performance of such investments is mixed.[24] However, the theoretical point here is clear: if people give up profitable opportunities to advance a cause, then their behaviour is genuinely moral. It involves a choice between alternatives, profits or ethics (though this should not be interpreted to mean that profit is itself unethical). When shareholders' capital is used to advance the moral agendas of management (and others who do not have to bear the costs) and is diverted from profitable (but still morally permissible) outlets, the situation is actually unethical. The shareholders then are being used merely as a means to the ends of others.

No theorist has ever suggested that however successful the market was in generating prosperity that this exempted the personnel of the corporation from the obligation to observe the basic rules of just conduct. But the argument that they should go beyond this merely because of the (superficially) special features of the corporate form is not compelling. For corporations that do so are in essence arrogating for themselves the role of government and paying for it with shareholders' money. Indeed, when business people get involved in politics they rarely advance a genuine morality. They are more likely to seek exemptions from market constraints and protective tariffs (on behalf of the 'public good') than to work assiduously for the rule of law and the maintenance of competitive conditions.[25]

This is not to deny that business faces ethical problems even when it keeps within the positive law and tries to observe the injunctions of conventional morality. Indeed, because of the familiar public good problems, business agents are likely to face ethical dilemmas not encountered by the ordinary citizen. This is especially so in the problems over the environment, where a decision not to pollute, when it is legal to do so and when property rights are not decisive, can involve a company in avoidable costs. The dilemmas here occur because the business community has not been all that successful in developing conventions that encourage self-restraint.

A special problem occurs in the manufacture of dangerous products. The normal moral constraints on risky activity are less effective when the manufacturer does not know the consumer of a potentially lethal product. Sometimes the argument for personal responsibility for action, an essential feature of any version of liberalism, may not be effective in conditions of consumer ignorance. The serious ethical problems for business arise when producers exploit their superior knowledge, to the detriment of consumers – that is, when the conditions of the market provide no incentive for moral behaviour. The exploitation of special knowledge may be an example of genuine entrepreneurship or it may be sheer opportunism. It is in the latter circumstances that arm's-length morality is at its weakest.

The long-running saga over tobacco is a case in point. Manufacturers so far have resisted damages claims for the harm that their product causes, largely on the ground that consumers are fully aware of the consequences of smoking and in a free society persons should be treated as autonomous agents capable of choice. Although as this is being written, in the USA serious inroads are being made into the previous invulnerability of tobacco companies. Again, it is an example of the visibility of corporate moral failing, if that is what the sale and advertisement of tobacco involves.

The ethical question concerns knowledge. Did the tobacco companies, in the early days, fail to reveal all they knew about the harmful effects of smoking? Certainly advertisements in the 1950s emphasized the beneficial effects of the habit, even though evidence of adverse consequences of tobacco consumption was beginning to emerge. The success or failure of future legal action against tobacco companies will turn on the meaning of the complex relationship between knowledge and responsibility. Legal actions will succeed against tobacco companies if it can be proved that they deceived consumers about the true state of their knowledge of the effects of smoking on health. The plea of *caveat emptor* may not be so morally and legally compelling in cases of clear deception.

However, it should be pointed out in defence of the tobacco companies that their exploitation (if that was what it was) of consumer ignorance relates to the 1950s and early 1960s only. The harmful effects of smoking have been known for over 30 years. Surely the companies cannot be blamed for causing people to start smoking since then. Tobacco advertising is thought to be particularly venal but it would be strange state of affairs if it were to be forbidden while the product itself is still legal. What is also in doubt is the exact nature of the threat involved and the cost to the public purse that treatment for lung cancer victims involves. In fact, even leaving aside the tax contribution smokers make, smokers are not a financial burden. Death from cancer is often quick and, if smokers die earlier than non-smokers, as is always claimed, they are less of a burden on pension systems. In the light of this evidence, the current campaign to make tobacco companies liable for health costs is economically misguided as well as punitive and vindictive.

The disturbing thing about the campaign against tobacco companies, and other manufacturers of potentially dangerous products which people willingly consume, is the implicit threat to freedom and personal responsibility that it involves. There is an increasing tendency to burden business with responsibilities which should be borne by individuals in a free society. Because corporations are thought to have 'deep pockets' (which are apparently unaffected by costly civil damages claims) they are thought to be easy targets for those who would absolve individuals from responsibility for action. It is certainly legitimate to censure corporations who deceive the public but this is very different from making them surrogate defendants in fashionable moral campaigns.

But all this shows is that the morality that we ought to apply to business is simply the conventional morality of a liberal society. Too often the thesis of corporate social responsibility is used to impose additional, supererogatory principles on business agents merely because they are engaged in profit-seeking activity. The stakeholder theory of the corporation and the imposition of social duties on business are prime examples of this. These ideals are promoted not to make the market system work better but rather to compel it to do things which are alien to its *telos*. Business exists to satisfy the demands of consumers, to provide employment for workers and returns to investors. It is not the appropriate purpose of business to implement a set of contestable social goals which have no market, or even significant political approval.

5 Insider Dealing

On a visit to England in the eighteenth century the French Enlighten-ment thinker, Voltaire, was tremendously impressed by the morality and liberality which were mainly brought about by commerce. In his *Letters on England*, he gave this famous panegyric to the London Stock Exchange:

> Go into the London Stock Exchange – a more respectable a place than many a court – and you will see representatives of all nations gathered there for the service of mankind. There the Jew, the Mohammedan, and the Christian deal with each other as if they were of the same religion, and give the name of infidel only to those who go bankrupt. There the Presbyterian trusts the Anabaptist, and the Anglican accepts the Quaker's promise.[1]

What he was describing was a world in which traders knew and trusted each other, where there was little or no regulation and where the peace-engendering and conflict-resolving features of capitalism were manifest.

However, it is doubtful if modern stock exchanges would be described in such idyllic tones today. Of course, they are very different from their embryonic counterparts in the eighteenth century. Their extraordinarily wide extent, and the range of securities in which they deal, make it unlikely that the kind of trust that Voltaire was describing could be repro-duced in the late twentieth century. The very anonymity of much securit-ies dealing means that formal regulation has to replace the informal methods of monitoring that featured strongly in earlier times.

It is unlikely that an observer today would share Voltaire's opinion of the trust and honesty of the London Stock Exchange. And the same goes for New York and the other big financial centres. Indeed, it is in financial markets that the most publicized business scandals have occurred, in the USA especially, and it is in them that the most virulent hostility to capitalism is evident. This is partly because some discredited ideas about wealth creation still persist in the public mind and in the writings and pronouncements of religious and moral leaders. Real eco-nomic value, it is said, consists in the production of goods and services, not in the mere shuffling of paper. Little understanding is shown of the essential role in co-ordinating economic activity that asset markets play,

91

nor is there much recognition of the entrepreneurial and value-creating activities of those who specialize in these areas.

The opportunities for moral criticism arise out of the very complexity of financial markets and the opportunities they give for deception and fraud by experts who can easily exploit the ignorance of the public. Furthermore, and this is especially relevant to the problem of insider dealing, there is serious doubt about the ownership of information, the source of the wealth that is created in asset markets. Though property rights inhere in knowledge, it is not as tangible as it is in normal goods, and the title to it may depend on complex contractual arrangements. The whole issue, as we shall see, involves contested notions of justice and fairness and the attempt to 'moralize' financial markets has raised other ethical questions to do with the rule of law and the role of the state in commerce. Honesty in financial markets seems to be an especial problem of Anglo-American economies, since a large part of the money for investment in them is raised in the stock market. The ethics of the stock market seems to be not much of a problem for economies that rely less on this method.

Despite the recent passage of the Criminal Justice Act (1993) in Britain, which strengthened the law against insider trading, it is clear that the debate on the issue has not subsided. Most people involved in capital markets are convinced that the new law, so far from clarifying the issue, has actually made matters worse.[2] The consensus seems to be that not only will it not deter the real wrongdoers but it potentially penalises honest market traders, or at least makes the performance of their legitimate business more risky. This will in the long run have an adverse effect on efficiency since those agents, primarily analysts, whose activities tend to make stock market prices reflect more accurately the value of companies, will be deterred from the information gathering process. The new law was a response to a European Directive which had the superficially attractive aims of ensuring the smooth operation of capital markets and of guaranteeing fairness to all participants. Successive laws, and important judicial decisions, have not made the situation much clearer in the USA.[3]

Those who doubt the value of legislation (especially criminal) here must have enjoyed the irony in the fact that Europe's most successful (until very recently) post-war economy, Germany, was not only the last to adopt the directive but never had any law, either criminal or civil, against the practice (though zealous enforcers of the principle of prohibition would no doubt argue that the problem did not arise there because the country has a smaller proportion of private shareholders than

Britain and, especially, the USA). Still, other capitalist economies, such as Hong Kong's, have no laws against insider dealing. Within capitalist regimes that do outlaw the practice, legal prohibition does not extend to all asset markets; in the USA it is not forbidden in the futures market and not always in the bond market. The new law in the UK in fact widened the range of securities that were to be covered to include gilts and local authority stock, futures and options. The previous law, the Company Securities (Insider Dealing) Act (1985), was limited to controlling trade in the shares of listed companies.

What these cursory observations show is that there is a great variety in the way the activity is treated even though there does seem to be a consensus that there is something reprehensible about it. But if it is a crime, it is clearly not like murder, rape or robbery; primarily because the nature of the offence is in doubt and the identity of the victim sometimes hard to establish. Indeed, there is a considerable body of scholarship, to be considered below, which not only supports the claim that insider dealing should not be criminalized, or even made a civil offence, but that its existence is actually beneficial to the smooth running of capital markets. This argument is, of course, much stronger than the one that focuses on the difficulty of defining the offence and enforcing the law. Insider dealing is a civil as well as a criminal offence in the USA and this, it is claimed, has led to a more efficient monitoring of the activity.

WHAT IS INSIDER DEALING?

At first glance insider dealing is simple enough to define. It is trading on price-sensitive information, by company employees or others closely connected with the firm, which has not been disclosed to other market participants. It is thought to give them an unfair advantage. Of course, this is far too simple, because a myriad of perfectly legitimate market transactions take place in which information is asymmetric (that is, it is not equally available to all participants). What is relevant here is the argument that in certain transactions there should be strict rules (adopted either for moral or, less plausibly, for efficiency reasons) which determine who has the right to trade, what information is to be available and who has the right to the profits that arise from success in the deals. It is here that the problems of definition begin, the ambiguity of the offence emerges and the doubts about the enforcement of the law and the appropriate punishment surface. One cynical observer[4] has likened the current campaign against insider dealing to the historical persecution of witchcraft – the authorities did not know what it really was or who the witches were but were convinced that some women were guilty and should have no defence against the charge.

In fact, legal prohibition of insider dealing is something of a latecomer to securities regulation. In the UK it did not become a criminal offence until 1980. In the USA it was not specifically forbidden by the Securities and Exchange Act (1934) and it was only a somewhat convoluted interpretation (in the 1960s) of regulations made under this law that created the civil offence of insider dealing. The criminalization of it soon followed.[5]

Indeed, such is the uncertainty that surrounds the issue that there have been well-articulated fears of a threat to the rule of law arising out of the attempts to prohibit the practice. Uncertainty about court interpretation of the law, the discretion granted to officials in its enforcement and the way they go about their investigations have combined to produce a great deal of insecurity and unpredictability for market traders. This is to leave aside the efficiency problems that arise whenever the flow of information to any market is arbitrarily impeded. Any serious analysis of insider dealing involves problems of economics, law and, not least, ethics.

THE LOGIC OF CAPITAL MARKETS

Capital markets, more than any others, depend for their efficiency on correct information. If capital is to be allocated to its most productive uses, investors must have up to date information about company performance. Of course, much of this is obtainable from company reports and other public documents, supplemented by painstaking research. In an ideal world this information is embodied in the share price. It is true that for good commercial reasons a company will not want to reveal some information. Perhaps it has made an important discovery which it wants to keep from competitors, or there is an impending takeover. It is facts such as these that are likely to have a dramatic effect on share prices. That is why it is often said that a scrap of information, perhaps picked up through casual conversation or through sheer good fortune, is worth a year's solid research.

It is, of course, the circumstances in which such scraps are acquired that lead to problems. The vast rewards that can accrue to the lucky possessors of such knowledge offend against contemporary moralistic notions of 'just' earnings. Income that comes from sources other than traditional forms of endeavour is thought to be particularly unjustified, no matter how much it may contribute to the overall co-ordination of economic activities. The sometimes justified animus against insider dealing derives from the claim that the miscreant is not working for the company, least of all for the economy as a whole, but using the persons and assets of others for his or her purely selfish ends.

In conventional economic theory the 'Efficient Markets Hypothesis' presupposes that at any point in time the prices of securities contain all publicly-disclosed information about companies which is relevant to their future prospects. The key expression here is 'publicly-disclosed', for it is certainly possible that non-disclosed information is highly significant. This has the implication that the only useful economic knowledge is that which is technically inside information. Once that is released, the prices will more accurately reflect underlying economic values. It is this feature of capital markets that has led to the argument that insider dealing is essential if the market is to be efficient.[6] The faster the information flows, the more accurate will be the array of prices that confronts potential investors. For some observers, questions of morality are subordinate to the goal of efficiency. This is largely because they think that ethical questions are inherently intractable whereas the results of an efficient allocation of resources are readily observable. In a perfectly-competitive general equilibrium there is no problem of insider dealing because each transactor is fully-informed of every possible outcome. When the securities market is perfectly co-ordinated a 'random walk' is said to be produced – that is, the choice of an investment is a bit like tossing a coin; the market has already absorbed all the relevant information. This was never taken too seriously until modern technology began to bring about improvements in the gathering of information.

There is, of course, an argument between economists as to whether the Efficient Markets Hypothesis is an adequate guide to economic value. Critics of Anglo-American capitalism argue that the obsession with shareholder value, and the over-zealous concern that managements are compelled to show for it, leads to the problems of short-termism and under-investment in those long-term projects the value of which is not revealed in the current prices of shares. Indeed, in Germany[7] a rather smaller proportion of investment finance is raised on the stock market than is the case in the UK and, especially, the USA. Perhaps this is another reason why insider dealing was not considered to be a problem there. However, it is thought to be a problem in the USA and the UK because, rightly or wrongly, these economies rely mainly on the market for the raising of capital and therefore the way in which it reaches its

evaluation of shares does raise serious problems of ethics. But also efficiency is involved, since if the market is perceived to be tolerating bla-
tant acts of injustice in its allocation of rewards it will function less
effectively as a capital raising method. People will be deterred from investment if they suspect that the market is rigged.

Obviously people who invest in the stock market do so because they
think that they know more than the information that is revealed in current prices. There is a distinction between long-term investors who hold
a diverse portfolio of shares (their well-being depends little on the latest
rumour that sweeps the market) and pure speculators. The latter make
their living by trying to predict sudden changes in prices. They are, of
course, the people most likely to be tempted by the gains that can be
made from insider dealing, and also its potential victims. But in principle all forms of successful stock market investment depend on the ability
of the investor to 'beat the market'. If the market were in perfect equilibrium there would be no possibility of supra-normal profits, that is the
obvious implication of the Efficient Markets Hypothesis. The question
then is the permissible means by which market traders may push the system towards this desirable, though temporary, state of affairs.

JUSTICE AND THE LAW

The aim of securities laws must be to bring about some fairness in the
never-ending process of the gathering and circulating of information;
which, it is hoped, will lead to efficiency as well as justifying morally the
personal profit that accrues to the successful. That fairness is really
about the rules that should govern legitimate claims to property, the
contracts that govern the relationship between owners of companies
and their employees and the practices that contribute to a reliable and
orderly market. Of course, all market equilibria are temporary and are
likely to be disturbed by changes in the data that confront transactors.
Thus, although there can be no economic predictability, traders are entitled to some legal certainty and guarantees of fairness in the rules that
govern stock exchanges. A glance at the major cases in US and British
law gives us some idea of the problems involved in the issue.

For many years insider dealing was not technically prohibited under
US securities law (the bulk of which is contained in the Securities
and Exchange Act, 1934). It became so by judicial interpretation of
rules made under that legislation. The significant case was the Texas
Gulf Sulphur affair which was decided in 1968.[8] The employees of the

company had made a valuable mineral strike in Canada and had refrained from a public announcement until they had bought stock. Once the announcement was made they secured profits. They were eventually convicted of the *civil* offence of 'insider dealing' through an innovative interpretation of Regulation 10b under the 1934 Act, which forbids the 'employment of manipulative and deceptive practices'. Only later did it become a specific statutory civil and criminal offence. It is not at all clear that those involved in the activity were aware, or indeed could have been aware, that what they were doing was illegal. Many thought that the law simply forbade fraud and deliberate misrepresentation. The case clearly involved the question of who had the right to use information and also the problem of ensuring some predictability in the law.

Later cases did, however, establish some principles. It became clear that to be convicted of the offence the person had to be in a fiduciary relationship with the company – for example, a director or employee who held some position of trust – and he or she had to gain from the transaction. Of course, the temptation has been for the prosecuting authorities (in the USA, the Securities and Exchange Commission brings civil actions while the Justice Department brings criminal charges) to widen the scope of the fiduciary relationship. There must be some uncertainty here for the line of liability from the original insider and the 'tippee' (the person who first receives the information) is potentially endless.

However, the US Supreme Court, in some important decisions has to an extent clarified the issue. In the famous *Chiarella* case,[9] a printer for a Wall Street newsletter who cracked the code containing important news, on which he traded mildly, had his original conviction overturned on the ground that he did not owe a fiduciary duty to anybody. The mere fact of having the knowledge was insufficient. The Court held that no duty was owed to the market itself. This is important because many opponents of the practice cite a general duty on transactors to uphold the 'integrity of the market'. In the *Dirks* case,[10] a financial adviser, who knew that a company was about to be investigated for serious fraud and warned his clients, was convicted of insider dealing. However, his conviction was overturned on appeal because he did not personally profit from the revelation.

However, the law in America is by no means clear-cut. This was apparent in the *Winans* case[11], in which the writer of the *Wall Street Journal*'s 'Heard on the Street' column, who traded on the shares he himself recommended (based on no technical inside knowledge at all), had his original conviction for insider dealing upheld by the court. His sin was to 'misappropriate information' properly belonging to the *Journal*. The newspaper itself was content to dismiss him. This case raised questions of civil liberties and freedom of expression.

However, the really important convictions did not strictly involve insider dealing at all. They were about financial intermediaries, normally investment bankers, who were in a strict fiduciary relationship with their contracting partners. Thus Dennis Levine, who worked on takeovers for a number of investment banks on Wall Street, traded on the advance knowledge he was bound to possess.[12] He also sold information to Ivan Boesky, the Wall Street arbitrageur. Nobody protested about the propriety of their convictions and sentences, since Levine clearly was in a strict fiduciary relationship with the banks. His actions made him a thief and Boesky a fence. No bidder in a prospective takeover wants his intentions revealed.

In the UK there has never been a civil offence of insider dealing (although it is always theoretically possible for private actions under common law to be brought against company employees for breach of duty). Since 1980 the only serious sanction has been criminal. There is a parallel to the Levine–Boesky case in the conviction of Gordon Collier,[13] who worked on takeovers for the merchant bank, Morgan Grenfell, and traded on his advance knowledge. He received a heavy fine, and a suspended prison sentence. The only person to be imprisoned in Britain was Ivor Goodman, the director of a company who unloaded a vast amount of stock in the firm when he was in possession of privileged information about poor prospects.[14] This was a clear case of breach of fiduciary duty and the only interesting theoretical question is whether such wrongdoing should be disciplined by criminal or civil law.

There is, however, a case for insider dealing under certain circumstances that derives from a mixture of economic, moral and legal theory. But the various elements in such an hypothetical defence must be clearly distinguished. A person could argue, on economic grounds, for both the decriminalization of the activity *and* its immunity from civil law prohibitions of the type pursued by the Securities and Exchange Commission in the USA. This would still permit companies to forbid the activity in their normal contracts of employment (it would really be bizarre if a fanatical advocate of insider dealing were to recommend that individuals and companies should not themselves be allowed to take action against it). The more persuasive argument is to recommend that the activity should be decriminalized, largely because of the difficulty of securing convictions under the quite strict burden of proof required for criminal cases, and also because there is some difficulty in determining a clear notion of 'harm' as opposed to the demonstration of some unfairness in what is understood to be a necessarily risky activity. Those who recommend something like the creation of an SEC for the UK are implicitly appealing to the latter argument. They would like to make insider dealing a civil offence only.

I should like to consider first the argument for the complete removal of criminal and civil *statutory* law from the activity. But the upholders of this position would, of course, insist on the rigorous pursuit of those who use fraud, misrepresentation and other forms of deception in their dealings in securities.

THE CASE FOR INSIDER DEALING

Those who would both decriminalize insider dealing and make the activity immune from any civil action except those brought under private law, rest their case broadly on grounds of economic efficiency. They are not normally interested in ethics. Henry Manne summed up this position with admirable clarity with this comment: 'Morals, someone once said, are a private luxury. Carried into the area of serious debate on public policy, moral arguments are frequently either a sham or a refuge for the intellectually bankrupt.'[15] However, efficiency theorists unavoidably find themselves involved in moral argument, albeit of a negative kind, when they claim (with the occasional qualification) that no one is harmed by insider dealing. In their view any voluntary exchange is welfare-enhancing if no one is made worse off by it. Their commitment is to a minimalist morality. What they are concerned to refute is the idea that the distribution of income that emerges from voluntary transactions in securities is of any economic or moral significance. If they have a theory of justice it is limited to the strict enforcement of the basic rules of exchange – for example, those that prohibit fraud, misrepresentation, misappropriation of property and breach of contract.

The argument in favour of insider dealing derives entirely from the efficiency properties of unhampered markets, and this applies as much to securities as to any market in conventional goods and services. If the Efficient Markets Hypothesis is to function as a guide to the accurate pricing of securities, information must be allowed to circulate. The fewer restrictions there are, the faster this information will flow. Indeed, the profits of the insider will be lower the quicker the information is transmitted. To the argument that insider dealing leads to unjustified inequalities of income it is replied that not only are they not unjustified but also that the situation is more unequal under regulation and criminal-ization because then the really unscrupulous will make vast profits.

As a statement of pure economic theory this is unexceptionable. In equilibrium, which does assume perfect knowledge, there can be no ex-ploitation and profits that can be obtained by someone's possession of information are instantaneously competed away. Proponents of insider dealing maintain that this, admittedly imaginary, state of affairs is more likely to be approached, though never reached, in real world markets, in a regime of minimal interference. Insiders trading on specialized know-ledge actually push the market towards this theoretical nirvana. Of course, companies may have special reasons for restricting the activity but, according to the theory, this should be a matter for negotiation between them and their employees. It should not be a matter for criminal law, or compulsory civil law enforced by a state agency.

What the proponents of insider dealing are objecting to is the idea of a 'level playing field' in securities markets, more particularly the idea that statute law should try to produce it. If this refers to the supposed ne-cessity of equality of information among transactors it is plainly absurd (outside the purely theoretical models of perfect competition in equilib-rium theory). Markets are only needed when there is inequality of informa-tion – otherwise there would be no reason why anyone should exchange. If there are no incentives for people who think they know more than actual markets to buy and sell then the exchange system cannot play its co-ordinating role. Compulsory law here simply inhibits the search for knowledge.

In this model, equality of opportunity means simply that there should be no restrictions on anyone expending the time and effort to ferret out the information. Equality simply requires open access. Disparities in in-formation can be competed away. Not all information is contained in company reports and other published material, but close study of the market will reveal facts not readily available to the casual observer. It is the role of analysts to discover it. Of course, it is difficult to imagine that all the advantages the insider has over outside shareholders can be com-peted away, as that argument would imply. After all, a public company is not going to reveal its future development plans to any enquiring and as-siduous shareholder. The somewhat limited notion of equality of oppor-tunity is apparently satisfied by the fact that it is always (theoretically) possible for the outsider to work for the company so as to whittle away the original disadvantage. This is somewhat implausible, though it does indicate that Anglo-American business is 'open' and much information is generally available to those prepared to make the effort to find it.

This superficial justification for the obvious inequality that the insider has over the outsider is sometimes strengthened by the invocation of features of the firm itself, especially the separation between ownership and control. The fact that in modern production systems the owners of enterprises do not normally manage them directly is simply a function of specialization and the division of labour. Owners hire managers to handle their assets more efficiently than they can. An implication of this would seem to be that the owners do not hire managers to exploit their ignorance in the stock market.

However, the case for the permissibility of insider dealing largely rests on the claim that the profits from this activity are simply a part of the justified emoluments of employees. In fact, the possibility of making such gains will, it is claimed, motivate employees to work harder for the firm. It is, of course, always possible for the owners to make contracts that forbid it, but the fact that very few firms did so before insider dealing became formally illegal strengthens the argument that it was an activity that shareholders thought was generally beneficial, or at least not reprehensible.

The justification for insider dealing that flows from this argument largely depends on an application of the theory of entrepreneurship to the earnings of company employees. In economic theory entrepreneurs, through their skill and foresight in spotting gaps in the market, in anticipating consumer demand and in introducing new products and production techniques, earn profits or income above that paid to the labour factor of production in perfectly competitive equilibrium. It is the entrepreneur's alertness to the potential difference between the price of resources and the final product price that justifies the extraordinary profits that can sometimes be gained. We normally think of entrepreneurs as the great innovators in industry, individuals who break up existing economic forms with their revolutionary discoveries or market flair[16] and their vast earnings do have a plausible justification. Many of the existing corporate structures that might be thought of as engaging in routine production processes, and whose personnel receive payment according to conventional marginal productivity theory, are usually the products of original acts of entrepreneurship.

However, the concept is increasingly used to describe innovative activity within the firm. So what was conventionally thought of as routine productive activity by employees is often said to be a form of entrepreneurship – as a certain type of creativity to which the authors are entitled to at least some of the rewards.[17] In other words, a wide range of economic activity is value-creating in the original sense of that word. If it is just that acts of discovery in the market at large should be rewarded with profit, then why should not innovators and creators in the firm get their profits through share dealing? Insider dealing would be one way of achieving this.

This position is given an initial plausibility by a consideration of some comments made by Joseph Schumpeter, himself a pioneer of the theory of entrepreneurship. He thought that capitalism would spontaneously slip into a form of socialism precisely because of the drying up of opportunities for entrepreneurship in the modern world.[18] For him the entrepreneur was the destroyer of existing industrial structures rather than the person who contributed to overall co-ordination by discrete acts of adjustment to ever-changing circumstances. In fact we know, for a number of by now well-known reasons, that Schumpeter was wrong about the future course of capitalism, but it is important to focus on his implicit claim that entrepreneurship did not take place within the firm. Yet if it does, as most observers now concede, then there might well be an argument to the effect that the innovators are entitled to rewards that go beyond the payment that is normally made to a factor of production according to its marginal productivity.[19] Permitting the discoverers and innovators within the firm to trade in the stock market on privileged information is thought by some writers to be a legitimate form of income, in the absence of which entrepreneurship would dry up. Why should the shareholder, who merely lends the capital, be entitled to all the gains that accrue from discovery and creativity? Should not those employees of Texas Gulf Sulphur who made the initial mineral strike have a claim to some of the 'profits' from their entrepreneurship over and above the normal emoluments in the form of salaries, bonuses and so on?

In fact the main thrust of the argument for insider dealing does not really turn on quasi-moral notions of entitlement to these earnings but rather on the utilitarian claim that entrepreneurship within the firm can only be encouraged if there is some prospect that individuals will be able to secure some reward for their efforts. However, companies have developed a number of schemes to promote innovative activity which do not involve the risks, such as the cheating of stockholders, that can occur if employees are permitted to trade on inside information.

Perhaps the more interesting question really is about the morality of those gains that can be made from insider dealing, irrespective of utilitarian considerations. Is the use of privileged information a form of theft? Do the stockholders own every asset that is created in the commercial actions of the firm or are some of them, which are created by a particular person's ingenuity, at least partly owed to him or her? Can a distinction be drawn between stealing the office furniture and the appropriation of knowledge which a person may have been instrumental in creating?

This is really a question about property ownership and may partly turn upon the state of the positive law. In a regime with no statutory law about the use of company property, or indeed its definition, the assignment of property rights will depend on the particular contractual arrangements between the firm's owners and its employees. In some cases, even without statutory law, the ownership of property is clear. For example, financial intermediaries are under strict fiduciary duties not to reveal information about forthcoming takeovers because they do not own it. If they do trade they will not add any value to the firm, they will simply steal from it.

However, in matters involving company employees who may have made a discovery and effected an innovation the matter is a little more complex. What statutory law in relation to insider dealing does is reassign property rights. This provides a formal resolution of the problem but it leaves open the theoretical question as to whether such a reassignment is a good or a bad thing. Does not it take away from the employees something that is rightfully theirs?

We can ask, therefore, whether it is right or efficient that the shareholder should capture all the entrepreneurial gains that are made by company employees. From an efficiency point of view allowing insiders to trade would increase the welfare of the shareholder through the rise in prices that would occur from any innovations. Everybody would gain. It is doubtful, however, that insider dealing is needed to motivate employees, since company owners are adept at developing methods for influencing good performance. Stock options, bonuses and attractive pension schemes are among the devices which are used, in addition to normal salary.

The only possible objection to this is the argument that the company does not technically own any of the new property values created by internal entrepreneurship. But if this is owned by enterprising and innovating individuals within the firm, it could well be argued that the shareholders, as mere lenders of capital, have no claim on any of the new value thus created. Yet they do secure some of this through the rise in share prices that internal entrepreneurship causes. From this perspective the separation between ownership and control is complete, so that managers are entrepreneurs who claim all the profits that accrue exclusively from their activity. They could be rewarded with large bonuses and other cash payments rather than the permission to trade on the company's stock. They may not want that because if they did so trade then some of the value they create would leak to shareholders in the form of higher share prices.

This analysis produces the ironic result that so far from the theory of entrepreneurship within the firm validating insider dealing, it in fact generates the opposite result, for to the extent that insider dealing takes place it entails a diversion of profits to the passive shareholder who does nothing to create them.[20] All he or she would be strictly entitled to would be the normal rate of return on shareholding. Still, it could always be said that since the employees cannot guarantee that their entrepreneurial activities will be fully rewarded with bonuses and other forms of compensation, they ought to be motivated by having the permission to trade in company shares even if that does result in some of the their profits unjustifiably going to shareholders.

These rather abstruse arguments are really about efficiency – what is the best method of motivating management? The moral question is really about whether insiders do indeed have a valid title to the value they create (in whatever form it is distributed). This is a problem to which no precise answer can be given. From one perspective it will depend on the state of positive law. Perhaps the proponents of insider dealing want the law to allow contracts to be made which assign all property rights in new information to employees, though it is hard to imagine that they would do so. The traditional view of the joint-stock company is that the owners have more or less exclusive rights over the use of property. It might be theoretically possible to make the case for owners and employees contracting out of a positive law that prohibited insider dealing if they thought that this was the only way of encouraging entrepreneurship but this is unlikely, given the other methods available for achieving the same result. The risk that would result from insiders trading on bad news would be sufficient to deter owners from taking such action.

The case that insider dealing is essential for the encouragement of internal entrepreneurship remains unproved. However, a large claim made by the opponents of regulation is that it makes for unreliable and unpredictable law and that the activity itself is quite unsuitable for control by statute law, criminal law especially.

INSIDER DEALING AND 'HARM'

A major part of the argument against statutory regulation of insider dealing concerns the vexed question of whether anyone is harmed by it.

As has been noted earlier, the elimination of harm is a major focus of business ethics. It has often been described as a 'victimless' crime. It follows from this that there is no clear and uncontroversial pursuer of the crime. Who has actually been hurt by the activity? Is it the company, outside shareholders or, as is increasingly asserted, the market itself?

The problem derives from the fact that securities transactions are normally conducted at 'arm's length': the transactors do not know one another and they buy and sell for a number of reasons, one of which might be connected with inside information. However, it is difficult to distinguish a transaction made for this reason from one that would have been made anyway. It may also be difficult to differentiate knowledge which is the result of genuine research from that derived from an unauthorized tip. Furthermore, if it is generally accepted that the securities market is a risky business, and one that is inhabited by people who think that they know better than the market, a certain amount of bad luck is to be expected.

Since there can never be a level playing field, unless the stock market is to be turned into a game of pure chance, it is almost impossible to explain, at least in terms that would satisfy the criminal law, the differing levels of information that participants will have. What makes insider dealing very different from the more familiar crimes is that one can never know whether a person's actions are at all influenced by the presence or absence of a particular rule.[21] It is certainly true that a transactor may be said to have been harmed in the trivial sense of not making as much money as he or she would have liked, as when a shareholder sells just ahead of a takeover announcement that would boost the price of the stock, but we can never know whether he would have sold anyway. Although he would presumably have sold at a different price had he known.

Allied to this difficulty is a problem of the almost impossibility of preventing one type of insider trading under the current (or any) law. Much of it may be a result of the decision *not* to trade as a result of inside knowledge.[22] Think of the company employee who, because of a pressing financial commitment, decides to sell her stock on Tuesday. Yet late on Monday afternoon she hears, quite legitimately, of some extremely good news for the firm and decides to hang on until the expected share price rise occurs. She has profited from inside information just as much as someone who actually trades on the information and is therefore equally culpable in a moral sense. It is difficult to imagine how such activity could be policed. No doubt, it will be said that because it may be impossible to prosecute one particular type of wrongdoing it does not follow that clear-cut cases should be permitted. Nevertheless the example, which is by no means hypothetical, does illustrate the difficulty of identifying both the victim and the perpetrator of the wrongful act.

It is often said by critics of insider dealing legislation that the long-term investor who holds a widely-dispersed portfolio is highly unlikely to be harmed by insider dealing, even in the narrow sense of harm alluded to above. Of course, speculators who hope to make quick killings may very well lose out from insider dealing but that surely is the price of speculation. The traditional rule of *caveat emptor* might be thought to be appropriately applied here.

However, even the most persistent critic of insider dealing laws, Henry Manne, does concede, in a rather oblique way, that some people may occasionally be hurt by the practice. He writes: 'To the extent that insider trading does in certain circumstances injure some particular individuals, unidentifiable in advance, financial advantages flowing to all shareholders more than compensates for this loss.'[23] He does not specify the category of losers, but presumably it would include those who buy shares from someone who possesses, through his position as an insider, bad news about a company. That person would surely have acted differently if he had access to the information. It is possible that there would be a breach of fiduciary duty here even in the absence of statutory law.

Whatever circumstances Manne has in mind, the general position he adopts could not illustrate better the conflicting demands of a utilitarian-based morality and one that derives from *deontology* – that is, one that places an absolute priority on duty, best exemplified in the rules of fairness. From the perspective of the latter ethics no efficiency considerations can ever compensate for an avoidable harm, however small, that is done to one individual. That person has been used merely as a means to the ends of another. Yet, the rigid enforcement of strict deontological rules would make some market exchanges impermissible. Of course, it would depend on which rules are chosen and there has been a tendency in some business ethics to extend the range of deontological rules precisely because they defeat all claims derived from utility.

Whatever Manne may say about the flaccid nature of much ethical discourse, especially that which occurs over securities trading, most people expect that certain rules of fairness should be observed, even if their rigid enforcement does sometimes result in a loss of efficiency. No doubt few of us live entirely by the rules of deontology, some of which if rigidly adhered to would make markets impossible to function. Does a deontological ethics require a seller of any good or service to reveal all that she knows about it? We do expect potential traders to do some research themselves. Still, it is no coincidence that the rules that govern trading in the Paris *Bourse* are called 'Les Principes des Deontologiques'.

The real controversy is not about the need for some utility-independent moral rules, *pace* Manne, but about their precise content and the domain over which they are enforceable. Should they be limited to the prevention of harm, the protection of justly acquired property or the enforcement of a fiduciary duty? Just how much information is required for a potential exchange to be just?

WINNERS AND LOSERS FROM INSIDER TRADING

However weak the deontological constraints are, it is easy to show how certain sorts of securities trading inevitably breach them. It may very well be the case that long-term investors are not harmed if insiders buy shares when the news is good, but what about when the news is bad? Surely outside shareholders are harmed if a director sells his stock when he has exclusive possession of knowledge that the company is heading for bankruptcy. The two types of insider dealing may be logically indistinct, but their practical differences are potentially enormous. When the news is bad the outsiders have been harmed in the sense that they have to bear all the loss. This is surely a breach of fiduciary duty.

It is important to mention that in this case of insider dealing efficiency considerations are not inconsistent with conventional ethics. If the news is good, that is quite probably because of some act of value creation within the company, the extra rewards of which the innovator might have some moral claim, but if it is bad, it might be a consequence of bad management or some other failing. If insider dealing is allowed, then employees can avoid the penalties of their incompetence. In no way can this be said to be justified on the ground of the need to encourage entrepreneurship within the firm.

Other things follow from this observation. If insider dealing were permitted, a different set of incentives would now be faced by the employee. She no longer has an immediate incentive to work for the firm in the development of new products and making other sorts of innovations. She is encouraged to play the market. She might even be tempted to circulate bad news about the company. The opportunities to 'short' the stock once a person has inside knowledge, or can 'create' it, might well be irresistible. In this scenario the claim is not simply that the outsider is harmed by not making as much money as he would have liked, but the more manageable complaint that he has been used merely as a means to the ends of the insider. The latter is not working for the company in a contractual sense (and least of all in a moral sense) but is simply working for herself. Although defenders of insider dealing claim that the market would eliminate such unscrupulous behaviour, there would be victims before the market had time to work its therapeutic effect.

No matter how fast the information circulates, so that prices soon reveal the bad news, someone will have been hurt by the activity. Manne's claim that even if some are hurt the situation is better because of the overall improvement that takes place is not convincing. In the strict (scientific) economic sense there has been no efficiency improvement because at least one person has been harmed. Manne's claim is the crude utilitarian one that utility is maximized merely because the benefits exceed the (allegedly) minor losses. He merely *asserts* that the overall gains compensate for these misfortunes. Would an outside shareholder, seeing that the company's finance officer had sold all his stock because he knew that the dividend was going to be cut, be happy with this form of compensation? Hardly.

There is a further argument against insider dealing which is worth considering: it derives from efficiency rather than moral considerations. Market-makers, fearing insiders in the market, may price securities so as to protect themselves. They will widen the 'spreads' between the offer and bid prices. This, of course, leads to inaccuracies in company evaluations and a loss of confidence in the market. It cannot be known in all cases if fear of insider dealing causes these inaccuracies. Still, the case for prohibition should not rest on this. There will inevitably be asymmetric information in the markets and there is little that intervention via statute law can do about it. Most observers deny that a serious loss in efficiency occurs because of this. Market-makers want very strict laws against insider dealing to protect themselves rather than to preserve the integrity of the market. Certainly the law should not be designed to cater for their interests.

The objections to insider dealing discussed above relate entirely to the breaches of trust that it entails. It is interesting that in the Chicago commodities market[24] where insider dealing is allowed, there are no market-makers: the traders deal entirely face-to-face. However, in the highly anonymous world of conventional stock markets, where dealing is almost entirely at arm's length, it is the outside investors who require protection against dishonesty. Here people normally do not know each other, so trust cannot develop.

It should be apparent from the above considerations that there is a plausible case for some legal restraints that go beyond those that are possible under private law. It is important, however, that such restraints should distinguish carefully between the legitimate and illicit use of information. Such restraint should not make it impossible for genuine research into company performance to go on. It must be recognized in the law that there will always be inequality of information in this area and that attempts to establish a level playing field in knowledge are not only impossible, and are likely to be counter-productive, but they are also destructive of the efficiency properties of free competitive markets. In addition, they deprive those prepared to use their skill and ingenuity in the evaluation of future performances of companies of their just rewards.

HOW SHOULD INSIDER DEALING BE REGULATED ?

Given that there is case for the prohibition on the use of unfair practices in the stock market the question then becomes one about the appropriate methods for their elimination. The important point to bear in mind here is that such regulation should not inhibit the main function of the securities market, which is to circulate information about companies through the price system. The regulatory arrangements should not aim at equality of information but at the removal of those practices that put one person at an unfair advantage to another because of the breach of some justiciable duty. There is no evidence that potential investors are deterred from making stock market investments because they fear that some people know more than others. They will be inhibited if they think that the game is fixed in advance, that fraud, misrepresentation, breach of duty and exploitation of privileged position within an organization make it impossible for them to compete on reasonably fair terms.

There are a number of ways in which unfair practices can be eliminated. One, which is attractive to doctrinaire market theorists, is self-regulation. The self-interest of market traders might drive them to enforce informal rules on participants, not merely to create an environment of fairness which makes stock market investment appealing, but also to prevent excessive regulation by the state; which might have a quite destructive effect on the working of the system. This argument has some plausibility in relation to the behaviour of financial intermediaries. Investment (or merchant) banks have a clear self-interest in enforcing compliance rules on their employees. Their reputations will suffer grievously if, for example, employees reveal highly sensitive information about takeovers: hence the presence of 'Chinese walls' in these institutions.

Still, people are not content with this form of self-regulation. The fact that someone can be dismissed for a breach of duty is not felt to be an adequate sanction, either because elementary principles of justice demand a greater punishment or because such a mild retribution is inadequate to guarantee a reliable market. The question is really whether the criminal or the civil law is the more appropriate method for dealing with obvious wrongs.

The case of genuine insider dealing, the unauthorized use of company information by an employee, is a little more complex. Undoubtedly, in the past, directors who breached their fiduciary duties quietly left the firm. In the absence of criminal and civil sanctions there was little else that could be done. One possibility was the use of the common law. It is always logically possible for the company, through its board of directors, to bring a private action against a person who had acted improperly. This holds, whatever the state of statutory law. However, history shows this not to be a reliable method of discipline. The leading cases seem to suggest that courts are not willing to enforce particularly burdensome duties on, for example, company directors. The classic case is *Percival v. Wright* (1902). Here a shareholder had sold his shares to the directors of the company (which was unlisted) in advance of a takeover bid, of which he was ignorant though the directors were not. He sued on the ground that they owed a duty to all shareholders to make such information available. In this case the action did not succeed. It was ruled that the officers of the company owed no such fiduciary duty.[25]

Thus although most observers agree that there are complex fiduciary duties owed by employees to shareholders, especially where the information is confidential, the exact nature of these is by no means clear and the likelihood of legal redress uncertain. In any case, critics of insider dealing seem to think that the cost and the cumbersome nature of the private law process mean that it is an inadequate sanction for what is agreed to be a wrong. The informal methods of dealing with it, such as dismissal and the shunning of the culpable individual by the commercial community, are similarly thought to be insufficient sanctions. This is probably true, although one should not dismiss out of hand informal methods of policing wrongful activity. It is quite likely, however, that the desire to encourage a wider spread of share ownership has fuelled the demands for a more rigorous approach.

The difficult question is whether the formal sanctions should be criminal or derive from a strengthened civil law. In the UK the statutory sanctions have since 1980 been entirely criminal. In America, however, the Securities and Exchange Commission is responsible for bringing civil actions against insider dealing, and it has a battery of sanctions at its disposal. The country also a court system that has been prepared to interpret the nature and range of fiduciary duties somewhat generously. Furthermore, the rules created under the auspices of the 1934 Securities and Exchange Act have systematically widened the scope of the law. However, as we have seen, the Supreme Court in some cases has restrained the zeal of the prosecuting authorities.

In the legal moves against insider dealing in Britain dissatisfaction has been expressed at the fact the only serious sanctions have been criminal. This has had two unfortunate consequences. First, the more rigorous demand of the criminal law, which requires that the case be proved beyond reasonable doubt (whereas civil cases are decided according to a balance of probabilities) has meant that prosecuting authorities are wary about bringing cases. Undoubtedly, insider dealing goes on but it is hard to detect and prove. Second, and possibly more important, in response to the disappointing record, legislatures are tempted to make the law even tougher. Britain was given a perfect opportunity here with the requirement to implement the European Directive on the subject.

The problem here is that the enactment of even more Draconian laws poses a threat to the functioning of the securities market. If participants are put off dealing through fear of prosecution then information will circulate more slowly, to the detriment of all transactors. Furthermore, since this is such a vague area, in which the definition of the offence is difficult and identification of the victim almost impossible, some of the rules will emerge from judicial interpretation. That produces considerable uncertainty and a threat to the rule of law.

This doctrine is a very important feature of liberal democracies. It requires that laws be known in advance, not applied retrospectively, and that they should not allow too much discretion to prosecuting authorities. The demands of morality nicely complement those of efficiency here, for not only is it intrinsically unfair if individuals cannot predict reasonably accurately how the law will affect them, but it also inexpedient: it adds another layer of uncertainty to an already uncertain world.

A further point should also be added. Draconian laws in the securities market do not always stamp out a perceived wrong. What they do, though, is raise the rewards for those prepared to take the risk of disobedience. People will always deal on inside information, especially as the offence does not have quite the opprobrium that the more conventional crimes do, and they will therefore make vast profits. The parallel between tough securities laws and Prohibition in the USA has often been commented on.

The changes in the British law are worth commenting on in the light of these considerations. Under the 1985 legislation, proof of the offence of insider dealing depended on there being a clear relationship of trust between the defendant and a company. It was illegal for someone either to trade on confidential information that had not been made public or to pass on such knowledge to a third party. The main purpose of that Act was to prevent people abusing positions of trust; it was not an attempt to establish equality of information and did not, apparently, deter analysts going about their normal business of ferreting out information. The obvious targets of the law were people who traded on information about takeovers in advance of the announcement of the bid, or directors who sold shares knowing that a fall in profits was about to be announced.

These are clear enough, but there are many grey areas where it is difficult to distinguish between intelligent research (or inspired guesses) and a genuine breach of duty. Certainly it was not unlawful merely to possess superior knowledge, even if it were acquired from an insider. Such was the technical nature of the offence, and the difficulty for the prosecution to demonstrate a clear illegality in all but the obvious cases, that people were convinced that the activity went on and, more important, that it was harmful to the market even if identifiable individuals did not often suffer. Sudden sharp price movements were recorded just ahead of important announcements. But even if these phenomena were absent, that would not indicate that the activity does not take place. Insiders can make gains in undramatic ways. Between 1980 and the coming into force of the new Act in April 1994, the Stock Exchange referred only about 180 cases to the prosecuting authorities, only 26 prosecutions were mounted and there were a mere 10 convictions.

The 1993 Criminal Justice Act brought in significant changes.[26] The range of securities covered by the prohibitions was extended and the definitions of insiders and inside information were widened so as to make it easier to secure convictions. The new Act no longer requires the information to be confidential nor does it require there to be a breach of trust for a prosecution to succeed. There seems to be a desire to create an expanded notion of 'fairness' in securities dealing.

In brief, the new law focuses on a number of main areas: the accused must have had information as an insider (a shareholder, a director or someone closely connected with the firm, such as a financial intermediary), the action has to take place on a regulated market, the suspected dealing must be in a specified and broadened range of securities and the information must be specific or precise and not public. Some of the meanings of the terms used will depend on judicial interpretation.

Thus under the new law a person immediately becomes an insider if she happens to hear a piece of relevant information from a company employee, if it can be proved that she knew it was non-public information, and that she knew it came from an inside source. It is illegal to trade on the information, to pass it on to a third party or to encourage others to trade. The information does not have to be confidential.

All this should make it easier for the prosecution to identify insiders. The prosecution, for example, no longer has to show that an insider passing on information knew that someone would deal. The onus appears to be on the defence to prove that he did not expect a deal to occur. The offence is not limited to dealings in shares of a company with which the accused is connected but covers all share transactions in regulated markets. Since company employees will always know more about the market in general than outsiders, they are likely to find themselves under suspicion if any unexpected price movement occurs with which they can be connected.

The law will have a particularly deleterious effect on investment analysts, whose role it is to dig out information which they use in their advice to clients. People invest in the stock market precisely because they think that existing prices are inaccurate and they can profit from their superior knowledge. And, as was pointed out earlier, that information is almost certain to be non-public, or at least not readily available to the public, if it is to be useful. Information may not be confidential but not easy to come by, especially by non-professionals. The question of what is or is not public will not be easy to determine and we may well have to wait for judicial interpretation. Because of the uncertainty about the meaning of the law (itself an important departure from the moral ideal of the rule of law) analysts are likely to be deterred from doing the research, and disclosing information to clients, through fear of becoming insiders.

Although the law has widened the definition of an insider and extended the range of securities covered, it has introduced a number of defences for the accused. But again this is bound to introduce uncertainty, as the meaning of them will depend on judicial interpretation. Market-makers can use knowledge (which is technically inside information) in their normal bona-fide pricing activity, as long as they do not make a personal profit. But what is bona-fide may well be disputable. Furthermore, it will not be illegal for a company to build up a stake in a target company in advance of a takeover announcement: but 'front running' (a person buying shares on his own account) presumably will be. A particularly contentious defence is certain to be that which allows deals which a person would have made anyway, even without the inside information. Someone may have decided to finance a house with the proceeds of a share sale and subsequently became the possessor of inside information which is relevant to the transaction. Her dealing will be legitimate if it can be shown that she would have proceeded with it irrespective of the state of the market. It is not difficult to imagine how an unscrupulous person could manufacture plausible but dishonest explanations of her conduct. A further, somewhat vague defence, is that which permits the use of information that an individual has through being an insider but which does not prejudice the interests of others.

It turns out then that, because of the possible defences, the new law is not as Draconian as it appears at first glance. But this is the problem. Convictions may be as hard to secure as in the past, which means that the real perpetrators of wrongs are not likely to be deterred; but risk-averse people, engaged in the normal activity of researching the prospects of companies, probably will be. A valid criticism is therefore that the law may not catch the real villains but it will impede the rapid flow of information to the market. Already it is being said in the City that analysts will not talk to company chairpersons without the presence of witnesses who can provide a guarantee that no non-public information is passed.

We should remember that the new law was enacted in response to a European Directive which set certain minimum standards with which we had to conform.[27] Unlike UK legislation, a European law, or projected law, is preceded by a preamble which broadly states its purpose. The purpose of this directive is to guarantee investor confidence and ensure the smooth running of the market. They are anodyne enough aims but they reveal a certain *naïveté* about securities. No evidence has ever been produced to show that investor confidence is undermined seriously enough by insider dealing to justify the measures the directive made obligatory on member states. Nor was it considered whether the recommendations themselves might inhibit the smooth functioning of the market. The imposition of very similar rules across member states means that competition between different securities markets to offer better conditions for potential investors has been virtually eliminated. Furthermore, the fundamental principles of insider trading law, that relationships of trust should be honoured and genuine fiduciary duties maintained, appear not to be part of the rationale for European law. They are implicitly covered by it but only at the cost of the imposition of serious disabilities on transactors.

RECURRING PROBLEMS

The major difficulty of the regulation of insider dealing is that of deterring obvious wrongdoing while not at the same time deterring genuine research into company performance which is relevant to market pricing. The ideal situation would be one in which the private law duties of employees to company owners could be efficiently enforced. They are likely to be the victims of illicit activity. Such nebulous and inherently contestable entities as the 'community' or the 'market' should not be invented as 'victims'. Immoral and illegal insider dealing is an action committed by *individuals* against other *individuals*, difficult though they may be to identify.

The problem would perhaps be less pressing if companies could regulate their own employees efficiently. It is true that most publicly-quoted companies do have internal rules specifying the conditions under which trading in the firm's shares is permissible. Perhaps a more active shareholders' movement, led by institutional investors, could improve compliance with the rules. However, critics are not satisfied with this and want both more restrictive rules and their more efficient enforcement.

Most reform suggestions centre on the possibility of decriminalizing the activity; mainly because of the difficulty of securing convictions. An alternative to the criminal law would be the creation of a public body charged with the responsibility of bringing civil actions, for which convictions could be more easily secured, imposing heavy fines on the guilty and ensuring just compensation for the victims (where they can be identified). Free-market purists may demur at the suggestion that public funds should be expended on policing what is in principle private activity. But it is clear from legal history that nothing much will be done if it is completely left to individuals. It may be less costly for firms not to proceed with formal legal processes, especially in view of the difficulty of securing redress under private law, but this may have an adverse effect on investor confidence. As long as the authority of the public body does not exceed the range of legal remedies that are theoretically available under the currently ineffective private law the efficiency of the market need not be impaired. It would mainly be concerned with enforcing relationships of trust between market participants.

The body, however, should be seen to be independent. Public confidence in the arrangement will not be advanced if it is staffed exclusively by City practitioners. Still, the very complexity of the issue means that legal procedures appropriate for normal civil matters might be inadequate for the task of policing insider dealing. One further problem with institutions of this type is that they might become 'captured' by those whom they are designed to regulate. The main danger in this area is that market-makers might have an undue influence over the legal arrangements. Yet they have an obvious self-interest in tough securities law since they are the potential victims of both illegal activity and genuine skill in the market for information. They are quite likely to encourage the development of a regime in which the distinction between these two phenomena is subtly blurred. This is, after all, the problem with the current criminal law. Still, it is quite probable that in the future market makers will not be required and direct trading between transactors will be feasible. This is already the case in the USA.

Connected with this point is the argument that these sorts of public bodies have a habit of acquiring new powers over time. This has been one of the objections to the Securities and Exchange Commission in the USA. This may be as much caused by natural bureaucratic aggrandisement as it is with the aim of achieving efficient regulation of the market. Yet the accumulation of new powers is bound to have an adverse effect on the rule of law. It introduces uncertainty and a loss of predictability. But at least a single regulatory body of the type proposed would be an improvement on the myriad of agencies and authorities that we have at the moment.

The precise organizational form of the proposed body will, no doubt, be controversial but its rationale should not be in dispute. It is to prevent harm to investors perpetrated by those who abuse the trust placed in them. Its existence would avoid the need for the criminal law. The difficulty of securing convictions here has meant that it is not a serious deterrent. Yet any further tightening up of criminal procedures would constitute a threat to the rule of law, increase the likelihood of unfair convictions and have a deleterious effect on the working of securities markets. In principle, the regulatory body should aim at making efficiency improvements on the private law procedures that have always been available to persons who feel they have been victimized because of a breach of fiduciary duty by responsible agents. In the past such procedures have been quite ineffective.

What the body should not aim at is the creation of some highly contestable condition of substantive equality in securities markets. Not only is this an impossible ideal, its pursuit would drastically reduce the efficiency properties of securities markets.

6 Takeovers: An Economic and Ethical Perspective

The 1980s was the age of the takeover boom in Anglo-American economies; although it was by no means the most extreme example in the USA's economic history.[1] It was an era in which considerable disruption was caused to economic organizations; in plant relocation, management restructuring, considerable layoffs and localised unemployment. In ethical terms it was thought to be an example of rampant self-interest and unrestrained individualism.

The process of restructuring seemed to be brought about not by the normal processes of economic change but by the short-term desire for profit displayed by corporate raiders in hostile, and usually costly, bids for major corporations. Friendly mergers might be acceptable but predatory raids were not. It seemed to illustrate perfectly the anonymous nature of Anglo-American market societies; societies in which individuals meet entirely as strangers without long-term obligations or social commitments. Acting under impersonal and abstract rules, they are concerned solely to maximize their immediate advantages at the potential cost of a social good, which they may or may not be aware of sharing. Many of the apologists for the economic practices of the era denied that there were such things as a 'common good' or the 'public interest'; or, at the most, would claim that they came about unintentionally rather than by deliberate design. This, of course, had the implication that policies that interfered with the market process could not be justified by reference to a contentious notion of the social good.

It is noticeable, then, that the criticisms of that era were both moral and economic; as if immorality at the micro level would always lead to inefficiency at the macro level. As if the individual (or institutional) shareholder, selfishly trading his stock to a corporate raider or predator, were somehow responsible for an alleged national economic malaise. This apparently led to short-termism, lower investment and the emergence of excessive debt-financing of companies. This is the conventional view of the 1980s. However, there is now considerable evidence that the takeover process was actually conducive to overall economic efficiency, and also that it did not involve any serious immorality.[2] In retrospect, the 'decade of greed' looks a more benign era despite the

117

apparent frenzy. This is true of economics (considerable and necessary restructuring was brought about in the USA, from which almost everybody is now benefiting) and even ethically, at least as measured in terms of charitable giving, which increased markedly.[3] This may have been done for personal moral vanity but to the recipients of charity the motivations of the donor are not important.

WHY TAKEOVERS?

Still, it is certainly not the case that free market economies have to be organized in the Anglo-American way. Two of the most successful market economies in the world, Japan and Germany, are characterized by rather different economic arrangements. In these two countries firms appear to be engaged in more 'intimate' economic relationships in which instantaneous gratification for the shareholders is subordinate to long-term considerations. Obligations (implicit and explicit) in these countries between contracting parties extend beyond immediate financial time periods and seem strong enough to resist the *immediate* impulse of the profit motive. Indeed, takeovers are rare in these countries, and that discipline over management which is required in a market society is brought about by other methods; notably the close supervisory role played by banks as major shareholders. In the USA banks cannot by law hold stock in quoted companies[4] and in Britain they do not do so by convention. It is perhaps partly the explanation of that apparent 'short-termism' on the part of financial institutions there; an attitude which is said to be a major factor in the *alleged* relative economic decline of the USA and Britain. But in the past few years this last thesis has been falsified by serious research and Anglo-American economies are now admired for their flexibility.

The differing economic institutions in Anglo-American economies go a long way towards explaining their differing economic styles. It has been noticed, since Berle and Means's[5] pioneering study of the US corporation, that ownership and control of large-scale corporations have become separated since, at least, the beginning of the twentieth century. The demise of the owner-manager and his replacement by dispersed stockholders who, in effect, hire managers to run the enterprise that they (only) nominally own, has according to the original theory, led to the domination of US industry by bureaucratic empires, responsible to no one and immune from competitive pressures. Writers in this tradition seemed unaware of the other market methods for the monitoring of apparently irresponsible corporate bureaucracies.

Competitive capitalism is not ultimately doomed, for the dispersed stockholders are by no means powerless. The USA is not destined to be run by industrial, managerial elites, as J.K. Galbraith[6] and others have supposed. The ultimate control of the stockholder over management is exercised through her ability to trade her shares. The stockholder is, in effect, only concerned about the price of her shares and if they are under-performing in the market she will sell to someone who thinks he can organize the assets better than existing managements. Therefore, the periodic bouts of extensive reorganisation that take place through the takeover mechanism function as surrogates for the close supervisory role that owner-managers play in small businesses, which banks play in Germany, or those complex interlocking directorship arrangements (the *Keiretsu*) achieve in Japan.[7] Those who would put limitations on the takeover mechanism are unwittingly allowing the power of corporate elites to be reasserted.

Yet, by a curious irony, the one instrument that the shareholder has for restraining the excess of corporate power, the threat to sell his stock, has become the single reason for the hostility with which takeovers are regarded in the USA and Britain. In buying up shares, at a premium, the corporate raider is then able to reorganize the company, sell off unwanted parts and (it is hoped) produce a viable enterprise. In doing so he will disrupt existing arrangements and bring about the disappointment of many expectations. Thus, on the one hand, entrenched managements are the subjects of moral obloquy for their irresponsibility to the market or the state and their failure to secure maximum shareholder value, yet on the other, the corporate raider is viewed with considerable disdain because he promises to break up the centres of corporate power and privilege.

The crucial point here is the fact that Anglo-American public companies are largely owned by institutional investors, pension funds, insurance companies and so on, which have no real interest in the day-to-day running of the companies that they nominally own. They have a contractual duty only to secure the best return for their investors: indeed, they are 'programmed' to buy and sell stock according to relatively small changes in price. In the large corporation, the managers are, in effect, the agents for the owners of capital and are entrusted with the task of managing it in the interests, not of themselves, but of the shareholders (owners). The argument is that only the takeover mechanism can solve the inherent problem of the 'principal-agent' relationship: how to make the latter serve the interests of the former? In the absence of firmly-established relationships of trust, the takeover device is the best method of controlling rent-seeking by employees.

However, from a strictly economic point of view, this is said to be dis-advantageous, since managements will be more worried about share price changes than actually running their companies and, hence, more likely to take a short-term view. It is frequently held that they will be par-ticularly disinclined to take on highly specific labour since its productiv-ity is likely to be realized only over the very long term. The corporate raider, it is alleged, is only interested in realizing short-run gains and is therefore almost certain to shed labour whose value is not immediately apparent. Indeed, it is noticeable that in Japanese and German firms, la-bour is employed over a long period, and often for life (though, of course, this causes a certain amount of labour rigidity). It is a feature of German and Japanese business that they invest heavily in human cap-ital; and this might have a social as well as a strictly economic rationale.

The important difference is that, outside the Anglo-American busi-ness world, corporations are often 'closely held' – that is, under the more or less direct control of a small number of individuals who are not motivated by the desire for instantaneous gratification. There is, therefore, close involvement of workers, owners and managers in the well-being of their companies: all are engaged in a collaborative enter-prise. This is supposed to contrast favourably with the individualism and short-termism of Anglo-American enterprise. Furthermore, in German firms there is considerable 'self-investment' via workers' pen-sion funds; a practice that would be highly risky in Anglo-American business.[8] In addition, the power of the shareholder is limited: the vot-ing rights of small shareholders tend to be exercised by the banks and much of the common stock is non-voting stock anyway. Banks, as ma-jor stockholders themselves, obviously have an interest in corporate efficiency. In Japan, the phenomenon of interlocking ownership by powerful industrial groups further strengthens the hand of existing managements. Takeovers are virtually unknown there and shareholders are excluded from management as well as being limited to derisory dividends.

There are at least two considerations in connection with takeovers that I would like to analyse. First, the utilitarian arguments that are ad-vanced, for and against this method of economic control, and second, the ethical issues that have arisen in the aftermath of the takeover boom of the 1980s: a phenomenon that aroused considerable disquiet, a number of critical Hollywood movies and almost frenetic legislative and judicial activity at the end of the decade in the USA. But the moral arguments were rarely informed by economics, and not often by reason.

TAKEOVERS AND THE SOCIAL GOOD

Arguments about the merits and demerits of takeovers range across a broad economic and ethical spectrum. It is true, though, that economists, with their broadly utilitarian approach, have dominated much of the debate and they have attempted to limit discussion to the broadly empirical features of this form of economic reorganization. However, a purely economic approach is misleading, if not impossible, since our evaluation of the takeover process must be embedded in the morality of the market system itself. Even arguments in favour of takeovers that focus solely on their role in the co-ordination of economic actions necessarily embody a controversial consequentialist claim: that is, that the *aggregate* well-being of the economic community is advanced if they are allowed to proceed (almost unregulated) despite the occasional harm that they may bring in their wake to individuals and, indeed, sub-sections of the community.[9] And this point surely holds even if the disadvantaged cannot be known in advance of the operation of the process. It is by no means self-evident that the utilitarian imperative should prevail against the competing claims of, say, social justice, or a welfarist conception of rights, or the demands of community. Yet direct evidence of the harm caused by takeovers is sparse.

Furthermore, corporate raiders and predators themselves could make claims that hold independently of utility (especially when this is interpreted in a broadened sense, one in which the claims of the disadvantaged are considered as a part of an over-all utilitarian calculation). Thus, the raider could claim that she is merely exercising her right to economic liberty when she buys companies, even if that is only for the purpose of breaking them up for profit. Again, shareholders who sell their shares at a premium in a tender offer could quite legitimately claim that the right to property entails just this eventuality, however harmful to some other individuals its exercise might involve. Those institutional investors who switch funds around according to (possibly) temporary movements in share prices are surely fulfilling a fiduciary duty to the ultimate owners of those funds, the contributors to pension funds and insurance schemes. Most of these people are, of course, by no means wealthy. Furthermore, it has yet to be shown whether takeover booms are logically different from any other type of market activity. Firms are constantly engaged in restructuring and refocusing their activities. Why should this be permissible when an exaggerated version of this, a multi-billion pound takeover, is condemnable?

Thus, when Henry Manne[10] and Michael Jensen,[11] to name but two protagonists of the takeover mechanism, defend this type of corporate restructuring, and the sometimes extraordinary returns that accrue to the participants, they are not relying on purely utilitarian considerations, despite what they say. Indeed, some takeovers, both in the USA and in the UK have not always had beneficial consequences. Their arguments are nested in the whole congeries of principles covering rights, property and freedom that make up the justification for the market process, however reluctant economists might be to make moral judgments.

What these writers try to show is that there is nothing *special* about takeovers; or at least nothing distinctive enough to attract the attention of government regulation or, indeed, moral philosophy. In other words, if one believes that the market mechanism is better than any other system for the allocation of resources one is committed similarly to its role in the determination of the uses to which capital is put. According to the theory, capital will always flow to where the returns are highest. A commitment to the process of normal exchange in assets entails a similar commitment to exchange in bundles of assets (that is, firms). Again, from this perspective, the liberty which is normally granted (if sometimes controversially) to the trader in conventional goods and services is not to be denied to the takeover specialist, even though his activities are commonly said to change, sometimes dramatically, people's lives. And clearly, in conventional ethics, if not economics, there are 'victims' of corporate reorganization.

A thoroughgoing advocate of this method would also maintain that the admission of the 'stakeholder' as an interested party into the debate is illegitimate. The stakeholder, in contrast to the stockholder, has no legal claim that would justify a diminution of takeover activity, even though his interests as an employee of an affected company, or as a resident of a locality which is dependent on the survival of a particular firm, are possibly harmed by it. Yet these considerations are only decisive to the extent that it is acceptable that the right to use property in any way the holder chooses is given priority over other social purposes.

One difficulty in admitting the claims of the stakeholder into a hypothetical category of people entitled to redress from the sometimes painful process of economic change is that it is conceptually impossible to distinguish victims of corporate reorganization brought about by takeovers from those disadvantaged by apparently 'normal' processes, such as a change in the demand for a product, or the invention of a new technology which renders some traditional method obsolete; at least it would be difficult to write a law that would, uncontroversially, make such a discrimination. Furthermore, from a more specifically ethical point of view, it is difficult to identify those stakeholders who might have a case for redress, to determine what that should be and, more importantly, to balance the various, and often competing, interests involved in disputed cases of industrial reorganization.

Takeovers, under the orthodoxy of market economics, take place as a normal process of market correction for inefficiency. The purpose of all economic activity is the efficient use of resources. In economic processes characterized by the separation of ownership from control, the management of a company is entrusted with the use of resources in such a way that maximized returns go to the owners of the capital. As the principals, the latter have the final say in how these assets are to be managed. The stock market, which is continually signalling information about the efficient use of capital on the basis of publicly available information, is the venue on which the decision as to the use of assets is ultimately decided. A fall in the price of a stock is obviously one possible indication that assets are not being managed to an optimal level of efficiency. Note, this does not mean that management is necessarily incompetent or slothful, it simply means that some alternative arrangement could lead to an improvement from which shareholders (and ultimately society at large) would benefit. The purpose of activity under capitalism is not merely to maintain a given level of productivity but to exploit resources so that maximum potential levels are achieved.

Now if in the (subjective) opinion of transactors a particular stock is not performing as well as it could, this perception is sufficient to motivate a bidder company to make an offer for the stock; and hence to acquire control of the company so as to realize the potential value of the assets by a reorganization. Of course, the incumbent management of the 'target' company will maintain that the market is systematically undervaluing the firm. They will claim, for example, that investment in research and development is essential for the long-term viability of the productive organization and that this takes time to be reflected in the share price. They will also argue that the predator shows concern neither for the ultimate interests of the shareholder nor for the workers in the enterprise. The bidder company will no doubt argue that all this is a deception on the part of management in order to conceal its inefficiency and to evade its responsibility for the fall in share value. The takeover mechanism may not improperly be described as the market for manager- ial talent.

Indeed, recent US corporate history might be interpreted as a perman- ent battle between shareholders and managements. They do not trust one another. However, this lack of trust, which is thought to be condem- nable by many observers, may not necessarily be harmful in an economic sense, especially if there are institutional arrangements, such as the takeover device, to mitigate its worst effects. Too much trust could, in fact, be harmful, because it might inhibit entrepreneurial activity within the firm. Too many stakeholder groups might resent the change it brings about. It is almost certain that they will use quasi-political methods to resist change.

However, it should be pointed out that not all takeovers are hostile. Some may be uncontested and involve mutual recognition of 'syner- gies'[12] that can be obtained through a merger of two organizations. Still, it is the contested bids that generate the controversy and which raise economic and ethical issues. For in these, the economic reasoning tends to get lost in the welter of moral, and often emotional, claims and coun- ter-claims that are made.

It is also important to note that a takeover can occur in two rather dif- ferent ways. One of these can be relatively benign. This is when an acquisi- tion of one company by another leads not to its breakup, but to a more rational use of the combined assets than was possible when they were separate. Although some disruption is caused by this, it would be diffi- cult to deny, without repudiating almost all of the claims of the market, that arrangements such as this increase economic value most of the time.

There is a second sense of takeover which describes a phenomenon which few people regard as at all benign. This is when a raider, noticing that the breakup value of the parts of a company is probably greater than the value of the current share price, proceeds to buy up the company's stock at a premium and then liquidate it for a profit. The controversy lies in the fact that the company may have actually been profitable, so that the result of the raider's action is apparently the destruction of eco- nomic value. Yet there is no theoretical difference between the two types. For even in breakups, assets are not destroyed, they are simply transferred from the present less than efficient managers to those who can extract more value from them in the future.[13]

The utilitarian argument for more or less unregulated takeovers de- pends, once again, almost entirely on the truth of the Efficient Markets Hypothesis. If the stock market is efficient, prices will signal to investors how well capital is being used, over the long term as well as the short.

The Hypothesis is used against those who maintain that the stock market is concerned with mere short-termism and cannot value long-term investment projects properly. Despite the vehemence with which this claim is uttered its plausibility may be doubted, for the implication of its denial is not only that investment projects exist somehow out there which will not be perceived by the market, but that some other institution, presumably government, has a better idea of these investment possibilities. It is surely unlikely that managements could render themselves immune from takeovers by choosing a series of short-term suboptimal investment strategies instead of the apparently higher valued long-term policy.

Thus, as we saw with the problem of insider dealing, the argument for takeovers depends on the claim that the stock market is the best guide to economic value. The Efficient Markets Hypothesis supposes that all relevant information about a company is embodied in its share price. It may not be perfect but the market is a superior transmitter of information than any known alternative, such as government[14] or some other agency (say, a coalition of stakeholders) that thinks it has a better idea of economic prospects than that indicated by current prices. In the controversial takeover of Trust House Forte by Granada,[15] in late 1996, critics of the deal concentrated on the fact that the success of the bidder was ultimately determined by the decision of one (albeit important) institutional investor. It was suggested that the well-being of an important company should not depend on the opinion of a probably ill-informed passive investor. But that criticism is misguided because the information about the company is contained in its share price, which is a function of a myriad of decisions by market participants. No one person or institution can determine the fortunes of a large company.

Nobody supposes that the stock market is an infallible guide to value, (least of all, future value) for if it were it would describe an economy in static equilibrium and no entrepreneurial activity would take place at all. Rather the Efficient Markets Hypothesis is an *ex ante* argument about the improbability of beating the market over the long haul. Market prices embody all the value that has been created from entrepreneurial activity, although it is impossible to know in advance of a market process what that value is. Corporate raiding is a type of entrepreneurial activity, for it depends on somebody spotting a difference in prices which can be exploited for profit. The case for takeovers rests largely on the belief in the stock markets capacity to reflect value; the raider creates value by reorganising assets in a more efficient way than his predecessors.

Furthermore, when empirical evidence is produced to show that mergers and takeovers do not greatly enhance value, the counter-factual is always germane to the issue – that is, what would have happened in the absence of the takeover mechanism? Often it is the threat of a takeover that spurs managements to produce more value. This same point is relevant to the much-disputed argument about who benefits from corporate reorganization. Is it the shareholders or the managements (and the financial intermediaries) who embark on these schemes?

The bulk of the empirical evidence[16] suggests, not surprisingly, that it is the shareholders of the target company that benefit the most. After all, a premium above the market price normally has to be paid in order to persuade investors to part with their shares. It is claimed that shareholders of the acquiring company gain very little, and sometimes lose, although over the long run they do probably gain (especially if account is taken of the previous performance of an acquiring company). And again, the counterfactual is relevant. How would they have fared in the absence of takeover activity which is, after all, just another form of investment? Indeed, it is worth pointing out in passing that in Britain, shareholders of Lord Hanson, the country's legendary predator, have gained significantly from his company's expansion, which has largely been by acquisitions rather than internal growth. But one suspects that at the heart of the objection is the moral claim that the verdict of the stock market is not the best guide to the true interests of the community, which are not to be defined exclusively in terms of efficiency. This moral argument rests on the claim that property rights should not be given pre-eminence in the appraisal of economic activity.

Even modest sceptics of the whole process, such as A.T. Peacock and G. Bannock,[17] do not claim that doubts about its economic benefits justify excessive government regulation. They prefer to point to the non-neutrality of the tax regimes in both the USA and the UK which encourage company growth through acquisition rather than by internal improvements.[18] Still, although a 'neutral' tax regime would no doubt have some effect on the market for corporate control, it is unlikely to alter radically the pattern of this traditional method of industrial reorganization.

I have so far taken a fairly benign view of the takeover process: ignoring fundamental moral questions to do with the rights and legitimate expectations of the participants and also the social question of the allegedly harmful side-effects that occur from a process which is unashamedly driven by self-interest. It is this egoism that has produced extraordinary profits for some of the actors and distributions of wealth and income that seemingly mock contemporary notions of social justice. Even if there were important utility gains from corporate restructuring via takeovers, as I believe there are, it is, superficially at least, hard to imagine that they *have* to be accompanied by enormous wealth for the few. This phenomenon cannot be explained without a proper theory of entrepreneurship, which is considered in the next section.

At the same time a largely mechanical description of the process does not do justice to the crucially important features of human action that generate it. Thus a more considered view of takeovers requires an explanation that takes account of what actually goes on in corporate restructuring and at least some discussion of the moral problems (especially those to do with distributive justice) that it generates. As in many other aspects of market behaviour, the Austrian theory of market process,[19] especially in the form elaborated by Israel Kirzner, is peculiarly apposite with regard to takeovers. Although in Kirzner's work there is no specific mention of takeovers, I believe that his arguments in favour of markets have a direct relevance to the economic and moral problems that they raise.

KIRZNER ON MARKET PROCESS AND ENTREPRENEURSHIP

Austrian economists maintain that to be plausible a market theory must capture essential features of real world economies. The most notable of these are: the relentless change and the uncertainty that characterize all economic action; the feature of entrepreneurship that must be present in economies if co-ordination is to be achieved; and profit (that is, income over and above marginal productivity) that accrues to the successful participants in real world economies. Most important, the Austrian idea of competition focuses on that phenomenon as a continuing and rivalrous (between the contestants for economic advantage) process. What is absent is an assumption of orthodox theory, which is that all agents in market economies have perfect knowledge of all possible states of affairs. However, according to Austrian theory, no economic agent can possess more than a fraction of the sum of knowledge that is available in a dispersed form throughout society. In this form the Austrian theory is basically utilitarian, though as I shall show below, it has been given an ethical twist which is peculiarly apposite to the explanation and justification of takeovers.

Economies progress to the extent that actors are permitted to use the little bits of dispersed knowledge for their own advantage: in so doing they contribute, albeit unwittingly, to a gradual equilibrating process which is to the general benefit. It is, however, a process that has no necessary end or destination since it is always likely to be disrupted by changes in data that confront transactors. In the orthodox neoclassical model, since every transactor is fully-informed of all possibilities of gain, an equilibrium is reached instantaneously, and without the constant experimentation that goes on in real world markets. With regard to takeovers this feature is crucially important because most corporate reorganization involves the correction of previous errors. The alert predator notices that assets are badly managed and that extra value can be extracted from them through a substantial reorganization.

One should notice that there is considerable creativity in entrepreneurship. The opportunities are not simply out there waiting to be discovered (if this were the case, then perhaps a sophisticated machine could be designed to perform the co-ordinating function) but their existence is partly a result of his skill and creativity. It is perhaps this feature that provides a moral grounding for the profit (income above marginal productivity) secured by the successful entrepreneur. Without her activity opportunities would not be realized. Thus profit is not a windfall gain, like an inheritance, but a reward for effort, though it sometimes looks like luck.

However, anti-market moralists fail to see the value-creating features of entrepreneurship, and the justified rewards that go to it, in takeovers. They might concede that profits are justly earned by the entrepreneur who discovers something new in a *physical* sense but would be reluctant to say same thing of what is dismissively referred to as mere 'paper churning' on Wall Street and in the City of London. A major criticism of the takeover boom of the 1980s was the claim that it did not add anything of value to the productive process. By value it was meant factories, inventions and other tangible innovations. Critics even found a reason to praise the notorious 'robber barons' of late nineteenth century and early twentieth century American history.[20] At least they produced something even in their 'monopoly' control of oil, the construction of railways, utilities and so on. The 1980s takeover artists apparently did not: they destroyed companies and burdened what was left of corporate America with debt.

But this physicalist conception of value on which the criticism is based, is completely mistaken; for economic improvement can come about just as effectively by a reorganization of existing assets. For example, there is an exchange of assets in the football transfer market but obviously the increased value is not a result of the teams possessing extra players.[21] In the industrial world extra value can be generated through a more efficient use of existing assets, and sometimes by the shedding of assets. People do not have a 'right' to permanent employment in the same position and it is only sentimental business ethics which supposes that morality can, or ought to, resist change.

The entrepreneur must be clearly distinguished from the capitalist (though their respective characteristics may be combined in the same human agent). The capitalist is a resource owner and his income derives from the earnings of capital. In contrast, the entrepreneur need own no resources (though it is hard to imagine one without anything) and her activity is, in principle, costless (apart from the opportunity costs incurred by the expenditure of her time and effort). In an ongoing capitalist system, the entrepreneur persuades the capitalist to advance her funds. This, of course, explains why takeovers tend to be debt-financed (leaving aside the encouragement to debt-financing brought about by the tax system.) It is important to note here that the entrepreneur's profits are not windfall gains or products of sheer luck, although on occasion it may look like this. They arise out of her discovery[22] of new ways of doing things. Indeed, discovery is involved in the creation of all economic value. In other words, gains from trade are not automatic but are a product of human action. However, the fact that the entrepreneur can borrow substantially (and does so in takeovers especially) means that profit can be earned almost out of nothing. It is precisely this that provokes the ire of the moralists. But it is not quite created out of nothing, since the entrepreneur provides considerable skill and alertness.

Using this intellectual framework it may be possible to explain (and morally justify) the activities of corporate raiders such as Carl Icahn, T. Boone Pickens, Sir James Goldsmith, Lord Hanson and others who disrupted corporate arrangements in the USA and Britain in the 1980s.[23] They were alert to the possibilities of the creation of new value by the reorganization of assets. That this could be done was signalled by the market. The existing corporate structures were not maximizing shareholder value, largely because the agents (the managers) had become detached from the interests of the principals (the shareholders). The market for corporate control is the institutional arrangement for overcoming this agency problem.

It is here that a vital distinction between socially-valuable and socially-costly takeovers must be made, for much of the corporate restructuring that took place in the USA in the 1980s was a response to previous misallocations that had taken place in the 1960s and 1970s. This had also been an era of takeovers, which were not taken in the interest of shareholders but had been pursued on behalf of empire-building managements.[24] This was the origin of the unwieldy conglomerates in the USA which had to be broken up if corporate efficiency were to be restored. Divestitures of inappropriate parts of a company are essential features of the takeover process. In fact, what is interesting about the takeover boom of the 1980s, as compared to earlier examples, was that it led to the deconcentration of industry. The previous fear about market-driven industrial reorganization was that it led to the rise of cartelization and uncompetitive monopoly capitalism. This is the origin of anti-trust laws. This important point was scarcely noticed in the febrile moral debate about takeovers.

According to Michael Jensen's 'free cash flow'[25] theory, cash-rich companies, when faced with the choice of paying back some of the cash to their shareholders had spent the money on unprofitable acquisitions and unnecessary expansion. One might have thought that from a purely moral point of view that they were in breach of a duty to their shareholders, which is to maximize owner value. Jensen noticed that in the oil and gas industries, especially, pointless exploration was embarked upon. It was T. Boone Pickens who noticed that this was not necessary and that extra value could be extracted by reorganising existing assets (another refutation of the physicalist theory of value) through strategic takeovers and breakups. In fact, managements in many US companies were behaving in a purely opportunistic manner (a point illustrated somewhat dramatically and misleading in the Hollywood films *Wall Street*, *Pretty Woman*, and *Other People's Money*).

In such circumstances, even buying companies in order to break them up is just as much as act of discovery, in Kirzner's sense, as any other form of value creation in the market. It is not often realized that capital structures are never actually destroyed (except in war) but are continually being reallocated in a never-ending market process. Thus, despite the pejorative language in which it is inevitably described, 'asset stripping' has a perfectly respectable economic rationale. It is indeed a good example of that correcting of error which entrepreneurship in the market produces.

The emergence of the highly-leveraged management buyouts in the 1980s can be seen as an example of this process in action. Borrowing heavily to buy out shareholders and take a public company private is, also, ironically, an example of the revival of what might be called the spirit of Adam Smith. He always had doubts about the joint-stock corporation and believed that economic efficiency was more likely to be brought about by owners directly managing their assets. The growth of management buyouts, with the managers becoming owners, is a tribute to this. The emergence of the buyout specialists, Kohlberg, Kravis & Roberts (KKR) is a good example of the creativity of the market even in its superficially most undesirable manifestations. For KKR took large equity stakes in companies, put in specialist managers who would therefore work directly to increase shareholder value. The much abused 'barbarians' became active participants in the running of companies.[26]

Of course, not all of them were successful, and a few really did become weighed down with debt, but an important lesson of Austrian economics is relevant here: success in the market can never be guaranteed because individuals are prone to error. Perhaps the best example is the notorious buyout of RJR Nabisco, the tobacco and food company. This cost $25bn and involved a large amount of debt. It did not perform that successfully (largely because of difficulties in the tobacco market) and eventually KKR sold most of it off. But this one misjudgement (if it were that) should not be used to disparage what is a significant innovation in corporate management. Indeed, although the original deal was the subject of enormous controversy, it is difficult to discover what was actually immoral about it. The shareholders did particularly well. Though the increase in debt, and the costs of paying it down, was at the heart of the controversy in this and other takeovers.

ETHICAL CONDUCT IN TAKEOVERS

However, there are some tactics that are used in takeovers that may be not implausibly said to detract from the entrepreneurial features of the activity. They relate to the procedural sense of justice – that is, the rules governing an activity – and are not necessarily connected to the 'social' justice of takeovers. Entrepreneurship is the perfectly legitimate finding of a profitable opportunity, the exploitation of a commercial possibility that is in theory available to anyone. However, it could also involve a different type of exploitation – that of the ignorance and vulnerability of others. When this happens it is not so much an example of the creation of new value but more a case of appropriating value that properly belongs to others.

An example may occur in management buyouts (MBOs) which occur when existing employees decide to bid for the company. If successful they take it private, reorganize it extensively and normally bring it back to market – for a considerable profit. There are perfectly acceptable reasons why this should take place. The managers may have seen a profitable opportunity which they understandably do not want passive owners to benefit from, they may operate a small part of a large enterprise and are inhibited by its structure or they may simply feel that they can do better on their own. In principle, there is nothing objectionable in this. The managers are taking a risk and are fully entitled to the returns.

Often management buyouts are highly leveraged (LBOs) and that has led to some criticism of the growth of a debt-financed economy (in the USA especially). However, there is nothing wrong in principle with debt. The appropriate debt–equity ratio of a company is not something that can be decided in advance of experience. Some economists argue persuasively that it has nothing to do with economic performance.[27] Indeed, debt is a good discipline on managements, since bondholders have first claim on assets in the event of bankruptcy.

What is ironic in all this is that those who admire the German and the Japanese style of economic management do not seem to realize that companies in these countries are normally heavily indebted to the banks; they are not, in comparison to the Anglo-American model, stock market-driven and therefore do not have to worry too much about shareholder value. Yet as soon as US companies began to behave a little like this their owners (and managers) were heavily criticized for loading up the US economy with debt.

However, ethical problems can arise because of the conflict of interests that face managements in buyouts. Their clear fiduciary duty is to the shareholders and in the event of a takeover they must secure the best price for the owners. But in an MBO they are the potential buyers and will be anxious to make the deal as cheap as possible. Do they have an incentive to so manage the company that its share price underperforms? They can then buy it cheaply, take it private and reorganize it properly and make a big profit when they bring it back to market.

The key point here is information and unethical conduct occurs when the managements refuse to reveal, or they dissemble, facts about the true state of the company. This would be condemnable as an example of exploitation of ignorance as opposed to the legitimate use of knowledge acquired through entrepreneurial endeavour. Of course, in the long run, the market will provide its own corrective mechanisms. Owners themselves will become alert to the possibility of their vulnerability being exposed and take appropriate action – by demanding a bigger premium for their shares. Of course, the long-run process may not satisfy the moralists who concentrate on the visible 'victims' who appear before the market has performed its prophylactic role. It is hard, though, to imagine that legislation could do any better. The most likely consequence of it would be to hamper genuine entrepreneurial activity and value creation.

A not dissimilar problem is the question as to whether there is deliberate promotion of takeovers by interested parties; normally lawyers, financiers and other intermediaries who are necessary for the process and are criticized for earning vast incomes. It is superficially hard to justify their activities on Kirznerian grounds. They do not make the entrepreneurial discovery which is essential for value-creation but may often delude investors into thinking that a discovery has been made. Once again the problems are about likely conflicts of interest and the possibility of the illegitimate exploitation of ignorance. And once again, the only feasible solution is greater openness on the part of all transactors if the sometimes harsh discipline of the market is to be mitigated.

However, perhaps the most controversial ethical aspects of the conduct of takeovers relates to the activities of the managements of target companies. They are the most likely to suffer from the attentions of a predator and can be expected to take defensive measures. Indeed, sometimes these tactics are in the interests of the shareholders because they may feel that long-term value will not be enhanced by a successful bid. Often, however, such tactics are entirely at the behest of management, who make it impossible, through various devices, for owners to secure the full value of their holdings.

The 'poison pill'[28] (or the closely related 'shark repellant') is the most notorious of the defensive devices and it is prohibited (as are most of the controversial anti-takeover devices) in Britain by the Takeover Code. However, the poison pill's legal status in the USA is a matter of continuing controversy and litigation. It is a method of making a takeover prohibitively expensive. The Articles of Association of a target company are changed so that a group of shareholders have special rights which are triggered by a takeover; these can include special voting rights and the right to buy and sell preferred stock at highly favourable prices. Since these are only exercisable in the event of a takeover they make takeovers prohibitively expensive. Through appropriate design companies can become effectively bid-proof.

What poison pills do is prevent an open competition between rival bidders for the shares and most often they make it easier for a suitor favoured by management to take over the company. In fact, it was the upholding of the first poison pill by the Delaware courts (in 1985) in the USA that was a contributory factor to the decline of takeovers at the end of the 1980s in that country. The real economic and ethical problems occurs when poison pills are put in place, and upheld (as can happen in the

USA), without the consent of the shareholders. For what occurs then is the effective transfer of the 'control rights' from the owners to the management. Under the business decision[29] rule in the USA managements are allowed considerable discretion in the handling of a company. They are assumed to be acting in the best interests of the owners and the courts have not attempted to second-guess them. The ultimate remedy for incompetence or venality is for the owners either to replace managements themselves or to sell their stock. However, if a takeover is inhibited by a poison pill then the entrenchment of management that results gives it *de facto* control rights.

In the USA that seemed to happen with the controversial merger of Time Inc. with Warner Bros. This was favoured by the management of Time even though Paramount Communications had made a better offer. The poison pill that had made this possible was upheld by the Delaware Courts in a decision which most critics thought was detrimental to shareholder rights. Curiously, Paramount itself was involved in a decision which seemed to reverse the previous ruling.[30] In a battle for the company between Viacom and QVC, Paramount's management put in a poison pill to favour a friendly merger with QVC. However, this was thrown out by the courts in order to ensure a contest for the company. As it turned out, Viacom won anyway. The difference between the two cases apparently turned on the argument that the Time–Warner merger was a genuine business decision in the interests of the company – though many commentators doubted that. Some US writers have come to favour the British Takeover Code, which does tend to bring about shareholder justice by ensuring a fair contest for a company: all shareholders are treated equally.

The only general conclusion is that poison pills are not harmful if they are designed with shareholder approval. There might be reasons why they should wish to deter a raider who might get control of a company and actually diminish long-term value. There is econometric evidence that pills put in place with the consent of shareholders do add to value while, not surprisingly, those without consent do not. Indeed, there might be reasons, both economic and moral, why all shareholders should not be treated the same; but the important proviso is that the arrangements should be done with shareholder approval.

The granting of 'golden parachutes', special severance packages for executives in the event of a successful takeover (there are sometimes 'tin helmets' for workers) can be analysed in the same way. Although managements are supposed to act always in the best interests of shareholders, they may sometimes need an extra inducement to do so effectively; after all, they are in the best position to make things difficult. Parachutes, with the consent of shareholders, provide a distinctive protection from possible managerial obstruction. Of course, a conflict of interest can easily arise when managements provoke an unnecessary takeover to secure highly favourable severance terms. Once again, it is only the vigilance of the owners that can prevent the abuse of such arrangements.

'Greenmail', with its connotations of blackmail, has provoked the most controversy.[31] Yet it is perhaps the least understood of all the anti-takeover devices. Invariably the wrong people are blamed when it occurs. The practice involves a potential bidder, who has established a stake in a target company, being bought out by an offer for his shares which is not available to other shareholders. It is hard to see why the greenmailer should be the subject of opprobrium. He is simply signalling to the owners that their assets are underperforming. When he is bought out it might be said that he is being bribed by an offer which others do not have; equal treatment for all shareholders is a common demand of reformers (though, as can be shown from many efficient takeovers, it is hard to see how, or why, that should be thought an absolutely necessary aim of securities law). The real culprits in greenmail are the managements who, anxious to protect their own interests, often weigh down companies with debt in order to ward off a predator. Of course, someone may go into the market for corporate control with the veiled intention of getting greenmail, but in such circumstances the management should simply refuse to pay up and wait to see what happens. In most cases of greenmail one suspects that managements pay it, without owners' consent, because they are worried about a potential genuine takeover.

JUSTICE AND TAKEOVERS

Enormous profits are earned by some participants in the takeover process; incomes which are almost impossible to justify in terms of contemporary theories of justice. It is true that one or two spectacular examples in recent US corporate history have come from criminal activity, but even in the absence of this there is little doubt that typical incomes of corporate raiders and their associated financial intermediaries still repel most people. Observers agree that the criminal offences to which financiers like Michael Milken (to be considered in detail later in this chapter) eventually pleaded guilty generated but the merest fraction of his total earnings yet he was still subject to intense moral criticism. The moral critics of takeovers often, somewhat disingenuously, linked the Milken case with that of Boesky, even though the latter's activities were much more venal. Milken's actions did add value, despite his (now very much-disputed) malefactions.

Even a utilitarian justification for the earnings of takeover personnel that purported to show that they are required for overall co-ordination of economic activity, and hence aggregate economic welfare, seems, superficially at least, to be implausible. Is an income of $550m (Michael Milken's reported 'salary' for 1987) required to induce an agent to unite a willing lender with a willing borrower? It is not surprising that such earnings are regarded as beyond the pale of moral justification and dismissed as the product of greed (if not crime). Still, what is 'greed'? And, more important, how could, for example, a redistributive tax rule discriminate between income that derived from pure avarice and that which resulted from a relatively harmless ambition? The onus is on the opponents of the market's allocation of income to demonstrate what a fair reward should be.

Still, however tempting it may be to regard twentieth-century corporate raiders as Mandevillian bees (see above, Chapter 1), and to be grateful for the (presumed) benefits that they bring to society, it is clear that such an attenuated vision of economic morality is not completely satisfactory. For one thing, if this is an appeal to utility, it is disabled by the insolubility of the problem of the intercomparability of utilities. Since, in some sense, people are harmed by the activities of corporate raiders, how is this to be accounted for, and how are the losers to be identified? Of course, in a rigorous interpretation of the Pareto principle no people in voluntary transactions are technically injured by an exchange process, subject to the rule of law, but in a broader sense of harm some interests are damaged by takeovers; after all, some unemployment does occur from restructuring and communal ways of life may be disturbed.

Furthermore, there are too many disputes about ownership of property, and entitlement to the gains from economic reorganization, for the moral argument to be settled by merely economic calculations. Who has a just claim to the fruits of a profitable takeover? What actions are properly called 'fair' in corporate restructuring processes? What are the property rights which are at stake in corporate raiding? To whom do they belong? These questions strongly suggest that appraisals of conduct in takeovers must incorporate some theory of justice.

Kirzner[32] has built a theory of distributive justice into his account of market process and this may have some application to the distributional problems raised by takeovers. He does not rely solely on a utilitarian justification for the market process (as, for example, most other classical liberals have done). He does not say merely that the private property/ market pricing system is superior in the co-ordination of human action to all known alternatives, irrespective of who actually gains from the process. In his view it is the entrepreneurs who are *morally* entitled to their reward. In his theory of entrepreneurship, it is not merely that profit is required to lure people into productive activity: that profit is morally justified (however high it is). His moral doctrine logically applies just as much to the takeover market as it does to intuitively more morally pleasing economic behaviour, such as more tangible innovative economic activity.

He makes a distinction between the income that is created by pure acts of discovery and that which accrues to individuals through their part in repetitive productive processes. The implication is that the more conventional notions of justice may apply to the latter form of income. Though it has to be noted that this distinction is not clearly drawn, or adhered to consistently by Kirzner. He often implies that there is an element of entrepreneurship in all economic activity, even of the most routine type.

Kirzner's theory of justice is entirely procedural and leans heavily on the moral theory of the seventeenth-century philosopher John Locke, and indeed, that of Nozick (though he takes his property arguments even further[33]). He rejects any notion of an end-state justice which depends upon there being a given pie which is available for distribution according to abstract moral principles (including those more sophisticated theories that link the size of the pie with the particular distributive rule adopted). For Kirzner, of course, almost all value is created by enterprising individuals and therefore it is their contributions, their discoveries, that ultimately determine the size of the pie. Hence, Kirzner is able to argue that his disagreement with alternative conceptions of justice is not really about ethics but about economics. It is a misunderstanding of the way that capitalist economies work, he maintains, that has led the authors of rival theories of justice astray.

Kirzner claims that a 'positivist' explanation of the way in which wealth is created, in combination with what he regards as a common (and uncontroversial) moral intuition, yields the correct theory of justice. That intuition is the 'finders keepers' principle.[34] The discovery of something new, be it a previously unowned object in nature or a new combination of resources to produce a wanted good, or a realignment of assets in a profitable takeover or merger, entitles the discoverer to ownership merely because he found it. Since no one else can have a claim to the valued object as it has not yet been created, only the discoverer has title, since he has insight that converts a physical object into an economic object. Thus, oil has no economic value until someone discovers a use for it. It is merely matter lying in the ground.

Still, despite Kirzner's insistence that entrepreneurial gains are not windfall gains it is clear also that they are not necessarily a product of what would normally be thought of as effort. Rivals may have been alert to its value. In his own example,[35] a person who discovers a valuable shell on a beach seconds before someone else, is entitled to exclusive ownership. Yet she may have been simply lucky in standing closer to the object (or perhaps she impeded somebody else in the discovery process). The profits achieved from takeovers are less likely to accord with conventional notions of justice, which tend to be suffused with often incoherent ideas about 'desert' and 'effort', precisely because who has discovered what is likely to be a matter of dispute.

While allowing for some initial plausibility to finders keepers, and conceding Kirzner's claim that it is deeply ingrained in our moral sentiments, it is not difficult to show instances in which its appeal rapidly diminishes. What if someone hit upon a resource vital to our survival and then proceeded to extract all of our income in return for its supply? Are there not, in many societies, commonly-held assets that resist any claim to individual appropriation? In general, the concept of alertness would seem to cover too wide a range of possibilities, from genuine acts of entrepreneurial discovery to what looks like sheer luck (or even seizure of an asset), for it to provide an exclusive theory of ownership. A person who appropriates the only water hole in the desert by running ahead of his rivals is entitled to the monopoly rents it generates. But what if there are traditional and communal, but ill-defined, property rights to such scarce resources? In the above example Kirzner adds that other moral considerations might tell against monopoly ownership; but it would still be valid in terms of justice.

However, I do not wish to explore further these puzzles and ambiguities but instead focus attention on an aspect of distributive justice that has relevance to the takeover issue. This is the problem that emerges when there are disputed claims to discovery, when the faculty of alertness does not seem to be exhibited by one person (or united group of persons) but by competitors. Although competition is rivalrous, there must be some method or rule that conclusively establishes a claim to the value that is created. We have to pose the question as to whether entitlement belongs to someone who is alert to an entrepreneurial opportunity or to that agent who actually exploits its economic possibilities.

The problem occurred in perhaps the most famous (or infamous) takeover battle in British industrial history: the struggle between Guinness and Argyll for the control of Distillers in 1986.[36] Guinness, under the chairmanship of Ernest Saunders, was ultimately successful, which might have been, in utilitarian terms, the best result; but that is hardly to the point, for this success was achieved by methods which ultimately led to the criminal convictions of Saunders and his associates. The facts are that the takeover was to be consummated by a swap between shares of Guinness and Distillers; hence it was imperative that Guinness shares be kept at a high level if the rival bid of Sir James Gulliver's Argyll Group were to be defeated. This Saunders managed to do by organizing a share price support scheme with the allegedly unauthorized use of Guinness money. His bid was ultimately successful.

There are serious moral problems with share price support schemes. They are, of course, incredibly risky; the price of the share might go the other way. That is why the participants in the arrangement were offered substantial indemnities. Indeed, in most commercial law systems the creation of a false market is an offence, though there are doubts about what constitutes one. However, the ground for successive appeals of those involved in the Guinness case was that the kind of practice they engaged in was a common feature of the City.[37] Apparently, it was conceded as such in a later instalment of the Guinness saga in which the defendant was found not guilty: the rationale for the support scheme was apparently accepted. There is also some doubt about the propriety of the investigation process. Saunders and his allies were compelled to give evidence without the conventional legal protection.[38]

Gulliver[39] has always maintained that he was robbed of the deal, and his shareholders deprived of the increased value that a merger with Distillers would have brought them. He had first noticed the opportunity and had done all the necessary research work only to see Guinness walk off with the spoils. Now, the interesting question is: would not Gulliver have had a claim in Kirznerian moral terms irrespective of the legal aspects of the takeover? In other words, even if Saunders and his associates had not broken the law (in fact, they continue to protest their innocence, with some plausibility) they perhaps still would not have a moral claim to the fruits of the takeover. The general point is that the person who notices a profitable opportunity, is alert to the prospect of gain, may not be the same person who actually achieves it.

As a matter of fact, compensation was paid to those who lost out in the deal. But this could only be the result of a very rough and ready calculation. There was obviously no suggestion that the original Guinness takeover should be unravelled, but does not a consistent Kirznerian theory of justice demand that it should have been done? In all this, there is a distinction between the *moral* claims to something that might be made in Kirznerian terms and what individuals may succeed in appropriating. And this distinction holds when the appropriation is lawful. Kirzner himself recognizes this problem with his example of the competing claims made to the possession of an animal that has been hunted by tribesmen.[40] Is the person who originally pursues the beast, or the one who finally slays it, entitled to ownership? He says that legal 'conventions' about ownership in such circumstances will have to be invoked in determining conclusively the rival claims. But this is extremely vague and, indeed, ambiguous. For if there are legal conventions about property ownership, does this not suggest that there are titles to resources that do not depend on entrepreneurship?

However, he gives the impression that, analytically, the person who seizes the opportunity is the same person as he who is alert to it; that the first person who successfully appropriates an economic discovery is necessarily the first person who is alert to it. Yet, as the Guinness example shows, that is not obviously so. An implication of Kirzner's analysis is that every outcome of a rule-governed process is necessarily just. But is it a moral rule or a legal rule that is relevant?

Martin Ricketts,[41] in an important critique of Kirzner, thinks that there is an ethically important difference between 'finding' an opportunity and 'grasping' it and, in relation to the Guinness affair, suggests that Gulliver had made the original entrepreneurial discovery. In a moral sense he was entitled to the profit. However, can a meaningful distinction be drawn between finding and grasping? After all, a deal has to be completed before a profit can be secured and the person who saw the opportunity first may not, for a number of reasons, be able to secure the gains. Is it plausible to maintain that merely seeing something, albeit through considerable research, is sufficient to constitute a property right?

It is true, as Ricketts stresses, that Kirzner's argument is weakened by the absence of a firm theory of property rights to ground a legitimate claim to a discovery (as is shown by his own example of the disputed right to the appropriated beast) but, in relation to takeovers it could be argued that the completion of the deal is the only feasible grounding of the property claim. Certainly it would be very difficult to design a legal rule which clearly distinguished between the 'finding' and the 'grasping' an opportunity, and which determined uncontroversially the appropriate rewards. Still, Ricketts has made an important theoretical contribution to the debate.

In general, there is an element of luck about some takeovers. A parallel might be those occasions when a driver notices that a parking spot is soon to become available, waits patiently for the other motorist to move out only to be beaten to the place by a rival who suddenly appears and 'steals' the place. Of course, takeovers are not quite like this, but despite all the research and effort they involve, the right person might not be successful. Furthermore, conventional moralists will always say that they are not necessary, that they offer opportunities for greed not just reward and involve luck rather than genuine effort. It is quite likely, though, that conventional morality is wrong, as it depends so much on the kind of physicalist theory of value criticized earlier.

JUNK BONDS AND MICHAEL MILKEN

Michael Milken has probably become the most controversial financier this century: praised by some for his undoubted flair[42] yet reviled by others for his alleged malign effect on the structure of the American economy through burdening companies with debt and apparently pushing ethical standards in financial markets to a new low.[43] Because of the hysteria created by his activities it has been difficult to have a rational debate over both his economics and ethics. Yet Milken is by no means a unique figure in US economic history: entrepreneurs in the past have cut through existing commercial structures, offended prevailing business power elites and earned, whether deserved or not, reputations for ruthless, unethical behaviour. Milken effected a revolution in US banking equivalent to that achieved by J.P. Morgan earlier in the century and parallel to the industrial innovators of the past who were castigated as robber barons.

One reason why Milken has suffered even more opprobrium, and has been subjected to even greater economic and moral censure than his predecessors, is that the vast increase in the regulation of securities markets and the criminalization of many actions which were once treated as minor civil wrongs, has made it superficially easier for moral criticism to stick. Added to that is the prevailing anti-capitalist ethos of the US intelligentsia: prominent Left-liberal spokesmen in the media found it easy to condemn Milken because he was spectacularly successful in an 'unjust' system. Leading figures in the business world were equally criti-cal, but for a different reason. Milken was a radical innovator in a conser-vative world and a threat to their power base. Important here was the established banking community of New York.

Milken pioneered the inaptly named junk bond. It was first used as method of finance for small and medium-sized adventurous companies deemed not to be creditworthy by the established rating agencies. Only later was it used by hostile raiders to take control of, and occasionally break up, large publicly-quoted corporations. What might be thought of as no more than a regular feature of capitalist development – that is, the emergence of new financial methods – became the symbol of all that was wrong in the USA's economy (that is, debt) and all that was immoral in US society (that is, greed).

The junk bond is no more than debt which is of lower quality than that issued by blue chip companies. To the extent that the majority of debt is not rated as investment-grade quality by the established agencies, the majority of debt is technically junk. Milken's skill lay in noticing that the default rate on so-called junk was quite low.[44] Since junk paid a higher rate of interest than investment-grade debt there was much money to be made. Even bonds that were close to default could be made to earn profits because they could be bought up cheaply. Milken noticed that bankruptcies were much rarer than most people thought, so that the risks were less than indicated by the credit agencies. Milken's activities led to a decline in bank lending to business.

In fact, much of Milken's behaviour is explicable by Austrian political economy. It was his alertness to the inaccuracies in existing valuations that generated profit and his uncanny ability to spot up-and-coming companies (often from minority communities) that were later to be very successful. Some now established names were originally discovered by him. One of the methodological problems with established rating agen-cies was that their rating of creditworthiness was based on *past* data. This leads to the overvaluation of blue chip companies and the under-valuation of newer enterprises. The credit rating agencies were crude empiricists and inductivists who assumed that the future would be like the past; a fatal error in business. Yet a sophisticated analysis of a firm's cash flow, an activity at which Milken excelled, proved to be a reliable indicator of future performance of companies which hitherto did not have good records. Milken's economic success actually illustrates a point in the philosophy of science. It is now accepted that scientific knowledge and laws are built up by bold conjectures and speculations on the part of the researcher. A scientific law is not established by empirical observation (as the positivists and empiricists thought) but by producing falsifiable hypotheses. In the takeover boom of the 1980s, the respectable credit rating agencies were the positivists, they merely worked on the past records of established companies and seemed to be unaware of the fact that the future is not always like the past. Milken was the bold innovator.

Furthermore, Milken's actions led to the revival of a style of business favoured by Adam Smith – the owner-managed enterprise. In fact, there was a considerable deconcentration of ownership in the 1980s, largely brought about by his revolution and the takeovers it inspired. What upset the establishment was the use of his methods in corporate raids. The highly-leveraged takeover put fear in the boardrooms of established companies. Managements that had not delivered owners (the shareholders) high value in terms of share price were under siege. The raiders were accused of showing no interest in the long-term interests of the company, in research and development and, least of all, the community. Most of these accusations are quite false. In fact, Milken financed some of the real innovators in the US economy, and the benefits of this activity are now beginning to come through. Corporate raiding did not itself cause extra unemployment – at the time of the Milken revolution established corporations were laying off workers at a greater rate than that caused by newly-created Milken enterprises. In a real economic sense communities gained from his activities. Unemployment in decaying industries was easily compensated for by new jobs in the growth areas.

It is difficult to see what was specifically immoral about all this, irrespective of the personal behaviour of particular participants (and Milken himself has lived a life of impeccable moral probity[45]). It is true that he earned a spectacular $550m in 1987, but this can be explained in Kirznerian terms as a reward for his extraordinary entrepreneurial flair. If any charges of immorality are to be levelled at anyone, it is to the people who brought about his downfall.[46]

This was partly due to the prosecuting zeal of the US attorney for New York, Rudolph Guiliani, who no doubt thought that his political career would be advanced (he was to run for mayor for the first time in the late 1980s) if he had a successful record in bringing unpopular financiers to heel. After a fairly brutal investigation Milken was originally faced with a 98-count indictment. He was, in effect, coerced into a bargain with the prosecutors and pleaded guilty to six fairly minor charges – none of which included insider dealing (which was in the first indictment). Some of the offences had only become criminal through highly controversial court interpretations of the law.

Yet even for the trivial charges to which he eventually pleaded guilty Milken was given an astonishing 10-year jail sentence. This was later much reduced but questions are still being asked about the behaviour of the authorities in the whole affair. It is clear that many well-established legal protection rules for suspects were disregarded and the rule of law was badly compromised. None of the methods used would have been admissible in regular criminal hearings. It seems that financiers are not granted the USA's legendary list of civil liberties. What was particularly reprehensible was the use the prosecutors made of the Racketeer Influenced and Corrupt Organizations Act (RICO). This is a tough statute which, among other things, allows the authorities to seize the assets of suspects before trial. It was originally aimed at the Mafia but was used much more frequently against business personnel. Its constitutionality has always been doubted.

One particular tactic used by the prosecutors, and the media critics of Milken, was to associate his activities with those of Ivan Boesky, whose wrongdoing was transparent and who received favourable treatment by the prosecution for his own offences. He was helped by the fact that he co-operated in the investigation of Milken. Furthermore, the Wall Street banking community had every incentive to encourage the hysteria, since he was a very real threat to their position. Milken neatly circumvented the formal and informal barriers that had been erected to deter outsiders.

It is really rather surprising that established opinion should have been so hostile to debt. United States companies have never been particularly indebted (they are mainly stock market-financed) and this did not increase during his era. All this is richly ironic since the critics of Anglo-American capitalism are sceptical about equity financing and admire countries whose investment projects are financed through bank debt – Germany being one good example. The whole Milken episode revealed considerable ignorance of economics and ethics on the part of the critics of free market, individualistic capitalism.

TAKEOVERS AND THE COMMUNITY

In current social philosophy the doctrine of communitarianism has a natural resonance in the takeover argument. Since it is explicitly directed against the individualism of liberal economics and its apparently anonymous world of arm's length traders (who have no long-term obligations of a non-economic kind), it is not at all surprising that it should be extremely hostile to the kind of corporate restructuring that takes place in Anglo-American economies: a form of economic reorganization that is no respecter of traditional ways of doing things or of established social and economic arrangements. The political Left and Right have always found common cause here, since both evince an almost visceral anti-individualism and an indifference to its economic success.

Communitarianism is partly a philosophical doctrine about personal identity and partly a set of social and economic public policies.[47] It denies that individuals can be properly understood in the terms of liberal economics (that is, as asocial transactors abstracted from those communal affiliations that give meaning to their lives and stability and permanence to their institutions). They need to be nested in given social arrangements if they are to be identified as persons: the market is too abstract to do this. It is for this philosophical reason that communitarians play down the role of the market: apparently it is always parasitic on other institutions. Its very existence as a choice mechanism depends on the preservation of those things that are not chosen, such as social arrangements, rules, practices and implicit moral obligations. An untrammelled market is thought to be corrosive of these traditional institutions.

At the more directly economic and political level, communitarianism presupposes that the state, through its regulatory or other controls, has a duty to protect society and its institutions from the ravages of the market. In fact, this critique is addressed to liberalism in general, even the more egalitarian versions of that doctrine.[48] It is not therefore merely about the distributive implications of corporate restructuring, though no doubt communitarians are repelled by the profits that are achieved by it, but about the methodological individualism that underlies it.[49]

Not surprisingly, communitarians have always favoured law and politics as devices to preserve communities against corporate raiders. They have secured support from business agents who have much to lose to predators. In the rush of state legislation that took place in the USA in the late 1980s to curb takeovers, business leaders joined with communitarian activists to influence individual state legislators.

Another argument, which is more prevalent in British and European anti-takeover writings, is to invoke the concept of the public interest to disallow certain takeovers. Under current British arrangements (the Takeover Code, which is not technically part of positive law but has the same effect), the requirement is that a takeover should not be *against* the public interest. It is obviously aimed at monopolists or those takeovers which would badly undermine competition by giving one company excessive market share. However, critics of corporate restructuring want to strengthen the requirement – potential bidders should demonstrate that the takeover should be *in* the public interest.

The concept of the public interest is highly contestable.[50] There are some things that affect everybody equally and are therefore to the advantage of the public: a common system of law and the supply of genuine public goods fall into this category. But beyond this minimalist conception, dispute occurs and what is presented as a policy for the public interest often turns out to be for the benefit of coalitions of interest groups. A generous interpretation of the concept would then make takeovers very difficult to justify. It would not be difficult for a critic to show why a particular takeover was not in the public interest – some politically-significant group might be adversely affected, the bidder might not be able to convince the authorities that his employment policies recognized 'diversity', or long-standing communities could claim that their traditional ways of life would be disrupted. All sorts of emotional and political factors would combine to disturb economic rationality. So far, successive British governments have resisted this strategy, but as the communitarian idea takes hold it is quite likely that legislation will eventually reflect these values.

It is the use of takeovers that best distinguishes the Anglo-American economies from their rival capitalist systems. But all types of capitalist regimes face the same problem of ensuring good and efficient behaviour by managements. Given the open nature of the economies of the USA and Britain (and some other English-speaking countries) the takeover method is the only device that can ensure this. There are simply fewer communal bonds that bind people, though it might be more accurate to say that these social arrangements are spread across a number of *communities*. It is not that trust and loyalty is absent but it is consistent with significant pluralism. In such circumstances the co-ordinating process of the market are excellent surrogates for the consensus and community spirit that might make hostile bidders unwelcome in other countries.

Most of the fears about the effect of takeovers in the 1980s were grossly exaggerated. They did not set community against community or even devastate local areas. Indeed, most of the 'victims' were not workers but layers of management, who may have been responsible for the inefficiencies in the first place. And the personal behaviour of a minority of the personnel involved must not be taken as an example of all that is wrong in Anglo-American economics and ethics. Of course, there were considerable resource costs incurred through payment to lawyers and financial intermediaries but it is difficult to see how they could be avoided, given the legal and social environment of Anglo-American economies. If there were efficiency savings to be made, an alert entrepreneur would have spotted them.

In retrospect, the 1980s seem relatively benign. The Anglo-American economies have now acquired an almost legendary reputation for flexibility which other countries, formerly hostile to their methods, are now beginning to envy. Indeed, the fear of unemployment, which was an important rhetorical weapon in the anti-takeover movement, is now dominating economies that spurned that method of industrial organization. Unemployment has soared in economies that hitherto tried to guarantee lifetime employment.

Even outside the Anglo-American business world, takeovers are recognized to be efficient. Ethical debate, therefore, will centre on particular takeovers. For example, many critics would like an egalitarian regulation that requires equal treatment for all shareholders (they should get the same price). In two-tier offers those who tender their shares first (normally big holders) gain a bigger premium than minority holders. For once control of the target has been secured the latter are 'coerced' to sell at a lower price. They are said to be 'looted'.

However, this is not unfair because the value of the share will not be always the same; it will vary according to the time of the transaction. And anyway, large shareholdres could be said to be morally entitled to a higher premium because of the contribution they have made to the sucess of the firm over time. Also, the attempt to produce equality by regulation generates the 'free rider' problem – with 'perfect fairness' assured to all no one has an incentive to initiate a takeover. Excessive regulation simply makes takeovers more costly. Equality of treatment should be *ex ante* not *ex post*.

7 The Environment and Business Ethics

Perhaps the most important ethical assault in recent years on the ethics of market capitalism has come from the environmental movement. It is assumed that the particular motivations of capitalism, self-interest and the desire for profit, must necessarily lead to a lack of concern for the environment, since each individual transactor cannot be expected to take care of a matter about which he has no *immediate* interest. Naturally the business community, and especially large-scale corporations, are assumed to be the major (indeed the only) culprits in the phenomenon of environmental depredation. Most of the ethical critics of business seem unaware of the direct role of government in the destruction of wildlife and damage to the atmosphere.[1] Equally important is its indirect role in these phenomena through its failure to provide the right incentive structure for the reconciliation of private and public interests.

It is claimed that the alleged egoism generated by market capitalism's spontaneous processes cannot take care of the environment, so that government has to have a decisive role in the protection of the air, water, natural resources in general, endangered species and any other phenomena which are vulnerable to the predatory actions of firms and other necessary features of capitalist organization. Moreover, it is assumed that without rigorous controls on production greedy capitalists will quickly exhaust the supply of oil and other valuable resources: a problem apparently exacerbated by unsustainable increases in world population.

Environmental ethics seems to demand, in addition to government action, that individuals voluntarily change their attitudes; that they become less concerned for profit and more solicitous of those values that they share with others. One of these is, of course, the common interest we have in environmental protection. It is unthinkingly assumed that a change in human attitudes and motivations is the necessary aim of an appropriate moral education for business agents. Of course, it has been well-known in classical liberal economic theory that it is futile to try to change human nature. It will always be more or less self-interested, in politics no less than in economics. However, what that doctrine has been concerned to recommend is the sustaining and occasional creation of institutional forms which harness this not reprehensible feature of the human condition for the public good. Protection of the environment fits in with the traditional market explanation of how the public interest is the unintentional outcome of the pursuit of private interests. Indeed, environmental 'goods' are increasingly demanded by inhabitants of more prosperous societies and their supply can even be made profitable for business agents. Thus they are not 'educated' to do this by moralists but induced to do so by appropriate institutional forms.

As will be shown, the major mechanism here is the design of efficiency-promoting property rights structures. Indeed, they do not often have to be constructed from first principles but can be inferred from traditional common law entitlements. Environmental damage can be treated as a particular type of harm for which redress is available. Of course, there are special problems that arise in certain circumstances, notably that arising out of the difficulties that 'large numbers' make to the securing of remedies for environmental wrongs. Small face-to-face societies use informal methods to secure compliance to common standards but such methods are not normally available in modern, anonymous capitalist orders. When large numbers of people are involved, whatever corrective measures are proposed should be built on the principle of liability for wrongs which is enshrined in classical liberal economic and political theory. Difficulties arise when the familiar 'public good' problems make private solutions infeasible.

There are a number of different and competing responses to the environmental problem and they tend to rest on divergent ethical foundations. The standard view is that all the familiar issues and 'crises' can be blamed exclusively on capitalism and can be solved only by a drastic alteration (or elimination) of the goals that a capitalist society typically strives for, such as economic growth, ever-rising living standards and the efficient exploitation of the earth's resources. The target of environmental extremists is the almost exclusive concern that market capitalism shows for human needs. It is also said that the system shows an undue commitment to the demands of the present inhabitants of the earth and is indifferent to the needs of future generations. But the critics of capitalism tend to divide into extreme and moderate reactions to the same problems.

The extremists[2] adopt an ethic which is specifically anti-human: in their view it is the hubris of humans, particularly civilized humans, which is responsible for the alleged degradation of the environment. As merely temporary occupants of the planet humans have no prior entitlement to its resources and nature itself (and non-human animals) have valid claims against their predatory actions. As I shall show, this type of environmentalism takes on the form of a religion[3] and is indeed resistant to the claims of science whenever they arouse scepticism of the extremists' claims. The latter are also unreceptive to any suggested improvements to the property rights structure of capitalist society which may alleviate some of the familiar problems because these (even if they were effective, which is denied) would simply allow the continued exploitation of the earth's resources. An efficient legal system that prevented degradation would merely perpetuate the immorality of capitalism. The business community is *a priori* unethical and no reforms to its structure will appease the zealots.

The more moderate environmentalists[4] are not against progress and civilization, sometimes they claim to be not ideologically adverse to capitalism itself. What is distinctive about their position is the pre-eminent role they give to government itself in the management of the environment. It is a form of socialism in that it assumes, like old-fashioned central planning, that the market could not spontaneously correct the errors that the pursuit of profit is alleged to create. Hence the familiar technique is the 'command and control' method of environmental management.[5] Environmental problems are identified by government and that body should have the power to direct the activities of business agents so that the pre-determined goals are achieved. It is assumed that the government has some special omniscience in the setting of those targets which are supposed to reflect shared values. The typical methods are statutory prohibition of certain activities, excessive taxation of firms that produce pollution, various charges and other strategies designed to generate the public interest by design. The ethical foundation of this is a version of utilitarianism that is supposed to be superior to the self-correcting mechanisms of both markets and common law. Of course, it is alert to the fact that some environmental problems are obviously cross-national so that command and control methods tend to take the form of 'international socialism' as applied to the environment. The fact that different countries may have different environmental goals is ignored; international environmental regulation imposes compulsory, uniform standards and bureaucratic action which are not limited to the control of external effects in a particular country. A total planning of the world environment is implicit in 'command and control' methods.

However, a different form of environmentalism favours capitalism and the development and spread of business enterprise. Its solution to pollution and other problems does not lie in religion, or even a new ethics, but in the refinement of the property rights structure of market capitalism so that it does not pay individual transactors to despoil the habitat. It is not indifferent to morality since all theorists of the market believe that the system depends on certain moral predispositions in the participants – the capacities for trust, reciprocity and co-operation being pre-eminent. But it certainly does not demand superhuman moral qualities in individuals and it is assumed that in the appropriate institutional setting protection of the environment can be quite consistent with the pursuit of profit. Indeed, it is empirically the case that advanced capitalist societies have better environmental records than those in any other form of economic organization.[6] In advanced capitalist societies a clean environment is itself a consumer good and, with the right legal framework and well-defined property rights, the market can produce it. Furthermore, the business community has every incentive itself to pay heed to the ever-rising public demand, in advanced economies, for good stewardship of the environment.

RELIGIOUS AND EXTREME ENVIRONMENTALISM

Unfortunately much of the argument about the environment has been dominated by an attitude which can only be called religious.[7] By this is meant an approach which is impervious to science, to economic reasoning and to facts: it is also completely insensitive to the subtle tradeoffs between productivity and the need for environmental protection that have to be made if a rational solution to the typical problems is to be achieved. With religious environmentalism *nature* itself becomes a god to be worshipped and man is seen to be an unnecessary intruder. Of course, a pristine nature is especially threatened by capitalism, the purely instrumental rationality[8] of which is the prime cause of the alleged deprivation of the environment. In this extreme environmentalism a higher form of rationality would eliminate the necessary calculation of means to ends, which the participants in market capitalism regularly do, but determines objectively the ends themselves. The form of instrumental rationalism in capitalist society which carefully balances concern for the environment with the need for productive efficiency is rejected because it privileges man. This form of rationality takes account of the sometimes competing and always subjective human purposes. According to religious environmentalism technological innovations that have improved the well-being of humans are condemnable if they have the minutest effect on nature. The long campaign against insecticides (especially DDT) is the prime example of this religious approach, for it asserts that there is no moral basis for assuming that humans as a species should have a privileged position in the eco-structure. Nature itself embodies a kind of objective morality which must always take precedence over our merely human concerns. The elimination of DDT has produced an increase in deaths from malaria (in Sri Lanka, particularly[9]). But what does that matter for a religious environmentalist for whom nature is to be worshipped and mankind scarcely tolerated? It is not surprising that pharmaceutical industries should be a particular target of religious environmentalist: after all, they do much to save humanity from deadly diseases.

The famous Gaia philosophy[10] is an example of the quasi-religious approach. In this doctrine it is presupposed that the universe is governed by a cosmic law which orders every part of it. There is a kind of spontaneous order in the universe which has its own mechanisms of coordination and, if it is left undisturbed, nirvana will result. However, humans, and especially capitalist humans, disturb this delicate ordering mechanism with regular and disruptive departures from what is known as 'the Way'. It is difficult to know what to make of this heady metaphysics. Most environmental problems are about really mundane matters, such as the appropriate structure of property rights, the assignment of liability for damage and so on. Religious, metaphysical and most notions of extended ethical environmentalism have little to contribute to these problems.

It is clear that religious environmentalism has nothing to do with Christianity (or indeed any of the great religions of the world) for this specifically enjoins humans to tame nature and to make the world a better place for God's chosen people. We were not put on this earth to be stewards of a permanent wilderness. Religious environmentalism would appear to have little to say to the pressing concerns of business and the natural world. As a religion it cannot be proved wrong; it depends on faith and is impervious to economic evidence.

One clear example of the incompatibility of religious environmentalism and science is the current hysteria about global warming: allegedly caused by the excessive emission of carbon dioxide in the atmosphere which prevents the natural cooling processes from operating effectively. This phenomenon is apparently entirely a result of modern industrial processes, which are themselves the outcome of unrestrained capitalism. The plausibility of this thesis depends entirely on the claim that temperature variation (in particular, increases in temperature) are related unequivocally to the use of cars, modern consumer goods and appliances fed to a compliant population by profit-maximizing business.

But the evidence[11] is now becoming well-established that temperature variation is a product of natural changes in the atmosphere and that the increases in temperature that have occurred over the past decade are really insignificant. All this has been established by the use of sophisticated measuring devices. Roger Bate, who has made an extensive study of the literature, maintains authoritatively that: 'The mild warming that has occurred over the past century is well within the natural temperature range, and mostly happened before the emissions of man-made gases intensified'.[12]

However, this tends to be ignored by extreme environmentalists, who either reject the scientific approach as just another example of instrumental rationality or, only slightly less plausibly, adopt the 'precautionary principle', which says that even though the scientific evidence about global warming may not be compelling we should refrain from industrialization just in case it should turn out to be right. If applied consistently throughout history this would have prevented any economic improvement. Anyway, it is an illusion to think that all risk can be eliminated.

ENVIRONMENTALISM AND RIGHTS

However, there is a form of the environmentalist doctrine (which is just as extreme as the religious variety) that has a certain superficial plausibility in ethical terms because it uses not quasi-religious symbolism but instead exploits a language which has a peculiar resonance in modern thought – the language of *rights*.[13] In invoking this discourse it has distorted the traditional understanding of rights and prevented rational argument. In liberal social philosophy of the past to have a right meant that a person had a claim not to be unjustifiably interfered with in an exercise of his faculties which did not impede a similar exercise by others. Rights holders were thought to be a carefully defined class of agents, normally sane adults (or, perhaps more controversially, children) – not animals, nature or the environment itself. We may have moral duties towards non-human entities but these are subject to the qualifications of conventional morality (including utilitarianism). Certain sorts of duties (especially those towards children) are especially compelling.

But rights, properly understood, have a peculiarly compelling force – their invocation defeats all other moral considerations. Thus no amount of improvement in social or economic well-being justifies arbitrary imprisonment or the violation of the right to free movement or free speech. At one time economic liberties were included in this category but the prevailing collectivist opinion in the twentieth century led to their exclusion from the same protection that the familiar civil liberties have come to enjoy. What is distinctive about these rights is that their possession by one person is compatible with other people's similar claims. This is not so with environmental rights which, if implemented, almost always result in a diminution of rights for some, especially those of property holders.

The business community has always encompassed a limited notion of rights. The right to fair treatment in trading, to honesty and so on are integral features of good business practice and are not obviously inconsistent with utility – which has always been the major ethical validation of business. Of especial importance are the rights that derive from property and contract, although perhaps these more properly belong to the more tractable category of positive law than to the nebulous category of moral and natural rights. Even though there are hypothetical and real cases of conflict between rights and utility in business they are rare enough not to cause major concern. Indeed, the business world tends to develop a notion of right conduct that may often inhibits short-term utility-maximization: a practice which is to the long-run advantage of all participants. There is no reason why this should not occur in environmental matters.

However, the vast extension of the range of rights to be claimed and the similar extension of the category of putative rights-bearers, both of which have occurred in the last 30 or so years, has made discourse about rights inherently controversial. For example, welfare rights, which require extensive state activity, are now assumed to be logically equivalent to the traditional rights, that (unlike welfare claims) normally demanded little more than *restraint* by the state and by other individuals. The same thing has happened with regard to the environment where rights arguments are frequently used. Rare species, especially animals, are said to have rights which defeat all claims derived form utility. Humankind is morally prevented from pursuing profit-maximizing activities which might threaten their existence. To assert the over-riding needs of humans is now regarded as 'speciesism', an apparently grievous moral wrong.[14] The inanimate environment itself is a kind of rights-bearer, the claims of which are decisive in matters which might have hitherto been thought to be exclusively economic. Indeed, in extreme rights-based environmentalism no economic facts are allowed to impinge on the purely ethical claims.

And this is the problem with a rights-based environmentalism: by making use of the traditional rights argument (which defeats all claims derived from utility) it cuts off debate in which competing values are highly relevant. Once we say that the environment, or some agents acting on its behalf, has rights we preclude the tradeoffs that are otherwise suggested for dealing with both public policy problems and the particular choices that face individual actors in markets. It is true that the traditional civil rights are sometimes inconsistent with utility and are still upheld uncontroversially – for example, the right to a fair trial is not normally suspended on grounds of cost, or because of a threat to public order that might occasionally occur when it is honoured. But there is little dispute about the importance of these claim rights. This is not so with environmental rights. Can the claim that rocks or trees have rights be even said to be meaningful, let alone equivalent to the arguments in favour of the rights of free discussion, property, contract, due process and liberty of movement?

Furthermore, the seemingly endless proliferation of rights claims (and the increasing number of minor environmental harms that are labelled as rights-violations) has the unintended effect of actually eliminating all rights. For if the distinguishing feature of a claim right, that it highlights a crucially important human demand, is applied loosely and indiscriminately, then rights become mere *interests* that have to be negotiated through the political process. Environmental groups become pressure groups, albeit particularly strident and articulate ones, and even genuine concerns about the earth and its resources become diluted in the welter of conflicting (and irreconcilable) interests. Prominent environmental groups are well-funded and politically active.

Any utilitarian calculations derived from instrumental rationality are immediately excluded when rights are asserted. It has been shown, for example, that the massive sums of money spent on environmental protection through the Clean Air and Clean Water legislation and anti-toxins regulation in the USA saves no more than a handful of deaths from cancer a year.[15] Many environmental hazards are less frequent and rarer than the risks we encounter in everyday life and about which we do not show excessive concern. The right to life cannot be guaranteed against all dangers. Moreover, increasing investment expenditure on the environment produces, as one would expect, diminishing returns. Beyond a certain point, it costs a great deal more in forgone income to secure ever fewer gains. Extreme environmentalists almost deliberately ignore, or downplay, the significance of such elementary economic propositions. It is as if they would prefer to shut down the whole of economic life for infinitesimal environmental advantages.

Equally important is the well-documented fact that capitalism is itself responsible for little environmental damage compared to socialistic planning. The record of the former Soviet Union and its satellites, especially Eastern Germany is dismal in comparison to conventional market economies.[16] River and sea pollution reached catastrophic levels and the intensive use of old-fashioned industrial production techniques caused grave air pollution with a consequent serious rise in avoidable health problems. Also, inefficient energy consumption was a feature of those regimes. The superiority of capitalism in energy use is a result of economic progress which has led to much more economical production techniques.[17] Competitive pressures in a market economy induce producers to reduce costs. Although comparable amounts of energy were used in capitalist and socialist regimes output was vastly superior in the former.

The environmental crises created by central planning closely parallel the insoluble efficiency problems in the production of ordinary goods and services in those economic orders (or disorders). For just as the absence of a market to indicate economic value and scarcities precluded an efficient allocation of resources for the production of consumer goods, its elimination also prevented a rational appreciation of the relative importance of prosperity in comparison to preserving an habitable environment. This, plus the impossibility of the citizenry expressing any meaningful choice between competing ends, meant that the central planners had complete and unfettered sovereignty over the environment. Given the obsession with 'production' in socialist societies there were no incentives for the central planners to make the finely-balanced judgements that are required.

Yet, in a more benign way the 'command and control' methods of environmentalism practised in nominally capitalist economies reflect the strategies of these malevolent regimes. Environmental targets are set and economic agents are compelled to follow them through coercive law, liberty-reducing regulation or ruinously expensive tax policies. Furthermore, producers are induced to produce environmental 'bads' up to the level permitted by the regulations so that here is a disincentive to introduce innovations that might maker greater environmental improvements. Business agents cannot be morally blamed for this; their behaviour is consistent with the law. The state has, in effect, taken over the morality of the environment.

What command and control methods normally preclude is any real competition between environmental authorities. Regulations are uniform and coercive. But it might be the case that poorer regions of a particular country are prepared to tolerate some environmental disadvantages in return for more employment-creating investment. Then, as the region gets richer, the demand for tougher laws may well outweigh the preferences for more industrialisation. In such cases it is not the immorality and greed of the business agents that are responsible for the adverse conditions. They are simply responding to the demands of consumers; demands which are not immutable.

Yet the ethics of environmentalism often expresses a demand for 'justice' – every one should be subjected to the same laws and regulations, there is an 'equal right' to clean air and clean water. It is argued that poorer areas are typically the favoured site for potentially harmful industrial development, landfills and disposal facilities. But this again ignores the fact that these very same areas gain from economic development and will suffer worse conditions in terms of employment and general well-being if it is forbidden by arbitrary regulations formulated in the name of environmental justice. What the ideologues do not appreciate is the fact that the demand for a cleaner environment is largely a function of income; as people get richer they value it more. That is why prosperous economies have safer and cleaner environments. There is no irreconcilable conflict between efficiency and the preservation of a pleasantly habitable planet.

Furthermore, in a regime of well-defined property rights it is possible for particular communities to sell the right to develop in their areas. Only in those circumstances can a tradeoff (which must be subjective) be made between competing values. However, environmental ethics too often proceeds on the basis that there is an objective measure of necessary protection from the effects of economic progress.

Of course, this does not solve the problem of 'external effects' that harm the interests of third parties who have no opportunity to express a preference at all; and this is what a sensible discussion about the environment should really be about. It is especially important when pollution spreads across regions and countries. These effects do not recognize international boundaries and the large numbers of people involved may make it difficult to generate a property rights solution. In such circumstances it might be impossible to identify particular miscreants and to take corrective action.

THE FOLLY OF ATTITUDINAL CHANGE

Environmental ethicists make a serious mistake when they make specific recommendations to business (and indeed consumers and voters). They seem to assume that what is required is a change in *attitudes*, that people must be made aware of the adverse consequences of uncontrolled industrial development. People must either take direct action against businesses that breach their normally impossible high standards or they should boycott the products of firms that have dubious environmental records. The latter is of course a more acceptable approach as it does not directly undermine property rights. Still, environmental activist also try to influence political institutions so that regulatory solutions to problems rather than market approaches are encouraged. Here they make use of sometimes highly dubious environmental data. What is interesting here is the fact that these regulations appear to meet with the approval of dispersed and unorganized voters. Democratic theory predicts that strategically-placed, well-organized and well-financed groups with a direct interest in policy can normally resist such forces.[18] But business has been remarkably unsuccessful in countering environmental groups. But it can be doubted if the behaviour of the electorate reflects a genuine change in attitudes. Voting for fashionable environmental laws is a costless activity.

Significantly, environmental groups embark on massive propaganda campaigns, in an attempt to change attitudes, which often do more to increase the income and status of the activists themselves than to advance the cause of the environment.[19] The dominant environmental organizations rarely take part in activities that actually benefit the environment or preserve some wild species. Yet they could do so by buying up land, perhaps to protect it from some unwelcome industrial development, or by embarking on schemes to preserve things of value, such as are birds threatened with extinction. No change in attitudes is required here.

In fact, the whole idea of changing people's attitudes is a pointless exercise . Human motivations are pretty much universal. Nothing much has really changed since Hume, in the eighteenth century, wrote that: 'as it is impossible to change or correct anything material in our nature, the utmost we can do is to change our circumstances and situation, and render the observance of the laws of justice our nearest interest and their violation the most remote'.[20] We do not go far wrong if we understand people to be driven by the desire for profit (which can harm the rights of others, for example when pollution becomes a costless activity for the perpetrator), the desire for political power and (increasingly) the desire to be well-thought of by our fellow citizens. In the modern world, with the heavy politicization of economic life, the last motivation has degenerated into moral vanity; the desire to be well-thought of at no personal cost to oneself, to strike the right attitudes in public and to engage in a certain amount of posturing. The campaign for political action, via prohibition of industrial development, involves just this exaggerated notion of self-esteem. The costs of such political action are rarely borne by the activists themselves. The victims are normally workers who become displaced by the regulation and property owners who see the value of their land and buildings depleted by excessive regulation. Although the activists might eventually have to bear the costs in terms of higher prices, this is usually far enough in the distant future to outweigh the utility they get from striking the right attitudes. But what it essentially involves is the imposition of environmentalist values on others.

The environmental zealot assumes that people's attitudes can be changed and that it is actually harmful to adjust law and other social arrangements so that the permanent mainsprings of human action are not destructive of order. The extreme environmentalist morality assumes that the claims of the environment defeat all others and this is, of course, why the demands are increasingly put in the form of rights. But no one has yet satisfactorily demonstrated that there is such an objective morality beyond the minimum requirements of civility and personal protection that every humane order requires. And regimes rarely bring about a voluntary sacrifice of personal interest for the common good. Force, of varying degrees of severity soon replaces moral persuasion.

The problems of the environment involve a plurality of values. The rights of property compete with the preservation of acceptable public standards and the natural desire to 'better our selves' should not be achieved at the cost of other people's legitimate claims. The monistic pursuit of a single end, preservation of the environment in some predetermined form, should not license a prohibition of economic progress. All that this requires, as I shall see below, is a careful appreciation of the way in which laws and other social institutions can be so developed that the almost instinctive desire for profit does not impinge on other people's values. What is required is an acceptance of a necessary subjectivity and pluralism in human values. Thus no government or regulator can know *a priori* what is the precise relationship between environmentalism and economic prosperity or how much of one should be given up for the pursuit of the other. It is of course the market, subject to appropriate law and characterized by well-defined property rights that is the most feasible social institution in most cases (but not all) for making these necessarily subjective judgements. It is a mechanism that, in the right legal context, can delicately order a plurality of values.

It would appear that there is actually no need for a special environmental ethics, especially one that would sanction massive governmental discretionary power. For traditional rules and practices and the growth of a certain amount of co-operative behaviour (which does not involve the sacrifice of personal interest) are capable of developing in such a way as to cope with most issues that have now reached the public agenda. Co-operative activities on the part of business is especially important since its personnel have a clear interest in developing self-restraint because in its absence commerce exposes itself to really heavy regulation. However, what is required is not a change in attitudes but the inculcation of rules and practices that encourage restraint from those acts of immediate gratification that are costly in the long run. The only thing which is special about the environment is that some circumstances may make it difficult for business to develop and internally enforce these rules of restraint. Certain obvious facts make it hard to identify and punish the violators of these putative rules. Without some guarantee of compliance, business personnel are vulnerable to acts of exploitation which ultimately harm the commercial world as a whole. The original violator has made his profit and escaped detection before corrective processes can take effect. Still, in all cases we should follow Hume's advice and search for changes in circumstances (especially the incentive structure that maximizing individuals face) to bring about a harmony between an unchanging self-interest and the common and uncomplicated morality that we all share. We must not look for a change in human nature and should welcome the fact that the world is not irredeemably divided between the morally enlightened and the eternally damned.

BUSINESS AND THE ENVIRONMENT WITHOUT ETHICS

This subtitle does not, of course, mean that business is absolved from ethical duties in environmental matters – a Mandevillian abstention from normal moral standards in the vain hope that private vice might eventually produce public virtue without any help from morality and the law – but it does imply that the ethics which is appropriate for the environment is different from what is normally recommended by environmental activists. Business ethics requires of commercial personnel the capacity to co-operate and to abide by common rules, even if an agent could gain a temporary advantage by a breach of them. It does not require the suspension of the profit motive, or any other of the self-interested mainsprings of human action, but it does insist that business agents follow those conventional rules and practices that are essential for the long-run advantage of all. But most of all it requires a common set of predictable public rules that harnesses self-interest for the common good, a body of private rights that enable transactors to know who are the potential victims of any wrongdoing. This applies to the environment no less than elsewhere in business life. It is the case that people look after that which own privately much better than that which is owned collectively. Aristotle, who had some unflattering things to say about commerce, nevertheless was aware of this. He said: 'What is common to many is taken least care of, for all men have a greater regard for what is their own than for what they possess in common with others.'[21]

The difficulty with this area is that it involves most crucially those 'public good' problems encountered elsewhere and which are theoretically described in Chapter 2. A public good is one which is not supplied by normal market action, since the price mechanism does not properly indicate where the costs of various actions fall. It is in no one's interest to keep the air clean or the roads clear of rubbish, as any one particularly virtuous act is not rewarded and any single act of non-cooperation is not punished. Again, there is a problem of the preservation of scarce resources if there are no property rights in the 'commons'. Over-fishing becomes inevitable if the sea is available, without restraint, for every fishing fleet to exploit. It is not an excess of greed that is problem, nor are 'command and control methods of regulation and 'quota setting' the necessary solutions. The latter are likely to produce arbitrary inhibitions to the development of an environment-friendly commerce. But even if business itself could voluntarily devise a body of rules that it would be in the interests of all to follow, the public good problems that beset the environment would make it impossible for them to be enforced in the absence of property rights and the related legal rules.

The difficulty here is simply an example of the 'large numbers' problem that is a feature of many social interactions: the anonymity of business and the fact that the many agents are involved make it unlikely that good behaviour will occur without an appropriate incentive structure. Also, the fact that issues relevant to the environment often involve business agents who do not regularly deal with each other is a further disincentive to the spontaneous development of rules of good behaviour. The polluter may have made his profit before the law and the market's correcting processes can take effect. He often cannot be identified. In the absence of rules of restraint it would be asking too much to expect any one business agent to behave virtuously when he has no guarantee that others will be so public-spirited. But in a free market the choice is not between shutting down business and ignoring the environment but between rules that encourage socially responsible behaviour (without some dramatic change in human motivation) and those that do not.

Environmental problems arise when a third party is uncompensated for some harm inflicted by the actions of others. This is, in a technical economic sense, inefficient. It produces an externality since the cost of, say, pollution is not reflected in the costs structure of the polluter but is borne by others. Someone is made worse off by the transaction. In more or less face-to-face business relationships this need not be too much of a problem, since the aggrieved party could always sue for damages; but in matters concerning the environment it is normally the community at large that is adversely affected and there are obvious disincentives for citizens to take corrective action. The large numbers affected means that there are organizational problems. Is it likely that aggrieved parties can all get together and sue? Is there not a free rider problem? Since everyone benefits from one person's legal action, whether they have paid for it or not, that action is unlikely to be forthcoming. The costs for one person will normally exceed the benefits to her. Equally important is the fact that sometimes it is not clear who has the property right. After all, a factory owner may be polluting the atmosphere but the problem also arises because it is one (or more) person's decision to live near the site. It is not obvious that the owner should bear all the costs. It is something of a cliché to say that 'the polluter should pay' but it is not always clear who should bear the liability.

For a long time it was assumed in orthodox economics that this was pre-eminently a case for state intervention. The disjuncture between private marginal costs and social marginal costs should be closed by government action that forbade the harmful activity, taxed the perpetrator, laid down strict conditions of production or in some other coercive way limited the harm. The difficulty here is that no government can ever know what corrective action is appropriate. The damage cannot be measured accurately and public authorities cannot know what people's subjective preference is for pollution control over, say, production methods that generate cheap goods and more employment. There is no guarantee that government action will protect the environment better than the market would under efficient rules. One does not have to refer to the horrific examples of central planning to doubt the efficacy of government, for even when political action is taken in capitalist countries subject to property rights and the rule of law it may be worse than spontaneous methods. For example, when pollution controls are imposed they merely encourage producers to pollute up to the maximum limits, whereas some alternative legal arrangement may well provide incentives for producers to install pollution control devices which might actually generate less harm than that permitted by government controls.

Still, no alternative to direct political action was seriously considered until a famous article by the economist, Ronald Coase, was published in 1960.[22] Since that groundbreaking article there has been a great expansion of work on the environment by free market economists.[23] Coase argued that if transaction costs were zero it was always possible for parties to bargain their way to an optimal solution whatever the distribution of property rights was and to whomsoever the liability for damage is attributed. Thus if a person were living in a area where a producer was damaging the environment and the resident owned the property right, the producer could always compensate the resident(s). If the factory owner had the property right then aggrieved parties would have to bribe him to desist, or at least reduce his activity to a mutually agreeable level. The amount paid in either case would represent the various costs involved in reaching an efficient solution – one that properly accounted for the difference between marginal private and marginal social costs. People could always negotiate an efficient solution without invoking contestable notions of justice or highly elaborate theories of extended rights. From a purely technical perspective the liability rule should be so assigned that the responsibility falls on the person who can avoid polluting at the lowest possible cost. But in theory an optimal solution could be reached whatever the assignment of liability.

Indeed, there is some evidence from legal history[24] that damages paid under various common law rules contributed to the internalization of external costs. It is important to note that solutions reached by this method reflect the subjective evaluations of the parties, if people cared enough about pollution they would pay to have it abated. It would not be an arbitrary decision of government, a decision that is based on the assumption that some external observer can know the efficient environmental strategy. Moreover, it is not the case that all pollution is automatically bad; indeed it would be hard to imagine an economy that does not generate side-effects that are unwanted by some. But pollution is efficient if the cost of the damage is less than the cost of preventing it. The difficulty is that fanatical environmentalists rule such calculations out of court. They do so precisely because they adopt an absolutist ethic that forbids such marginalist evaluations. From their ethical perspective, every case of pollution that disturbs a hitherto industry-free environment is condemnable and any attempt to make a calculation based on relative costs is a further abject example of instrumental rationality.

Of course, the key question is transactions costs. For in large-scale pollution activity it will be difficult for the aggrieved parties to organize and the costs involved may have an adverse effect on the distribution of income. Who is to sue whom when the pollution affects large towns? What do we do about situations when the distribution property rights is not known or feasible? What can be done about smog in Los Angeles or Tokyo (although even here road pricing and other disincentives to excessive car use could be introduced)? Aircraft make a lot of noise when they fly over residential area but do the inhabitants automatically have the right to peace and quiet? One solution might be to distribute the property rights in such a way that it encourages those who can avoid the harmful effect at least cost to take action; but this can only be a rough and ready approach. The importance of transaction costs effectively reduces the theory to a tautology[25] since obviously an efficient solution (one that balances the demands of the environment with cost-reducing production methods) can be found if these are zero. But they are not, competition is almost always imperfect, and it is never easy to see how we can make it perfect so that all costs are fully internalized.

But we should not despair of this general approach, for just as the absence of perfect competition in the market for ordinary goods and services does not necessarily justify state intervention, its absence in the problem of the environment does not automatically validate command and control methods. The point here is that the market is a discovery procedure which encourages human ingenuity. In the nineteenth century the absence of enforceable property rights over wide territory was thought to be a barrier to the protection of live-stock – then barbed wire was invented. Because of the public good problem it has always been assumed that the polluter whose activity covers a wide area would go undetected, but there is now encouraging progress in the development of tracers that can pinpoint the culprit. Of course, it is always the additional polluter who causes the problem and it was assumed that because he could not be identified private solutions were impossible, but this may not be the case in the future. 'Fingerprinting' and tracing might develop so that the control of externalities can return to the legal system.

The most promising developments in environmental protection will increasingly come from a more refined appreciation of the roles of law and the market, not from some potentially authoritarian attempt at the moral re-education of the business agent and the consumer. It is these institutions that are most effective in harnessing self-interest for the public good. Although English common law was slow to develop and expand the law of nuisance (which could protect victims of industrial innovation) in the last century the legal approach should not be dismissed. There is at present a good example of it operating in relation to water pollution in Britain today.[26] Anglers have for some time been taking legal action against polluters. Landowners have the riparian rights to rivers that flow over their land and they sell licences to anglers, who have then the legal right to sue for damages if an upstream polluter damages their fishing areas.

In the USA similar common law remedies are much more difficult to secure: there is proportionately much less private ownership of rivers and, equally important, the Clean Water Act (1972) effectively ruled out common law remedies. Before that legislation was passed a number of important common law decisions went in favour of the riparian owners. One case (Walden *v*. Union Bag and Paper Co., 1913) involved a perfectly legitimate use of a claim right.[27] In upstate New York a paper mill discharged effluent that damaged a riparian owner's water. The investment of the company was quite significant and the damage not great but the court ruled that this was not the point, the firm should have found out whose rights were affected by its actions and negotiated a settlement. However, since 1972 there has been much more pollution under the rules laid down by the authorities than would have been the case if common law remedies prevailed. The important point is that the common law develops in a case-by-case manner and each decision reflects individual circumstances. It is through this method that rationality can be achieved for each litigant transmits special knowledge and also indicates the value placed on the environment. It is noticeable also that in important cases victories have been secured over polluting public authorities.

A lot of attention has been drawn to the development of pollution permits in the USA since 1990.[28] Under this system permission to pollute up to a certain level is sold in the market. This has the great advantage that it encourages businesses to develop pollution-reducing techniques. They can then sell the permits on the open market. People genuinely concerned about pollution could always buy up the permits and prevent industrial development. A number of the well-known environmental organizations are, in fact, extraordinarily well-financed but they prefer to spend their money on well-publicized propaganda campaigns. Like all human organizations, environmental groups are prone to rent-seeking and their activities are just as likely to increase the income and well-being of those who work for them as they are to improve the environment.

The major theoretical and practical flaw in pollution permit schemes is that the actual levels of pollution permitted are determined by central authorities. The approach is not properly subjectivist, for it is assumed that government agencies have special knowledge of appropriate tradeoffs between protection of the environment and the need for industrial development. How can a government know what the proper environmental goals are? Still, if public decisions about the environment were taken at the lowest level of government, a better transmission of people's preferences would occur than that achieved by the prevailing uniform and centralized approach. Until a system of property rights in the atmosphere is established, little progress can be made towards a proper accounting of environmental measures. At present the problem is compounded by the fact that some negative externalities cross boundaries and their internalization will depend on international co-operation.

Certainly within countries progress can be made in balancing the needs of the environment with economic progress through negotiation. Firms often consult local communities about their development plans. If the inhabitants of an area genuinely value their amenities they can demand a high price for their co-operation. But they may not, the area may be poor and badly in need of the employment the projected development brings. This is another example of the subjectivism (and marginal adjustments) that are required in a rational approach to the problem. All too often the environmental movement lays down absolute standards which must be adhered to at all costs. Of course, such usages work to the advantage of richer areas (including countries) which tend to value the environment higher than poorer ones do. The latter are compelled to adopt universal standards which are to their detriment. A better policy would be to encourage economic growth so that beyond a certain point it begins to be less valuable. Then the demands of the environmentalists are more likely to be spontaneously met without the need for too much government intervention.

A lot of progress can be made, however, in the related problem of the preservation of scarce resources. It is blithely assumed that capitalist development will automatically exhaust the earth's valued commodities. But as their scarcity intensifies, the price mechanism will operate – their prices will rise and that will lead both to their more efficient use and to a relentless search for close substitutes. In a famous example, the environmental optimist, Julian Simon, took a bet (in 1970) with a well-known doomsayer that 30 of the most well-known resources (including oil) would be cheaper in 10 years time.[29] He won the wager. In many other areas the optimists have been proved right: increases in population have not led to famines (the price of food is continually falling in real terms), health is improving and longevity (especially in advanced capitalist societies) is increasing.

The point is that private ownership encourages the efficient use of resources. A person will preserve an asset if it will yield an income over the long run. When faced with the prospect of losing it through, for example, government confiscation, she will extract its full value now. At one time there was a fear that elephant tusks would disappear through excessive exploitation. Yet those countries in southern Africa that allowed trade in them conserved elephant much more successfully than those that banned it. So far from capitalist avarice destroying scarce resources, it is their saviour. Given the right legal environment, self-interest promotes the common interest far more effectively than government regulation.

There is still a problem, however, which is posed by traditional ethical theory and it involves the question of what one generation owes to another. Even if the above analysis were largely correct, that a proper legal and property rights system handles the environment better than 'command and control' methods, it might still be protested that the continued exploitation of the earth's resources leaves an inferior world to future generations.

The seventeenth-century philosopher, John Locke, claimed that property accumulation was permissible provided that 'enough and as good' were left for others. Taken literally, this is an impossible demand (he was talking about the appropriation of land) and to meet it would require impossibly severe restrictions on the use of resources. But interpreted moderately we can ask the question whether the technological improvements and higher productivity of capitalism which future generations enjoy compensates sufficiently for the significant changes in the environment that they bring? An optimistic answer would be in the affirmative.

CONCLUSION

It is clear that the problems that business faces with environmental activists will not go away. While it is true that the property rights solution discussed above will eventually have some impact on the debate, and possibly policy, the moral pressure on business will increase. It is the case that the heady environmentalist idealism has little to offer rational argument on the issue but there are still moral arguments that have some relevance even if the property rights and common solutions were to be widely adopted. For one thing, transactions costs will remain an important impediment to the reaching of some kind of equilibrium. A person may have legitimate rights to compensation for harm but it may be too costly for her to pursue her case. Big companies will always have the advantage here. And, of course, large numbers of citizens may be difficult to organize in comparison to the ease with which companies can get together to resist the legitimate demands of genuine rights claimants. But the power of large companies can be exaggerated. Such is the moral hysteria created by pressure groups that criminal actions in pursuit of environmental goals are tolerated. Still, an additional, but crucially important, reason why purely spontaneous processes may not always be effective is that some environmental damage does not become apparent for some years after the original violation – by which time it has become harder to identify the perpetrator.

As has been suggested before, for reason such as these business will find it to their long-term advantage not to exploit any powers they have. This will only lead to ever-increasing and more oppressive regulation. Still, already the pressure of public opinion (albeit sometimes ill-informed) is having an effect on business. Companies are now producing environmental audits and executives are being appointed who are specifically responsible for these matters. The difficulty will always be securing industry-wide co-operation and disciplining violators of putative agreements. A measure of self-regulation (under what became known as the 'Valdez Principles') was projected in the early 1990s[30] for the oil industry after the Exxon spillage disaster in Alaska. But the really big companies were reluctant to participate in this. However, recently they have been very much aware of the controversy their activities provoke and have been anxious to advertise their good behaviour.[31] In fact, oil companies have always been the major target for environmental groups but much of the criticism has been misguided and their actions unlawful and based on unsound environmental science. The continued exploration for oil is quite consistent with 'sustainable development' and the externalities produced are not greater than those generated by other fuels, and sometimes much less (especially in comparison with coal). But such is the frenzy and emotionalism on this issue that business will find it to its long-term advantage to develop and perfect viable forms of self-regulation.

8 Conclusion

The argument of this book has been addressed to some of the claims of business ethics as that is conventionally understood; and indeed taught in business schools and philosophy departments. The idea seems to be that the activity of business is essentially morally neutral (or even in certain respects immoral) and that ethical value must be imposed from outside the activity itself. Business must meet certain external criteria, derived from moral philosophy if it is to be legitimate. It is not normally accepted that there is a morality that is intrinsic to business itself; an ethic that drives from the virtues of free exchange, valid claims to property and the sanctity of contract. The values that are implicit here are thought to be insufficient for a genuine business morality.

The reluctance to accept the intrinsic morality of business derives, no doubt, from the fact that self-interest is its major, if not its only, motivation. From Mandeville onwards, the critics and admirers of business seem to make this assumption: the former maintain that commerce must be constantly held up to standards that emanate perhaps from religion, or some other tuistic value system, if it is to have a moral validity, the latter argue that most of what passes for morality is actually a restraint on business enterprise and should be resisted; it is also said, by the same people, to be little more than hypocrisy. Either way there appears to be a conflict between ethics and business and the assumption seems to be that business, and the market system in general, do not generate autonomously a morality. To the extent that business morality exists, it is parasitic on some other set of values.

Even writers noted for their approval of commerce are often too anxious to over-emphasize the apparent neutrality of the market, or its failure to generate coherent moral principles. Thus a leading (and persuasive) exponent of German Ordoliberalism, the social and economic doctrine that underlay Germany's post-war success, Wilhelm Röpke, once wrote that:

> The market, competition and the play of supply and demand do not create ethical reserves; they presuppose and consume them. These reserves must come from *outside* the market … Self-discipline, a sense of justice, honesty, fairness, chivalry, moderation, respect for human dignity, firm ethical norms – all of these are things which people must possess before they go to market and compete with each other.[1]

Since the market and capitalism do not generate moral standards, the implication is that in the absence of a morality imposed by an outside agency (Which is that? Religion, society, the state?) the exchange system would be morally nihilistic.

However, there are problems with this scepticism about the moral capacity of market capitalism. First, it ignores the evidence of the development of moral standards in markets independently of any external agency (the City of London's creation of ethical conventions discussed in Chapter 5 is an important example of this but there are others). People in trading relationships do create moral reserves. Second, as soon as it is admitted that moral standards have to come from outside the market, then opportunities emerge for the encouragement and imposition of values which are antithetical to efficient markets. Germany itself is a good example. For the gradual undermining of the hitherto immensely successful post-war market system was brought about by the importation into the system of values which are not conducive to successful capitalism. A lot of these came from the state, notably a costly welfare system, but some were the result of developments in the German social system itself, notably the rejection of the takeover mechanism and the reluctance to care about shareholder value. Of course, much of these inhibitions to efficient markets came about almost naturally, and believers in the virtues of spontaneous social order cannot complain if this happens. One suspects that they will be eliminated by evolution, as Germany begins to imitate the now more successful Anglo-American model, but it is the case that their persistence is partly a result of a certain 'moralizing' of the market brought about by influential spokesmen.[2] The original pro-capitalist Ordoliberal system became the 'Social Market Economy',[3] with a myriad of state interventions and redistributive policies. This climate of intellectual opinion had an effect on German business whose spokesmen still show a reluctance to accept the full implications of Anglo-American capitalism.

Similar phenomena are visible in nominally Anglo-American economies where the influence of business ethics has led to the imposition of statutory inhibitions on the natural processes of capitalism. Even in the USA, the takeover process has been subject to legal restraint (especially at the state level), largely at the behest of legislators under the influence of business ethics. But often such measures are brought about by interest groups seeking protection from competition rather than by proponents of a genuine moral mission. An additional problem with the view that ethics must be imposed on business from outside is that the standards here are always higher and more demanding than those that apply to people in everyday life. Indeed, as we have seen, the social responsibility of business ideology is predicated on the assumption that commercial agents need a kind of 'moral licence' to practise their activities. The way to earn such a permission is to demonstrate one's success in suppressing self-interest. The natural inference from all this is that business personnel require some kind of education in the higher ethical codes that are apparently appropriate here rather than a full appreciation and understanding of the normal ethical practices that govern everyday life.

CONVENTIONAL ETHICS AND BUSINESS

There is a different tradition in business ethics from the familiar one described in orthodox textbooks, and it is one which is more consonant with the practice of commerce. It is well described by the eighteenth-century philosopher, and early advocate of the market system, David Hume. In his description of the trading relationship between two farmers, he wrote:

> Your corn is ripe today; mine will be so tomorrow. 'Tis profitable for us both, that I should labour with you today, and that you should aid me tomorrow. I have no kindness, and know you have as little for me ... Hence I learn to do a service to another, without bearing any real kindness, because I foresee, that he will return my service.[4]

What is important here is Hume's claim that a morality can develop automatically in the trading relationship which does not depend on a kind of change of personality or is the result of an enlightened education. People do not have to display 'kindness' to behave morally, or to show benevolence in order to fulfil the demands of the rules of just conduct. In his example, both parties gain from a certain kind of *co-operative* activity and they learn the advantages of such co-operation by repeated 'plays' of the trading game. All that is required is that they refrain from actions which could lead to immediate gratification by, for example, breaking a promise or not fulfilling the terms of a deal, but which, if repeated, make everyone worse off.

But in these relationships the victims of opportunism can punish the violator of the implicit agreement or moral convention. If they play the business game long enough they soon learn the benefits of co-operation (and the game does not have to go on for too long for this to be apparent). In this sense morality and business are compatible in that conventions develop which, although they act as side-constraints on egoism, are consistent with self-interest in the long-run. Perhaps the most important moral capacity the players have to acquire is *reciprocity*, an understanding of the fact that all sides to a business deal benefit to the extent that they recognize that the honouring of an agreement requires something in return. This has nothing to do with altruism but drives from a mutuality of interest. This conventional morality would have been incomprehensible to Mandeville, who could conceive of no constraints on immediate gratification (apart from the force of law). Yet trading developed through medieval fairs, which had their own rule structures, without the force of positive law.[5]

What emerges from this is the idea that there is no special moral 'sense' appropriate to the attitudes and behaviours which constitute civilized living. People learn the rules and conventions of social life through experience. This is especially true of business, where the cultivation of extraordinary virtues is obviously less likely than in other human activities. Even Adam Smith on occasions appeared to be under the illusion that commercial morality was something different from conventional rules and practices and worried that a too extensive development of trade and the division of labour might threaten morality.[6] In fact, he thought that benevolence was the highest moral virtue but it was merely impracticable. Hume would probably have thought that it was not a special virtue and that its pursuit would impoverish a nation. He had none of the qualifications to market individualism that Smith sometimes expressed.

There is one serious qualification that must be made to the theory that business has every incentive to develop its own rules of conduct: there may be inhibitions to their growth within the business system itself. The most important of these is the anonymity which tends to be a feature of some aspects of modern commerce. If business agents in Anglo-American economies deal normally at arm's length, their relationships may be too ephemeral for 'trust' and conformity to informal rules and conventions to develop. Someone be tempted to break a moral rule if he knows he is never to meet his victims again; indeed, he might never see them at all. There is something to this: the world of twentieth-century commerce is not the same as that described by David Hume (and Adam Smith). But the effect of this anonymity should not be exaggerated. People may deal at arm's length but they do so under rules that have developed over time out of small-scale relationships. Thus even in large, more or less anonymous, markets the participants transact under rules that are as obligatory and persuasive as those that characterise small associations. Only on very rare occasions will a business agent be confident that he can breach a rule and not be detected. But when this occurs it is likely to result in great publicity in the open market societies of the English-speaking world.

Of course, the major complaint about this form of capitalism is that it encourages excessive individualism and greed. But not all self-interested action is greed and it would be foolish to discount the social significance of the former motivation in all commercial societies. As the distinguished American lawyer, Richard Epstein, comments;

> This characteristic of wanting more is universal. It applies with equal force to both greedy and rapacious firms and self-interested individuals. Indeed, wanting more is not a characteristic for which we should want to condemn people. The desire for more is one of the few features that is indispensable for human progress and advancement. The right question to ask is not why we want more. It is how are we prepared to go on getting the more that we want.[7]

The important implication of this is that we should not look for ethical improvement through changing the predispositions of the players in the commercial game but instead search for those institutional structures which encourage the desire to better ourselves to be directed to socially worthwhile ends. Too much of contemporary business is concerned with motivational questions. We saw all this most clearly in the question of the environment (Chapter 7), for the problems only arise here because of the ill-defined property rights structure of capitalist economies that produce socially harmful acts out of not itself reprehensible self-interest. Anonymity becomes a problem because often it is difficult to identify those who breach a rule or convention. Once again it is appropriate rules rather than morally exquisite motivations that are important.

The problem of greed is all too often analysed in the context of some apparently acceptable distribution of income. Someone whose income departs too dramatically from this is labelled greedy merely because her income is higher than some arbitrary norm. Michael Milken was assumed to be driven by greed because of his vast income ($550 million) in 1987, although it was not actually the highest personal earnings of that year in the USA. The real question is: how did that income come about? In his case, even if he were guilty of the charges for which he was convicted, the total value of these acts added very little to his income. Most of this was a product of genuine entrepreneurship, the creation of new value through acts of discovery. In contrast, greed is a product of someone's breach of rules (both legal and conventional), a flouting of the standards of just conduct in pursuit of personal gain without the addition of value to society. The presence of greed is not measured by the size of someone's income but by how it is achieved.

It is true that some of the earnings of corporate employees may not reflect genuine entrepreneurship, they may sometimes be a product of rent-seeking, and it is quite likely that shareholders are not very efficient at monitoring excessive pay of managers, but it is highly unlikely that the state (or moral philosophers) could make any improvement on the allocation by the market, however imperfect that is.

ANGLO-AMERICAN BUSINESS AND RIVAL CAPITALISMS

The unfavourable comparison often made between the capitalism of the English-speaking world and the more communitarian regimes is hard to evaluate. Certainly capitalism in principle is by no means a threat to community as its critics often maintain. For the economies of East Asia are broadly capitalist even if they differ in the details from New York or the City of London. What is significant is that they appear to be quite compatible with community values. The allegedly relentless progress of market capitalism has not undermined community in those countries. The important point is that free market economies develop coterminously with communities: those closely knit social forms that characterize non-western market economies are natural developments out of the system of liberty. The generic moral code of capitalism is capable of sustaining a variety of free market forms. What communitarian critics of western capitalism want to do is to protect favoured social arrangements from the flux of economic life. This why attempts are made, by the artifices of statute and regulation, to protect favoured subsections of the community from the takeover process. But genuine communities are not created in this way. In fact, they are not created at all, but emerge from a long process of spontaneous development through freedom.

In fact, the much-vaunted morality of the communitarian capitalist economies does not score all that well when measured against the generic moral code of capitalism. As we have noticed, the business scandals in Japan have been much more venal than those on Wall Street or the City of London.[8] Indeed, the very openness of Western capitalism, especially its free press and belief in the rule of law, guarantees a kind of morality which is different from the largely exclusive morality of Asian economies. This relatively good performance is not in any way due to a supposed superior moral education of Western capitalists but is a consequence of the institutional structure in which Anglo-American business takes place. The partially closed and almost impenetrable corporate worlds of the Far East, and parts of Europe, mean that immorality there can go undetected for some time.

BUSINESS ETHICS, CAPITALISM AND THE FUTURE

There are signs that both the efficiency and the morality of Anglo-American capitalism are experiencing a re-evaluation, and even imitation. For a long time, it seemed that its alleged short-termism, excessive individualism and unconcern for the collective good would make it unable to compete with its less atomistic rivals. The decline of the West was supposed to have been exemplified by the greed-driven 1980s in which immorality and economic decline apparently reinforced each other. But one can now detect a change in the intellectual sentiment, especially as the benefits of the corporate reorganization in the USA are revealed. It is doubtful if the quiet revolution in business life that took place there would have occurred if American business had followed the injunctions of American business ethics.

Nowadays that much-vaunted feature of Japanese business, 'trust', is seen to be something of a disadvantage. Throughout its golden period, workers in that country trusted the corporations not to make people unemployed and the employers could trust the workers not to be disruptive. This was thought to contrast favourably with Anglo-American capitalism, where nobody trusted anybody and the workplace became something of a battleground. However, in economic terms the Japanese model has produced great rigidity and Japan has become renowned for its inflexibility – partly made possible by docile and powerless shareholders. Again the comparison with the USA is instructive. In that country there is one revealing example of a lack of trust which is not harmful: the shareholders do not trust the managers, they think that they work exclusively for themselves not the stockholders, and the managers do not trust the owners, they assume that they do not have the interests of the company at heart and will sell their stock as soon as difficulties appear. Still, the normal sanctions of the market are remarkably successful in bringing some kind of harmony between these potentially antagonistic groups. The fact that both sides 'want more' is a sufficient motivation for their profitable participation.

None of this is meant to imply that trust, in principle, is not an important feature of business life. The more that agents can rely on each other to keep to deals and honour promises without the paraphernalia of formal law the more that transactions costs are reduced and business operations are smooth and predictable. Indeed, a justified complaint about American business is that its openness and relative anonymity has produced excessive legal costs; the vast earnings of lawyers and other intermediaries in takeover deals is an example (still, as Fukuyama[9] points out, America *in general* is a high trust society). There is a difference between the trust that is required between individuals if deals are to be conducted fairly and expeditiously and the trust that can emerge between collective organisations, such as labour combinations and groups of employees (or corporate cliques). The last feature is an example of the croneyism which is thought to be a characteristic of Asian capitalism. It is an especially deleterious aspect of the system if these informal groups become involved with government.

The attribute of classical liberal economic and moral philosophy that has relevance to the understanding of business ethics is its emphasis on individuals as *abstract* agents, entitled to the protection of universal law, and free to trade in unhindered markets irrespective of their identity as members of groups, religious movements or racial subcultures. These latter features of persons are mere contingencies which have no relevance to business arrangements. It is this aspect of traditional economic liberalism which provokes communitarians and is one reason why they have been so sceptical of the morality of business and critical of all attempts to demonstrate that there is a viable ethics in abstract individualism. But as economic and moral problems of the rivals of Anglo-American capitalism begin to emerge, the virtues of that system, which have been long-suppressed, will become more visible.

Notes

1. Business and Moral Philosophy

1. Quoted in R. Reidenbach and D. Robin, *Ethics and Profits* (Englewood Cliffs, NJ: Prentice-Hall, 1989).
2. See R. DeGeorge, *Business Ethics* (New York: Macmillan, 1982); A. Etzioni, *The Moral Dimension* (New York: Free Press, 1988).
3. See M. Albert, *Capitalism Against Capitalism* (London: Whurr, 1993).
4. DeGeorge, *Business Ethics*, ch. 3.
5. J.K. Galbraith, *The New Industrial State* (Harmondsworth: Penguin, 1988).
6. R. Nader, M. Green, and J. Seligman, *Taming the Giant Corporation* (New York: Norton, 1976).
7. See M. Friedman, 'The Social Responsibility of Business is to Increase its Profits', in T. Beauchamp and N. Bowie (eds) *Ethical Theory and Business*, 4th edn (Englewood Cliffs: Prentice-Hall, 1993) pp. 55–60; also, Elaine Sternberg, *Just Business* (Boston: Little, Brown & Co., 1994).
8. B. Mandeville, *The Fable of the Bees*, ed. F.B. Kaye (London: Oxford University Press, 1924) vol. 1, p. 364, first published 1705.
9. Adam Smith, *The Theory of Moral Sentiments*, edited by D.D. Raphael and A. Macfie (Oxford: Clarendon, 1976), first published 1759.
10. Smith, *The Theory of Moral Sentiments*, p. 346.
11. Friedman, 'The Social Responsibility of Business', p. 56.
12. H. Spencer, *The Man versus the State* (Idaho: Caxton, 1940), first published 1884.
13. See M. Novak, *Toward a Theology of the Corporation* (Washington, DC: American Enterprise Institute, 1981).
14. For the view that imperfect competition makes business ethics feasible, see M.G. Griffiths and J.R. Lucas, *Ethical Economics* (London: Macmillan, 1995).
15. I. Kirzner, *Competition and Entrepreneurship* (Chicago: University of Chicago Press, 1973).
16. For a definitive refutation of market socialism, see D. Lavoie, *Rivalry and Competition* (London: Oxford University Press, 1986).

2. Value Systems

1. For an introduction to the major ethical principles as applied to business, see W. Shaw and V. Barry, *Moral Issues in Business* (Belmont: Wadsworth, 4th edn, 1989) chs 1 and 2.
2. See A. Quinton, *Utilitarianism* (London: Oxford University Press, 1978); also R. Frey (ed.) *Utility and Rights* (Oxford: Blackwell, 1985).
3. J. Bentham, *An Introduction to the Principles of Morals and Legislation*, edited by J.H. Burns and H.L.A. Hart (London: Athlone Press, 1970), first published 1789.

4. See A. Hamlin, *Ethics, Economics and the State* (Brighton: Wheatsheaf, 1986) pp. 7–10.
5. For a discussion of utilitarianism in terms of preference satisfaction, see P. Pettit, *Judging Justice* (London: Routledge & Kegan Paul, 1980) ch. 12.
6. See A. Wildavsky, *Searching for Safety* (New York: Transaction Books, 1988).
7. *Foundations of the Metaphysics of Morals*, trans T. Abbott (London: Longmans Green, 1909) p. 15.
8. The doctrine of social justice, especially the version made famous by John Rawls, has been subjected to devastating criticism in A.G.N. Flew, *The Politics of Procrustes* (London: Temple, 1981).
9. Smith, *The Theory of Moral Sentiments*, p. 160.
10. F.A. Hayek, *The Mirage of Social Justice* (London: Routledge & Kegan Paul, 1976).
11. See M. Friedman, *Capitalism and Friedman* (Chicago: University of Chicago Press, 1963).
12. R. Nozick, *Anarchy, State and Utopia* (Oxford: Blackwell, 1973).
13. For a demonstration of the incompatibility of socialism and procedural justice, see Hayek, *The Mirage of Social Justice*.
14. In his famous Wilt Chamberlain example, Nozick shows how it would be impossible to maintain an equal distribution of income without coercion if people wanted to pay money in excess of the decreed figure to see the legendary basketball player perform.
15. This led to the passing of the Foreign Corrupt Practices Act, 1977.
16. See M. Keeley, *A Social Contract Theory of Organizations* (Indiana: University of Notre Dame Press, 1988).
17. There have been many scandals in the Japanese securities market, see *The Times* (4 September 1991).
18. R. Soloman and K. Hansen, *It's Good Business* (New York: Atheneum, 1985) p. 36.
19. For a description of the Prisoner's Dilemma, see M. Taylor, *Anarchy and Co-operation* (London: Wiley, 1976).
20. See R. Sugden, *The Economics of Rights, Co-operation and Welfare* (Oxford: Blackwell, 1986).
21. Sugden, *The Economics of Rights*, chs 5, 6, 7.
22. For description of the spontaneous development of commercial law in medieval times, see L. Trakman, *The Law Merchant: The Evolution of Commercial Law* (Colorado: Littleton, 1983).
23. Most of the evidence so far is journalistic but persuasive.

3. The Corporation

1. The science of catallactics was developed most cogently by the 'Austrian' school of economics, from Carl Menger. See N. Barry, 'Austrian Economics: a Dissent from Orthodoxy', in D. Greenaway, M. Bleaney and I. Stewart (eds) *A Companion to Contemporary Economic Thought* (London: Routledge, 1991) pp. 68–87.

2. I. Kristol, 'On Corporate Capitalism in America', *The Public Interest* (1975).

3. A. Berle and G. Means, *The Modern Corporation and Private Property* (New York: Harcourt & Brace, revd edn 1967).

4. For a pioneering analysis of the firm, see R.H. Coase, 'The Nature of the Firm', *Economica* (1937) pp. 386–405.

5. D. Robertson and S. Dennison, *The Control of Industry* (Cambridge University Press, 1960) p. 73.

6. M. Friedman, 'The Social Responsibility of Business', p. 56.

7. There is a vast number of books and articles on the social responsibility of business, see especially, C. Stone, *Where the Law Ends* (New York: Harper Row, 1975); T. Donaldson, *Corporations and Morality* (Englewood Cliffs, NJ: Prentice-Hall, 1983); R. Soloman and K. Hanson, *Above the Bottom Line: An Introduction to Business Ethics* (New York: Harcourt, Brace, 1983) and T. Mulligan, 'The Moral Mission of Business', in Beauchamp and Bowie, *Ethical Theory and Business*, pp. 65–75.

8. Dartmouth College *v.* Woodward (1819). For a critical discussion of this case, see R. Hessen, *In Defense of the Corporation* (Stanford: Hoover Institution, 1979) p. 9.

9. This was not so much 'creative' jurisprudence as the Court making explicit what was already implicit in the legal system.

10. See R. Pilon, 'Corporations and Rights', *Georgia Law Review* (1979) pp. 1246–364.

11. Adam Smith, *The Wealth of Nations*, edited by R. Campbell and A. Skinner (Oxford: Clarendon, 1976), first published 1776, vol. 2, p. 233.

12. Hessen, *In Defense of the Corporation*, p. 43.

13. Ibid., p. 20.

14. Reported in *Reason* (July 1996).

15. This is the claim of M.G. Griffiths and J.R. Lucas in *Ethical Economics* (London: Macmillan, 1996) pp. 64–5.

16. See O. Williamson, *Markets and Hierarchies* (New York: Free Press, 1975).

17. See K. Arrow, 'Business Codes and Economic Efficiency', in Beauchamp and Bowie, *Ethical Theory and Business*, pp. 118–21.

18. See the report, 'Air Wars', *Financial Times* (9 July 1996).

19. For a discussion of the German cartelization phenomenon, see N. Barry, 'The Political and Economic Thought of German Neo-Liberalism', in A. Peacock and H. Willgerodt (eds) *German Neo-liberalism and the Social Market Economy* (London: Macmillan, 1989) pp. 105–24.

20. For a defence of Ford in the Pinto case, see G. Schwartz, 'The Myth of the Ford Pinto Case', *Rutgers Law Review* (1993) pp. 1013–68.

21. See R. DeGeorge, 'Ethical Responsibilities of Engineers in Large Organizations', in Beauchamp and Bowie, *Ethical Theory and Business*, pp. 130–7.

22. Wildavsky, *Searching for Safety*.

23. F. Bastiat, 'What is Seen and What is not Seen', in D. Boaz, *Libertarianism: A Primer* (New York: Free Press, 1997) pp. 265–73.

24. N. Barry, *The Morality of Business Enterprise* (Aberdeen: Aberdeen University Press for the David Hume Institute, 1991) pp. 42–3.

25. See L. Nash, *Good Intentions Aside* (Boston: Harvard Business School, 1990) pp. 38–43.

26. P. French, *Corporations and Corporate Responsibility* (New York: Columbia University Press 1984,).
27. French, *Corporations and Corporate Responsibility*, chs 1–3.
28. See Novak, *Toward a Theology of the Corporation*.
29. 'Avoidable Human Errors Afloat and Ashore', *The Times*, 20 October 1990.
30. See the *Wall Street Journal* (3 May 1994).

4. Corporate Social Responsibility

1. For example, see N. Bowie, 'New Directions in Business Management', *Business Management* (July–August 1971).
2. See S. Littlechild, 'Misleading Calculations of the Social Costs of Monopoly Power', *Economic Journal* (1981) pp. 348–63.
3. A. Müller-Armack, 'Principles of the Social Market Economy', *German Economic Review* (1965) pp. 85–99.
4. Smith, *The Wealth of Nations*, vol. 1, pp. 26–7.
5. See H. Macdonald, 'Race Still Matters to Californian Companies', *Wall Street Journal* (11 November 1996).
6. F. Fukuyama, *Trust* (London: Hamish Hamilton, 1995).
7. America is reported to have over a quarter of all the world's lawyers. In countries like Japan, complex trust relationships seem to preclude the need for too many lawyers. Yet, curiously, Fukuyama regards the USA as a relatively high trust society.
8. K. Goodpaster, 'Business Ethics and Stakeholder Analysis', in Beauchamp and Bowie, *Ethical Theory and Business*, pp. 85–93.
9. W. Evan and R. Freeman, 'A Stakeholder Theory of the Modern Corporation: Kantian Capitalism', in Beauchamp and Bowie, *Ethical Theory and Business*, p. 82. For a critique of the idea, see Elaine Sternberg, 'Stakeholder Theory: The Defective State it's In', in D. Green (ed.) *Stakeholding and Its Critics* (London: Institute of Economic Affairs, 1997).
10. See M. Ricketts, *The Economics of Business Enterprise* (London: Harvester, 2nd edn, 1994) ch. 4.
11. Jeremy Bentham had a similar experience at Oxford not long after Smith's.
12. See J.K. Galbraith, *The New Industrial State* (Harmondsworth: Penguin, 1974). Though it should be noted that Galbraith did not expect corporations to display social responsibility.
13. See Evan and Freeman, 'A Stakeholder Theory of the Modern Corporation: Kantian Capitalism', p. 82.
14. J. Kuhn and D. Shriver, *Beyond Success* (New York: Oxford University Press, 1991) chs 2 and 3.
15. For a critique of Nader's proposal for federal chartering, see Hessen, *In Defense of the Corporation*, ch. 3.
16. In his *The Good Society* (London: Sinclair Stevenson, 1997) J.K. Galbraith presents a more reasonable analysis of competitive corporate capitalism than is to be found in his earlier work.
17. See Jim Levi, 'Shareholders from Hell', *Sunday Telegraph* (30 August 1997).

18. See Evan and Freeman, 'A Stakeholder Theory of the Modern Corporation', p. 82.
19. Shareholders in Germany are now beginning to press for Anglo-American business practices and to demand shareholder value; see *Financial Times* (6 August 1993).
20. This was very evident in the recent (unsuccessful) Krupp takeover bid for Thyssen. It produced great dissension among the various stakeholder groups, especially the trade unions; see O. August, 'Bid battle with Clausewitzian Echoes', *The Times* (20 March 1997).
21. Business ethics writers tend to concentrate on the moral failings of commerce, which are normally very visible.
22. See Manne's *The Modern Corporation and Social Responsibility* (Washington, DC: American Enterprise Institute, 1972) p. 29.
23. Marianne Curphey, 'Body Shop Stays in Public Ownership', *The Times* (5 March 1996).
24. See report, 'Investments from the Heart', *Sunday Telegraph* (3 March 1996).
25. See A. Shenfield, 'The Businessman and the Politician', in N. Barry (ed.) *Limited Government, Individual Liberty and the Rule of Law* (Cheltenham: Elgar, forthcoming, 1998).

5. Insider Dealing

1. Quoted in D. Boaz, *Libertarianism: a Primer* (New York: Free Press, 1997) p. 38.
2. The Criminal Justice Act, 1993. For an account, see J. Murray, 'The New Insider Dealing Law: A Critique', in H. MacQueen (ed.) *Insider Dealing* (Edinburgh: David Hume Institute, 1993) pp. 19–27. Also, from the same volume, N. Barry, 'Witchcraft and Insider Dealing', pp. 28–34.
3. For the legal background in the USA, see A. Brennan and N. Kubasek, *The Legal Environment of Business* (New York: Macmillan, 1988).
4. Pierre Lemieux, *Apologie des Sorcieres Modernes* (Paris: Les Belles Lettres, 1991).
5. In the USA the situation has been complicated by the fact that civil offences, on occasion, appear to have been made criminal by the courts, see D. Fischel, *Payback: The Conspiracy to Destroy Michael Milken and His Financial Revolution* (New York: Harper, 1995) ch. 2.
6. See H. Manne, *Insider Trading and the Stock Market* (New York: Free Press, 1966).
7. Instructively, the only serious insider dealing in Germany involved a typical Anglo-American business activity – a takeover. In a 1993 example a German trade union leader was censured for profiting from a deal, the details of which he had heard about through his membership of the company's supervisory board, see 'Union Man's Daimler Dealing Downfall Fuels German Woes', *Daily Telegraph* (31 May 1993).
8. The events surrounding this case are described in Barry, *The Morality of Business Enterprise*, pp. 51–2.
9. See Brennan and Kubasek, *The Legal Environment of Business*, pp. 300–1.

10. See N. Barry, *Insider Dealing: An Exploration into Law and Existing Practice* (London: Foundation for Business Responsibilities, 1996) p. 16.
11. Barry, *The Morality of Business Enterprise*, p. 52.
12. The whole story is graphically described in D. Frantz, *Levine and Co.* (New York: Holt, 1987).
13. See B. Hannigan, *Insider Dealing* (London: Kluwer, 1988) p. 24.
14. For the Goodman case, see *Daily Telegraph* (31 May 1991).
15. H. Manne, 'Insider Trading and the Law Professors', *Vanderbilt Law Review* (1970) p. 549.
16. J. Schumpeter, *Capitalism, Socialism and Democracy*, 3rd edn (London: Routledge, 1994: 1st pub. 1942) pp. 1–86.
17. See I. Kirzner, *Discovery, Capitalism and Distributive Justice* (Oxford: Blackwell, 1989).
18. Schumpeter, *Capitalism, Socialism and Democracy*, pp. 111–20.
19. Manne, *Insider Dealing and the Stock Market*, pp. 129–39.
20. Ricketts, *The Economics of Business Enterprise*, pp. 228–9.
21. H. Manne, 'Insider Trading and Property Rights in New Information', in J. Dorn and H. Manne (eds) *Economic Liberties and the Constitution* (Fairfax: George Mason University Press, 1987) p. 318.
22. Manne, 'Insider Trading and Property Rights in New Information', p. 322.
23. Manne, *Insider Dealing and the Stock Market*, p. 8.
24. R. Booth, 'Insider Trading, Better Markets', *Wall Street Journal* (4 July 1991).
25. Hannigan, *Insider Dealing*, pp. 113–15.
26. See A. Brown, 'Insider Dealing and the Criminal Law', in H. MacQueen (ed.) *Insider Dealing*, pp. 1–18.
27. Murray, 'The New Insider Dealing Law: A Critique', pp. 20–2.

6. Takeovers: An Economic and Ethical Perspective

1. The 1980s was not the most active era for takeovers. In the USA the turn of the century saw proportionately more takeover activity, see A.T. Peacock and G. Bannock, *Corporate Takeovers and the Public Interest* (Edinburgh: David Hume Institute, 1991) ch. 1.
2. An early intellectual defence of the takeover mechanism is H. Manne, 'Mergers and the Market for Corporate Control', *Journal of Political Economy* (1965) pp. 110–18.
3. So far from the 1980s being the age of greed in the USA it was an era of remarkable charitable giving, see R. Bartley, *The Seven Fat Years and How to Do It Again* (New York: Free Press, 1994) p. 5.
4. The Glass–Steagal Act, 1935.
5. See Berle and Means, *The Corporation and Private Property*.
6. Galbraith, *The New Industrial State*.
7. The Keiretsu in Japan, a complex system of interlocking directorships, prevents takeovers in that country. For the Japanese banking and financial systems, see M. Flaherty and I. Hiroyuki, 'The Banking-Industrial Complex', in D. Okimoto and T. Roblen (eds) *Inside the Japanese System* (Stanford: Stanford University Press, 1988).

8. Self-investment of pension funds is not thought to be good corporate strategy in Anglo-American economies, especially after the Maxwell affair. However, is quite common in Germany. But pension funds should clearly be ring-fenced.

9. For criticisms of the takeover mechanisms see essays by L. Newton and P. Steidlmeier, in W. Hoffman, R. Frederick and E. Petry (eds) *The Ethics of Organizational Transformation: Mergers, Takeovers and Corporate Restructuring* (New York: Quorum Books, 1989).

10. H. Manne, 'Mergers and the Market for Corporate Control', *Journal of Political Economy* (1965) pp. 110–18.

11. See Michael Jensen, 'Takeovers: Their Causes and Consequences', *Journal of Economic Perspectives* (1988) pp. 21–48.

12. A synergy exists when two companies pursing complementary activities can do better if they are combined.

13. See R. Almeder and D. Carey, 'In Defense of Sharks: Moral Issues in Hostile Liquidating Takeovers', *Journal of Business Ethics* (1991) pp. 471–84.

14. The record of government investment in economy in the UK is dismal, see J. Burton, *Picking Losers?* (London: Institute of Economic Affairs, 1983).

15. See John Jay, 'Money Defeated Sentiment at Forte', *Sunday Times* (28 January 1996).

16. See Jensen, 'Takeovers: Their Causes and Consequences', pp. 23–5.

17. Despite their doubts about the efficacy of takeovers, Peacock and Bannock do not recommend very heavy regulation, *Corporate Takeovers and the Public Interest*, ch. 8.

18. Certainly a neutral tax regime would reduce the incidence of takeovers.

19. The work of the Austrian economists has advanced our understanding of the market process, see especially, L. von Mises, *Human Action* (New Haven: Yale University Press, 1963); F.A. Hayek, *Individualism and Economic Order* (London: Routledge & Kegan Paul, 1948).

20. For a discussion of 'robber barons', see R. Bartley, *The Seven Fat Years and How to Do It Again*, ch. 15.

21. D. Boudreaux, 'Merger Paranoia', *Critical Review* (1987) p. 73.

22. See Kirzner, *Discovery, Capitalism and Distributive Justice*.

23. I. Fallon and J. Srodes, *Takeovers* (London: Pan, 1987).

24. Jensen, 'Takeovers: Their Causes and Consequences', pp. 25–6.

25. Jensen, 'Takeovers: Their Causes and Consequences', pp. 25–6.

26. See G. Anders, 'The Barbarians in the Boardroom', *Harvard Business Review* (July–August 1992) pp. 79–87.

27. See F. Modigliani and M. Miller, 'The Cost of Capital, Corporation Finance and the Theory of Investment', *American Economic Review* (1958) pp. 261–97.

28. See R. Ruback, 'An Overview of Takeover Defenses', in A. Auerbach (ed.) *Mergers and Acquisitions* (Chicago: University of Chicago Press, 1988) pp. 42–4.

29. Jensen, 'Takeovers: Their Causes and Consequences', pp. 42–4.

30. For an analysis of the Paramount case, see M. Dickson, 'Barbarians Waiting at the Gate', *Financial Times* (9 December 1993).

31. Jensen, 'Takeovers: Their Causes and Consequences', p. 41; Barry, *The Morality of Business Enterprise*, p. 73.

32. Kirzner, *Discovery, Capitalism and Distributive Justice*, ch. 7.
33. Ibid., pp. 133–43.
34. Ibid., pp. 97–128.
35. Ibid., p. 17.
36. Barry, *The Morality of Business Enterprise*, pp. 65–7.
37. The juries in other Guinness trials seem to have accepted this. There were no further convictions after those of Saunders and his accomplices.
38. The European Court of Human Rights ruled in favour of Saunders although his original convictions were unaffected.
39. J. Gulliver, 'How Scotland lost out to the Hammersmith Flyover', *The Times* (31 August 1990).
40. Kirzner, *Discovery, Capitalism and Distributive Justice*, p. 172.
41. See M. Ricketts, 'Kirzner's Theory of Entrepreneurship', in B. Caldwell and S. Bohm (eds) *Austrian Economics: Tensions and New Directions* (London: Kluwer, 1994) pp. 80–1.
42. R. Sobel, *Dangerous Dreamers* (New York: Wiley, 1993).
43. See for example, J. Stewart, *Den of Thieves* (New York: Simon & Schuster, 1991).
44. This was actually revealed in an obscure research publication (W. Braddock Hickman, *Corporate Bond Quality and Investor Experience*) which Milken studied.
45. See F. Bailey, *The Junk Bond Revolution* (London: Fourth Estate, 1994) ch. 4.
46. Their activities are described in D. Fischel, *Payback* (New York: Harper, 1995).
47. See S. Mulhall and A. Swift, *Liberals and Communitarians* (Oxford: Blackwell, 1992). For less philosophical view, see A. Etzioni, *The Spirit of Community* (New York: Crown, 1993).
48. The egalitarian liberal, John Rawls, has incorporated some features of communitarianism in the latest statement of his theory of justice, *Political Liberalism* (New York: Columbia University Press, 1993).
49. The Boeing aircraft corporation was made bid-proof by cleverly designed Washington state statute, see P. Linneman and E. Callison, 'Understanding Managements Role When Facing an Unsolicited Takeover Attempt', in Hoffman *et al.*, *The Ethics of Organizational Transformation*, p. 153.
50. For the public interest, see N. Barry, *An Introduction to Modern Political Theory* (London: Macmillan, 1995, 3rd edn).

7. The Environment and Business Ethics

1. See J. Shaw, 'Environmental Dangers', in *PERC Resource Book on Pollution, Trade and Aid* (Bozeman, Montana: Political Economy Research Center, 1991) pp. 1–4.
2. The first environmental 'scare' book was probably Rachel Carson's *The Silent Spring* (Greenwich, Connecticut: Fawcett, 1962).
3. It tends to link up with the radical animal rights and species movements in an onslaught on industrialism and capitalism.
4. These tend to derive from the work of the economist A.C. Pigou who developed the idea that there is a difference between marginal social cost

and marginal private cost. Since the publication of his *The Economics of Welfare* (London: Macmillan, 1920) economists of the Pigovian school have recommended taxation, and other direct measures, to solve externality problems.

5. See D. Pearce and R. Turner, *Economics of Natural Resources and the Environment* (Hemel Hempstead: Harvester Wheatsheaf, 1990) ch. 11.

6. J. Simon, 'More People, Greater Wealth, More Resources, Healthier Environment', *Economic Affairs* (1994) pp. 22–9.

7. See *Befriending the Earth: A Reconciliation Between Humans and the Earth* (Connecticut: Twenty Third Publications, 1991); M. Fox, *Original Blessing* (Santa Fe: Bear and Co., 1993). For a summary of religious environmental doctrines, see J. Shaw and R. Stroup, 'Environmental Crisis and Public Policy', *PERC Resource Book on Pollution, Trade and Aid*, pp. 23–5.

8. Instrumental rationality deliberately eschews discussion of the ends which ought to be pursued. It regards them as inherently contestable and not amenable to any definitive resolution. For a critique of instrumental rationality, see M. Bookchin, *The Ecology of Freedom: The Emergence and Dissolution of Hierarchy* (Palo Alto, Calif.: Cheshire, 1989).

9. J. Shaw and R. Stroup, 'Environmental Crisis and Public Policy, in *PERC Resource Book on Pollution, Trade and Aid*, p. 19.

10. The doctrine originated from the ideas of the scientist, James Lovelock, see S. Schneider, 'Debating Gaia', *Environment* (1990) pp. 5–9.

11. See K. Jeffries, 'Global Warming in Perspective', in *NCPA Progressive Environmentalism, Trade and Aid Resource Book* (Dallas: National Center for Policy Analysis, 1991) pp. 53–64.

12. R. Bate, 'Global Warming: Don't Believe All The Hype', *Wall Street Journal* (11 December 1995).

13. For an overall discussion of rights, see Barry, *An Introduction to Modern Political Theory*, ch. 9.

14. For a critique, see T. Anderson and D. Leal, 'Free market vs. Political Environmentalism', in *PERC Resource Book on Pollution, Trade and Aid*, pp. 40–7.

15. R. Stroup, 'Property Rights, Justice and Efficient Environmental Policy', *Journal des Economistes et des Etudes Humaines* (1997) p. 221.

16. M. Feshbeck and A. Friendly, *Ecocide in the USSR* (New York: Basic Books, 1992).

17. See *NCPA Progressive Environmentalism: Trade and Aid Resource Book*, p. 6.

18. R. Stroup, 'Property Rights, Justice and Efficient Environmental Policy', pp. 227–8.

19. See M. Ridley, *Down to Earth 11* (London: Institute of Economic Affairs, 1996).

20. David Hume, *A Treatise of Human Nature* (London: Fontana, 1972) bk 3, p. 220; first published 1740.

21. Quoted in J. Shaw and R. Stroup, 'Environmental Crisis and Public Policy', *PERC Resource Book on Pollution, Trade and Aid*, p. 27.

22. R. Coase, 'The Problem of Social Cost', *Journal of Law and Economics* (1960) pp. 1–44.

23. A standard work is T. Anderson and D. Leal, *Free Market Environmentalism* (Boulder, Colo.: Westview Press, 1991).
24. See R. Meiners and B. Yandle, 'The Common Law Solution to Water Pollution: The Path Not Taken', in *PERC Resource Book on Pollution, Trade and Aid*, pp. 88–98.
25. Pearce and Turner, *Economics of Natural Resources and the Environment*, chs 6 and 7.
26. See R. Bate, 'Water Pollution Prevention: A Nuisance Approach', *Economic Affairs*, pp. 13–14.
27. Meiners and Yandle, 'The Common Law Solution to Water Pollution', pp. 89–90.
28. See R. Stroup, 'Property Rights, Justice and Efficient Environmental Policy', pp. 215–18.
29. Reported in *NCPA Progressive Environmentalism, Trade and Aid Resource Book*, p. 38.
30. M. Ridley, *Down to Earth 1* (London: Institute of Economic Affairs, 1995) p. 50.
31. L. Kehoe, 'The Tide Has Turned after Exxon Valdez', *Financial Times* (27 March 1991).

8 Conclusion

1. Wilhelm Röpke, *A Humane Economy* (London: Wolff, 1960) p. 125.
2. Alfred Müller-Armack, who coined the phrase 'social market economy', was a significant figure in the theoretical and practical reorientation of the German market system. For a discussion of this, see N. Barry, 'The Political and Economic Thought of German Neo-Liberalism', in A. Peacock and H. Willgerodt (eds), *Germany Neo-Liberals and the Social Market Economy* (London: Macmillan, 1989) pp. 107–9.
3. See N. Barry, 'The Social Market Economy', *Social Philosophy and Policy* (1993), pp. 1–25.
4. D. Hume, *A Treatise of Human Nature*, ed. H. Aiken (New York: Macmillan, 1948) Book III, pp. 61–2.
5. See L. Trakman, *The Law Merchant*, for a description of the mergence of commercial law out of a common sense of morality.
6. In the famous Book 6 of the second volume of *The Wealth of Nations*, Adam Smith worried that too great a concentration on industry might affect people's capacity for morality.
7. Richard Epstein, *Simple Rules for a Complex World* (Cambridge, Mass.: Harvard University Press, 1995) p. 75.
8. The major stock brokerage firm in Japan, Nomura, has been the subject of continual investigation over the last five years. It has been accused of connections with gangsters, see *Financial Times*, 20 January 1998.
9. F. Fukuyama, *Trust*, pp. 49–57.

Index